# Master Your Maths

Mental maths and problem-solving activities

Eamonn Brennan • Meriel McCord
Deirdre Mulligan • Andrée Mulvihill

Published by

CJ Fallon
Ground Floor – Block B
Liffey Valley Office Campus
Dublin 22

ISBN: 978-0-7144-2173-5

First Edition January 2016
This Reprint September 2020

# Introduction

***Master Your Maths*** is a series of workbooks providing the most effective and structured daily mental maths and problem-solving programme. Each book is based on 30 weeks of the school year, comprising mental maths and problem-solving exercises for Monday to Thursday, along with a Friday test. The questions are varied and increase in complexity as the year progresses. ***Master Your Maths*** provides daily questions where children can develop problem-solving skills. It helps teachers create a classroom culture where children are encouraged to develop as independent mathematicians with strong problem-solving skills.

***Master Your Maths:***

- covers all strands and strand units of the maths curriculum.
- develops and reinforces mental calculation, concepts and skills.
- provides daily practice in problem-solving which is the key to maths understanding and higher scores in maths.
- provides real-life problems where children can see the role of maths in everyday life.
- provides Friday test pages to assess learning.
- provides assessment record sheets where children can track their own progress.

# Contents

# Individual Pupil Record

| Week 1 | | Week 2 | | Week 3 | | Week 4 | | Week 5 | |
|---|---|---|---|---|---|---|---|---|---|
| Date: | | Date: | | Date: | | Date: | | Date: | |
| Mon | 18 | Mon | 18 | Mon | 18 | Mon | 18 | Mon | 18 |
| Tues | 18 | Tues | 18 | Tues | 18 | Tues | 18 | Tues | 18 |
| Wed | 18 | Wed | 18 | Wed | 18 | Wed | 18 | Wed | 18 |
| Thurs | 18 | Thurs | 18 | Thurs | 18 | Thurs | 18 | Thurs | 18 |
| Fri | 25 | Fri | 25 | Fri | 25 | Fri | 25 | Fri | 25 |

| Week 6 | | Week 7 | | Week 8 | | Week 9 | | Week 10 | |
|---|---|---|---|---|---|---|---|---|---|
| Date: | | Date: | | Date: | | Date: | | Date: | |
| Mon | 18 | Mon | 18 | Mon | 18 | Mon | 18 | Mon | 18 |
| Tues | 18 | Tues | 18 | Tues | 18 | Tues | 18 | Tues | 18 |
| Wed | 18 | Wed | 18 | Wed | 18 | Wed | 18 | Wed | 18 |
| Thurs | 18 | Thurs | 18 | Thurs | 18 | Thurs | 18 | Thurs | 18 |
| Fri | 25 | Fri | 25 | Fri | 25 | Fri | 25 | Fri | 25 |

| Week 11 | | Week 12 | | Week 13 | | Week 14 | | Week 15 | |
|---|---|---|---|---|---|---|---|---|---|
| Date: | | Date: | | Date: | | Date: | | Date: | |
| Mon | 18 | Mon | 18 | Mon | 18 | Mon | 18 | Mon | 18 |
| Tues | 18 | Tues | 18 | Tues | 18 | Tues | 18 | Tues | 18 |
| Wed | 18 | Wed | 18 | Wed | 18 | Wed | 18 | Wed | 18 |
| Thurs | 18 | Thurs | 18 | Thurs | 18 | Thurs | 18 | Thurs | 18 |
| Fri | 25 | Fri | 25 | Fri | 25 | Fri | 25 | Fri | 25 |

| Week 16 | | Week 17 | | Week 18 | | Week 19 | | Week 20 | |
|---|---|---|---|---|---|---|---|---|---|
| Date: | | Date: | | Date: | | Date: | | Date: | |
| Mon | 18 | Mon | 18 | Mon | 18 | Mon | 18 | Mon | 18 |
| Tues | 18 | Tues | 18 | Tues | 18 | Tues | 18 | Tues | 18 |
| Wed | 18 | Wed | 18 | Wed | 18 | Wed | 18 | Wed | 18 |
| Thurs | 18 | Thurs | 18 | Thurs | 18 | Thurs | 18 | Thurs | 18 |
| Fri | 25 | Fri | 25 | Fri | 25 | Fri | 25 | Fri | 25 |

| Week 21 | | Week 22 | | Week 23 | | Week 24 | | Week 25 | |
|---|---|---|---|---|---|---|---|---|---|
| Date: | | Date: | | Date: | | Date: | | Date: | |
| Mon | 18 | Mon | 18 | Mon | 18 | Mon | 18 | Mon | 18 |
| Tues | 18 | Tues | 18 | Tues | 18 | Tues | 18 | Tues | 18 |
| Wed | 18 | Wed | 18 | Wed | 18 | Wed | 18 | Wed | 18 |
| Thurs | 18 | Thurs | 18 | Thurs | 18 | Thurs | 18 | Thurs | 18 |
| Fri | 25 | Fri | 25 | Fri | 25 | Fri | 25 | Fri | 25 |

| Week 26 | | Week 27 | | Week 28 | | Week 29 | | Week 30 | |
|---|---|---|---|---|---|---|---|---|---|
| Date: | | Date: | | Date: | | Date: | | Date: | |
| Mon | 18 | Mon | 18 | Mon | 18 | Mon | 18 | Mon | 18 |
| Tues | 18 | Tues | 18 | Tues | 18 | Tues | 18 | Tues | 18 |
| Wed | 18 | Wed | 18 | Wed | 18 | Wed | 18 | Wed | 18 |
| Thurs | 18 | Thurs | 18 | Thurs | 18 | Thurs | 18 | Thurs | 18 |
| Fri | 25 | Fri | 25 | Fri | 25 | Fri | 25 | Fri | 25 |

Week 1

## Monday

1. Round 4,836 to the nearest 10. ______
2. 3,214 + 6,836 = ______
3. 872 ÷ 8 = ______
4. Name the shape. ______

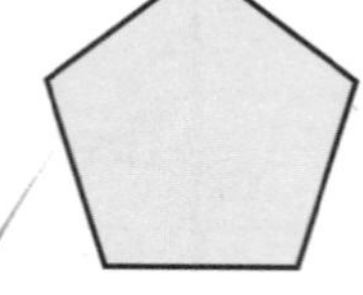

5. Name the shape. ______
6. What is the chance of a baby being born a boy? ______ in ______
7. Write the time shown in digital form. ______
8. hrs mins

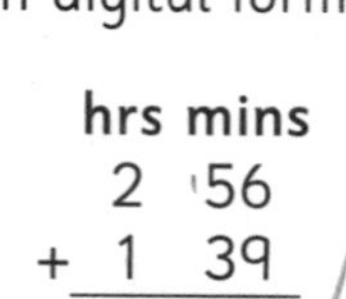

| | hrs | mins |
|---|---|---|
| | 2 | 56 |
| + | 1 | 39 |
| | | |

9. €18·40 + €3·35 + €1·20 = ______
10. 7m 62cm – 3m 52cm = ______
11. Find the perimeter of this shape. ______

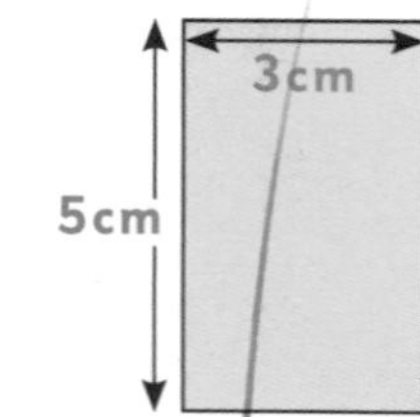


12. Find $\frac{1}{2}$ of 30. ______
13. 140 minutes = ______ hours ______ minutes
14. Complete the sequence.
224, 225, 226, 227, ______, ______, ______
15. What fraction of the shape is shaded? ______

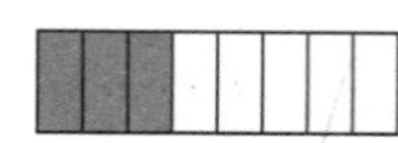

16. One train had 2,568 passengers. A second train had 1,486 passengers and a third had 2,159 passengers. How many passengers were on the three trains? ______
17. A new boat costs €3,683. A second-hand boat costs €2,223. How much more does the new boat cost? ______
18. A ticket to the museum costs €2·28 per child. How much would five tickets cost? ______

/18

## Tuesday

1. (9 × 7) + 8 = ______
2. Find $\frac{3}{8}$ of 40. ______
3. Write the missing number.
2, 9, 16, ______, 30
4. Round 2,485 to the nearest 10. ______
5. Name the shape. ______
6. Name the shape. ______

7. How many degrees are there in a right angle? ______
8. 346 ÷ 8 = ______ R ______
9. If one orange costs 15c, how much would 6 oranges cost? ______
10. 72 ______ 9 = 8
11. Find the perimeter of this shape. ______

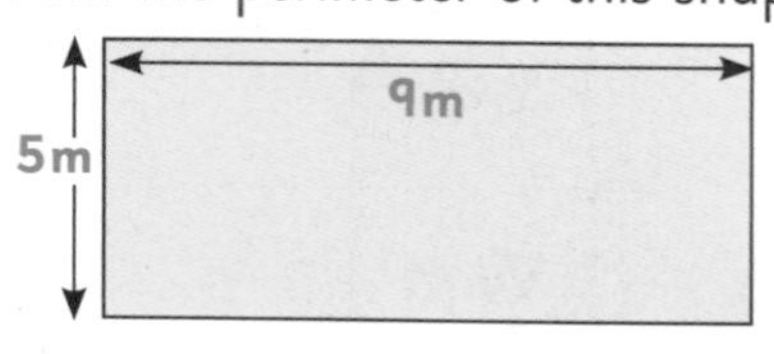


12. What time will it be 25 minutes later than the time shown on the clock? ______
13. Write 0·1 as a fraction. ______
14. 5kg = ______ g
15. 48 + 19 = ______

**A bicycle costs €245·95. Mary has saved €101·68.**

16. How much more does Mary need to buy the bicycle? ______
17. If her aunt gave her €71·26, how much would she need then? ______
18. The shop decided to have a sale and they reduced the price of the bicycle by €19·63. How much would the bicycle cost then? ______

/18

## Wednesday

1. $(6 \times 8) + 9 =$ ____

2. 
$$\begin{array}{r} 6{,}353 \\ -\ 1{,}569 \\ \hline \end{array}$$

3. Find $\frac{5}{6}$ of 36. ____

4. $571 \div 9 =$ ____ R ____

5. 96 ____ 12 = 8

6. Round 4,856 to the nearest 100. ____

7. What time will it be 35 minutes later than the time shown on the clock? ____

8. What type of angle is the smaller angle made by the hands of the clock? ____

9. Complete the sequence.
4, 10, 16, 22, ____

10. What decimal fraction of this shape is shaded? ____

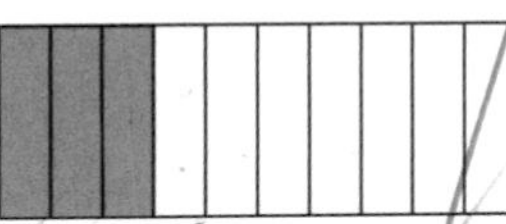

11. What fraction is not shaded? ____

12. Name the 3-D shape. ____

13. 3l = ____ ml

14. 
$$\begin{array}{r} 7{\cdot}256\text{kg} \\ +\ 3{\cdot}216\text{kg} \\ \hline \end{array}$$

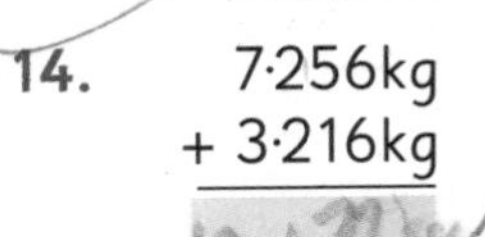

15. Measure the length of this line.
____ cm

16. Jane has 35 stickers.
John has 18 more than that.
How many stickers has John? ____

17. 6 apples cost €14·16.
How much would one apple cost? ____

18. A farmer had 63 sheep.
She sold $\frac{1}{7}$ of them.
How many sheep had she left? ____

/18

## Thursday

1. Round 6,833 to the nearest 100. ____

2. 2,457 + 700 = ____

3. $(8 \times 9) + 7 =$ ____

4. 0·7 of 70 = ____

5. What do we call the following angle? ____

6. Name the 2-D shape. ____

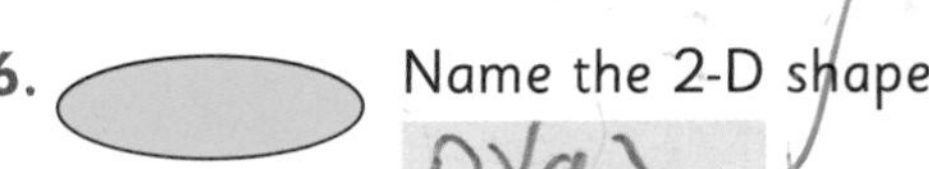

7. How many edges has a cube? ____

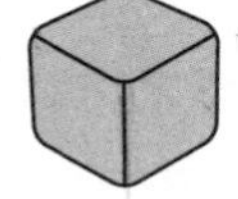

8. 8·95km ÷ 5 = ____

9. €5 – €2·45 = ____

10. Find the area of the following shape. ____

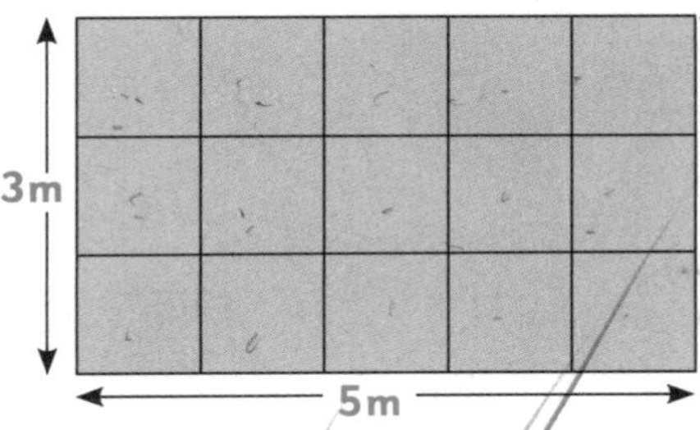


11. 40 + 25 + 60 = ____

12. 35 ____ 15 = 50

13. $45 \times 10 =$ ____

14. 2·8kg = ____ g

15. $1\frac{1}{2}$ hours = ____ minutes

A shopkeeper had a box with 164 apples in it at the start of the day and another with 185 oranges.

16. How many more oranges than apples had the shopkeeper? ____

17. If the shopkeeper sold $\frac{3}{4}$ of the apples, how many apples did he sell? ____

18. The shopkeeper sold $\frac{1}{5}$ of the oranges in the morning and then sold 42 more after lunch. How many oranges did he sell that day? ____

/18

See page 66 for test.

**Week 2**

## Monday

1. Complete the sequence.
   126, 127, 128, 129, ____
2. 250 + 450 = ____
3. Write the numeral one thousand and one. ____
4. Write this time in digital form. ____

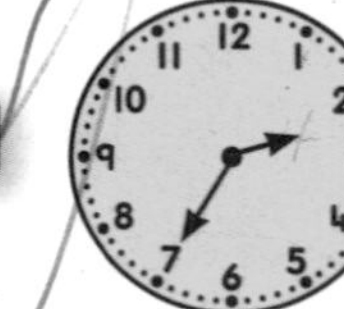

5. 156c = € ____
6. Measure the line. ____ cm
7. 8:00 =

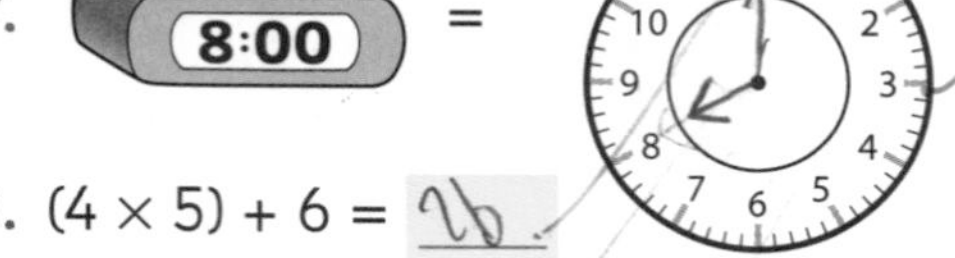

8. (4 × 5) + 6 = ____
9. $7\overline{)398}$
   ____ R ____
10. 20 × 30 = ____
11. $\frac{1}{2}$ ____ $\frac{1}{3}$ (>, < or =)
12. Name the shape. ____

13. Round 7,885 to the nearest 10. ____
14. $\frac{1}{3}$ of 36 = ____
15. What decimal fraction of the shape is coloured? ____

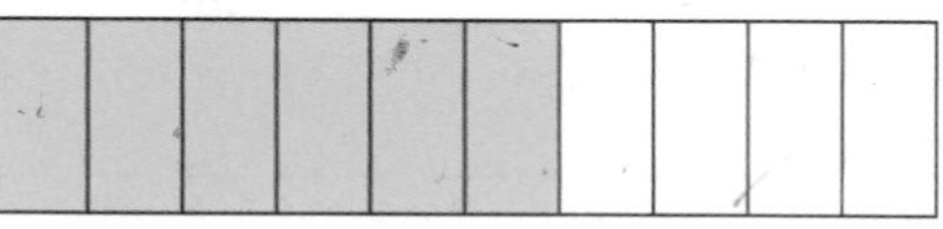

16. A kettle holds 4l 520ml of water.
    A bucket holds 7l 650ml more water.
    How much does the bucket hold? ____
17. John is 1m 45cm tall.
    Peter is 1m 37cm tall.
    What is the total height of the two boys? ____
18. One shirt costs €21·35.
    How much would 5 shirts cost? ____

/18

## Tuesday

1. Round 5,684 to the nearest 100. ____
2. Complete the sequence.
   4,217, 4,218, 4,219, ____

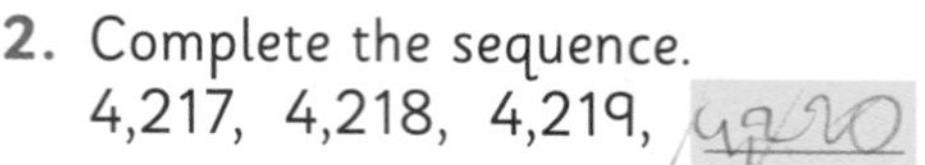

3. (7 × 6) + 9 = ____
4. 22 × 100 = ____
5. 0·1 = $\frac{\square}{10}$
6. How likely is it that you will go on a trip to space? ____
   (likely, unlikely, certain, impossible)
7. Name the shape. ____

8. What sort of angle is shown? ____
9. Which colour is the most popular? ____

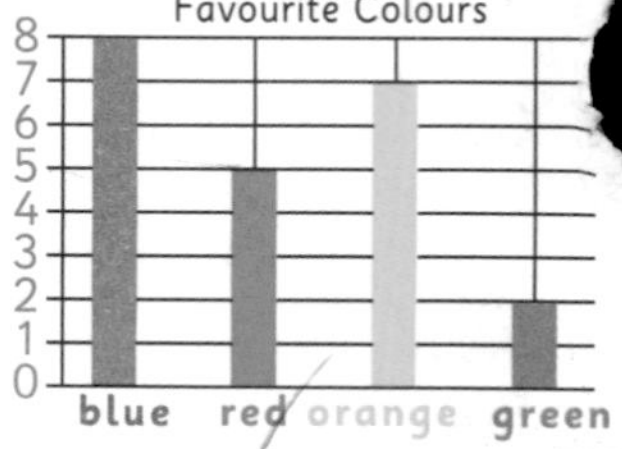


10. How many more prefer red than green? ____
11. How many like blue and red altogether? ____
12. 
    | | hrs | mins |
    |---|---|---|
    | | 3 | 42 |
    | + | 1 | 29 |
    | | | |

13. Find the perimeter of this shape. ____

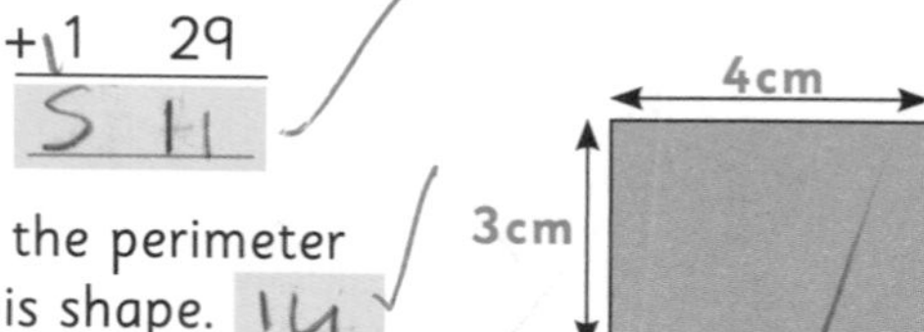


14. 3,200 + 1,000 + 100 = ____
15. €7·99 = ____ c.

A train leaves the Dublin station at 4:45 and is due to arrive in the Longford station at 6:34.

16. How long does the journey take? ____
17. If the train arrived in Longford 11 minutes earlier than expected, at what time did it arrive? ____ : ____
18. If the train was 15 minutes late departing Dublin, at what time did it depart? ____ : ____

/18

## Wednesday

1. Round 3,761 to the nearest 1,000. ____
2. (7 × 3) + 8 = ____
3. 62 × 10 = ____
4. Write this time in digital form. 
5. Name the shape. ____
6. 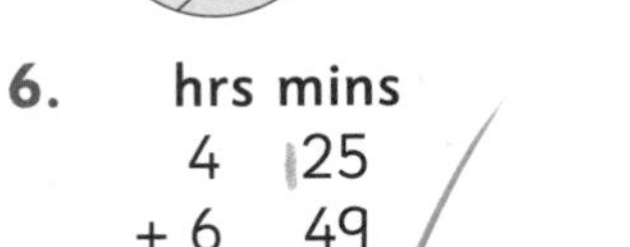

| | hrs | mins |
|---|---|---|
| | 4 | 25 |
| + | 6 | 49 |

7. 6,497 − 2,108 = ____
8. Complete the sequence. 4,007, 4,008, 4,009, ____
9. 5)342 ____ R ____
10. What fraction of the shape is shaded? ____

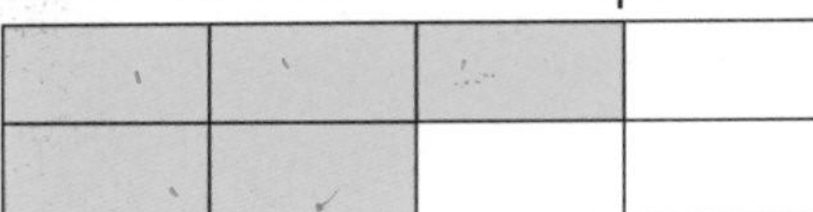

11. $\frac{1}{8}$ of 24 = ____
12. 6·2 + 8·3 = ____
13. 4·23m + 1·46m = ____
14. 6·155km ÷ 5 = ____
15. Is the letter **A** symmetrical? ____
16. Take 125 from the sum of 268 and 394. ____
17. Mary walked 4km on Monday, 3·5km on Tuesday and 2·75km on Wednesday. How far did she walk in the three days? ____
18. It is 79km from Dublin to Mullingar. It is 130km from Mullingar to Sligo. How far is it from Dublin to Sligo? ____

/18

## Thursday

1. $\frac{1}{4}$ of 32 = ____
2. 12·45 + 13·39 = ____
3. Name the shape. ____

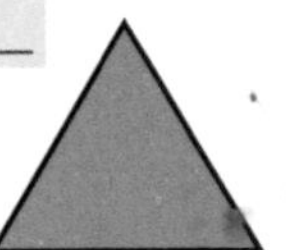

4. Round 6,245 to the nearest 10. ____
5. (6 × 8) + 9 = ____
6. 43 × 100 = ____
7. Are these lines perpendicular? ____
8. What fraction of the shape is shaded? ____

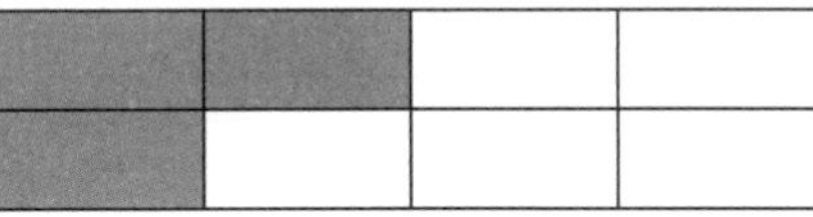

9. Complete the sequence. 2,017, 2,018, 2,019, ____
10. 15 × ____ = 75
11. 1kg 200g = ____ g
12. Write this time in digital form. ____ : ____

13. Draw this letter turned 90° clockwise: **A**.
14. Write the number five thousand six hundred and three. ____
15. 202c = € ____

There were 6,500 people at a football match. There were 1,654 women, 3,004 men and the rest were children.

16. How many adults were at the match? ____
17. How many children were at the match? ____
18. How many fewer children than adults were at the match? ____

/18

See page 67 for test.

## Monday

1. ____ ÷ 6 = 9
2. Complete the sequence.
   4,342, 4,344, 4,346, ____
3. What is the value of the underlined digit: <u>2</u>3,268? ____
4. Write $\frac{3}{10}$ as a decimal fraction. ____
5. $\begin{array}{r} 4{\cdot}67 \\ \times \quad 4 \\ \hline \end{array}$
6. 35 × 6 = ____

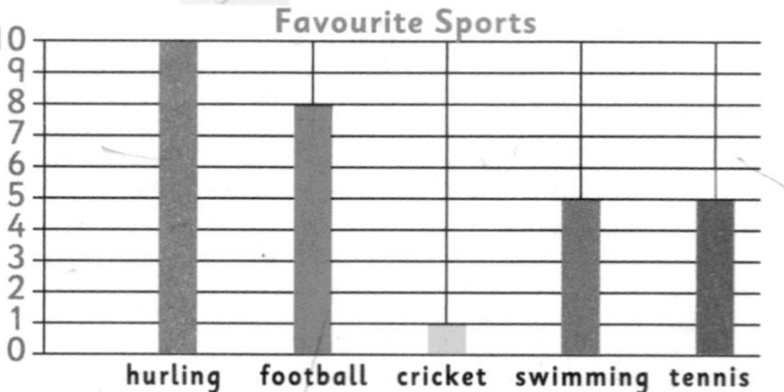


7. Which sport is the most popular? ____
8. How many more prefer football than swimming? ____
9. How many like tennis and hurling altogether? ____
10. Write this time in digital form. ____ : ____

11. 45,363 + 10 = ____
12. $\begin{array}{r} 2l\ 250ml \\ \times \quad 4 \\ \hline \end{array}$

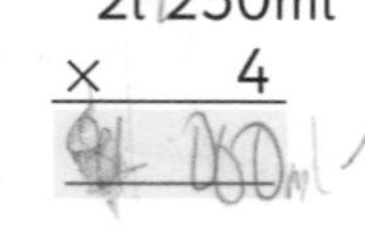

13. €1·02 = ____ c
14. What sort of angle is shown? ____
15. 16 + ____ = 35
16. Ann lives 7km from school. Her friend Joan lives 1·25km closer to the school than Ann. How far away is Joan's house from the school? ____
17. How much greater is the sum of 426 and 195 than 363? ____
18. Increase 1,063 by 327. ____

/18

## Tuesday

1. 281 × 10 = ____
2. 22 + ____ = 39
3. Complete the sequence.
   3,223, 3,225, 3,227, ____
4. (7 × 4) + 7 = ____
5. $\begin{array}{r} 4{\cdot}35 \\ \times \quad 5 \\ \hline \end{array}$
6. 2,428 + 3,000 = ____
7. Name the shape. ____
8. €3·45 + €2·11 + €1·25 = ____

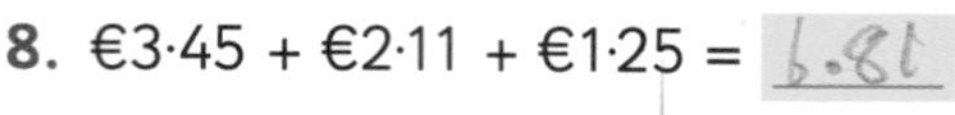

9. What is the value of the underlined digit: <u>4</u>6,223? ____
10. 44,268 + 100 = ____
11. What are the chances of you going into Sixth Class next year? ____
    (unlikely, likely, certain, impossible)
12. What sort of angle is shown? ____
13. Write this time in digital form. ____ : ____

14. $\begin{array}{r} 4kg\ 200g \\ \times \quad 6 \\ \hline \end{array}$

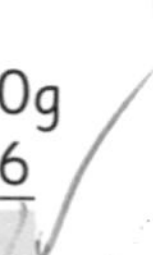

15. Write $\frac{1}{100}$ as a decimal fraction. ____

St Mary's School had a school concert and sold:
€2,430 worth of adult's tickets,
€360 worth of children's tickets and
€405 worth of senior citizen's tickets.

16. How much altogether did the school collect? ____
17. If a senior citizen ticket cost €5 each, how many senior citizens attended? ____
18. If an adult ticket cost €6 each, how many more adult's tickets were sold than senior citizen's tickets? ____

/18

## Wednesday

1. Complete the sequence.
   1,205, 1,207, 1,209, ____
2. (4 × 4) + 9 = ____
3. 26,423 + 1,000 = ____
4. 42 × 100 = ____
5. Write $\frac{3}{100}$ as a decimal fraction. ____
6. How likely is it that Christmas Day will be in December this year? ____
   (likely, unlikely, certain, impossible)
7. Name the shape. ____
8. 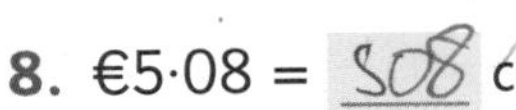
   €5·08 = ____ c
9. 4kg 250g + 3kg 900g = ____
10. 9)748
    ____ R ____
11. Measure the line. ____ cm
12. Find the area of this shape. ____

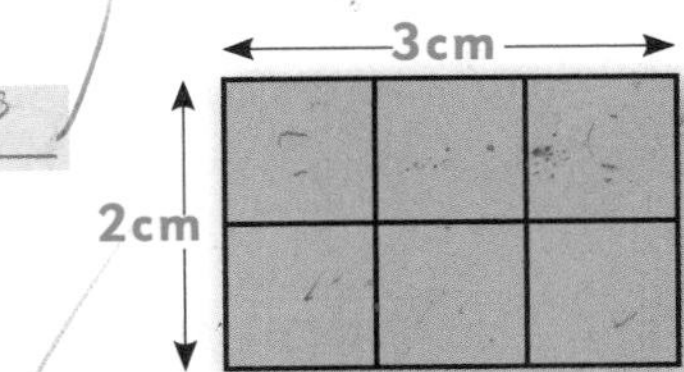


13. What is the value of the underlined digit: 16,5<u>8</u>5? ____
14. Write this time in digital form. ____ : ____

15. 57 ____ 35 (>, < or =)
16. A pole is 3m 45cm long. Another pole is 2m 28cm long. What is the total length of the two poles? ____
17. There are 12 eggs in a box. How many eggs would there be in 17 boxes? ____
18. A television programme started at 3:45. It ended 2 hours 45 minutes later. At what time did the television programme end? ____ : ____

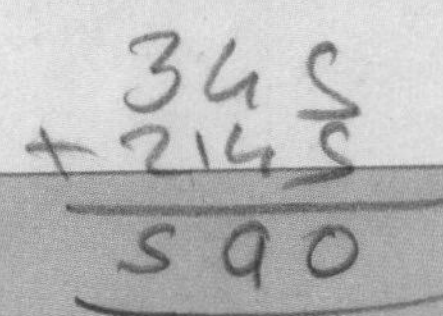

/18

## Thursday

1. 32 × 100 = ____
2. What is the value of the underlined digit: 28,<u>4</u>35? ____
3. Complete the sequence.
   6,294, 6,296, 6,298, ____
4. (9 × 6) + 7 = ____
5. 7·26 × 3 = ____
6. Write this time in digital form. ____ : ____

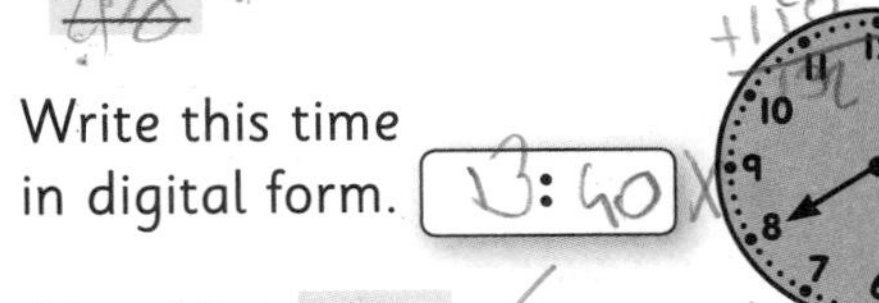

7. 11 × 12 = ____
8. Write $\frac{7}{10}$ as a decimal fraction. ____
9. Name the shape.
   ____

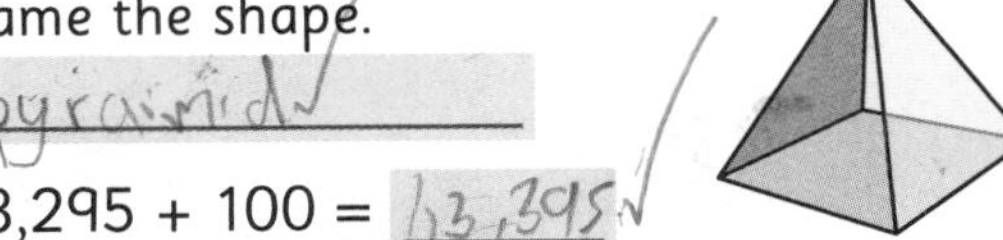

10. 63,295 + 100 = ____
11. 35 – ____ = 19
12. 503c = € ____
13. 6)12l 624ml
    ____

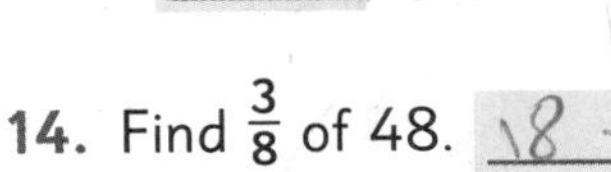

14. Find $\frac{3}{8}$ of 48. ____
15. What sort of angle is shown?
    ____

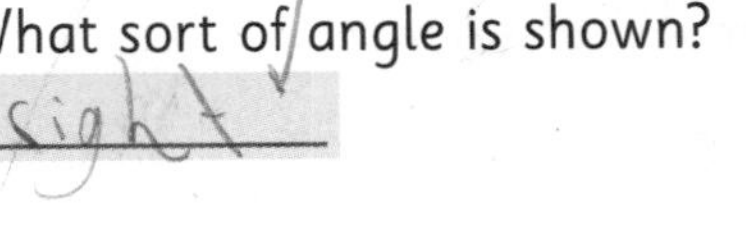

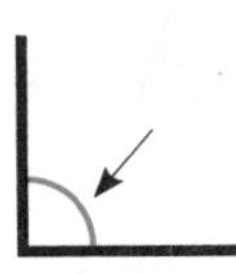

There are 220 pages in *Harry Potter and the Philosopher's Stone*. There are 600 pages in *Harry Potter and the Deathly Hallows*.

16. How many more pages are there in the *Deathly Hallows* book than the *Philosopher's Stone*? ____
17. If Jim read $\frac{1}{5}$ of the *Philosopher's Stone* on Monday, how many pages did he read?
    ____
18. If Jim read a further 35 pages on Tuesday, how many pages had he left to read then?
    ____

/18

See page 68 for test.

## Monday

1. Complete the sequence.
   4,284, 4,288, 4,292, ______
2. Put the following numbers in order of size, starting with the smallest:
   44,295, 16,383, 21,586, 89,312.
   ______, ______, ______, ______
3. Round 24,385 to the nearest 1,000. ______
4. 50% = 0·5. True or false? ______
5. Name the shape. ______
6. 56,425 – 100 = ______
7. Is this angle an acute, a straight or a right angle? ______
8. (7 × 6) + 4 = ______
9. 7 × ______ = 63
10. Find the perimeter of the rectangle. ______

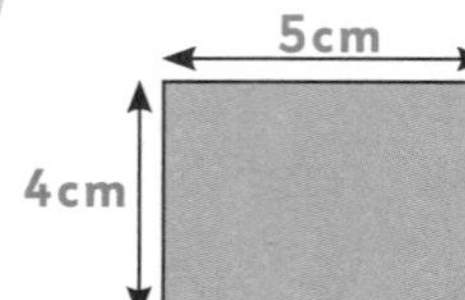


11. What time will it be 25 minutes later than the time shown on the clock? ______
12. How likely is it that tomorrow will be Tuesday? ______
    (likely, unlikely, certain, impossible)
13. 5m 44cm – 3m 32cm = ______
14.

| | 5km 275m |
|---|---|
| + | 4km 750m |

15. Write $\frac{7}{100}$ as a decimal fraction. ______
16. 

    Adam had €30. He bought the football jersey. How much had he left? ______
17. Brian spent $\frac{1}{4}$ of his money on a magazine. If he had €16 before he bought the magazine, how much money did he spend? ______
18. Alice had €20. She spent €9·80 in one shop and €2·45 in another shop. Mammy gave her €5. How much money had she then? ______

/18

## Tuesday

1. (3 × 8) + 12 = ______
2. 460 × 10 = ______
3. Put the following numbers in order of size, starting with the largest:
   17,428, 68,409, 12,633, 24,803.
   ______, ______, ______, ______
4. 1·240l = ______ ml
5. Round 75,568 to the nearest 1,000. ______
6. How many degrees in a straight angle? ______
7. Double 1·25g. ______

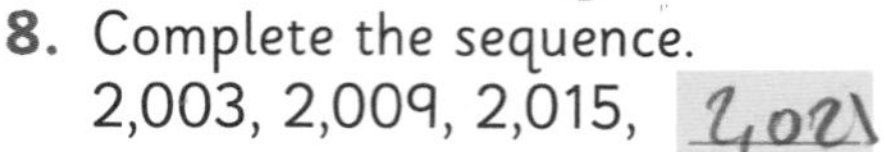

8. Complete the sequence.
   2,003, 2,009, 2,015, ______
9. Write $\frac{9}{10}$ as a decimal fraction. ______
10. 21 – ______ = 6
11. How many faces has a cuboid? ______
12. What time will it be 25 minutes later than the time shown on the clock? ______

13. Find the perimeter of the shape. ______

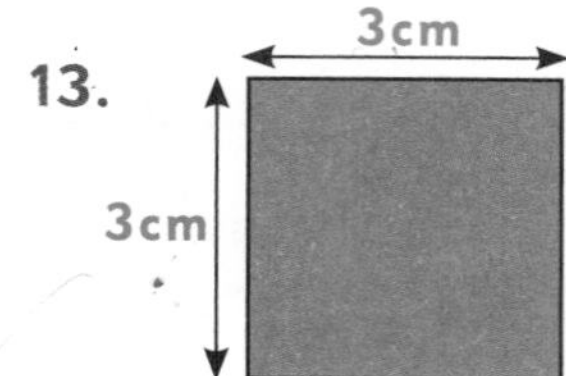


14. Is the capital letter **B** symmetrical? ______
15. A pentagon has ______ sides.

Mary spent one hour doing her homework last night. This time was divided as shown on the pie chart between Maths, English and Irish.

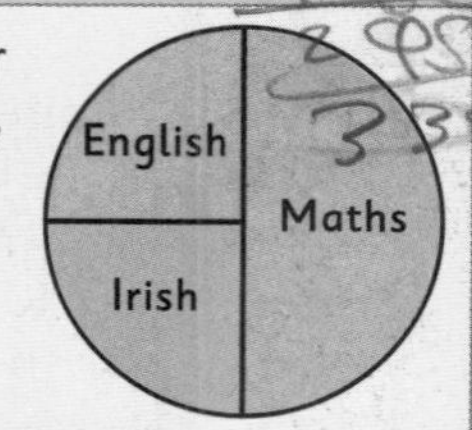


16. How many minutes did Mary spend doing her homework? ______
17. What fraction of time did she spend on Maths? ______
18. How many minutes did she spend doing her English homework? ______

/18

## Wednesday

1. Complete the sequence.
   4,085, 4,090, 4,095, 4,160

2. 66,435 + 100 = 66,535

3. Which number is larger:
   24,202 or 24,022? 24,202

4. 80,104 ÷ 100 = 801.04

5. 62 × 20 = 1,240

6. Which letter is not symmetrical:
   **A**, **C**, **E** or **F**? F

7. How many sides has an octagon? 8

8. 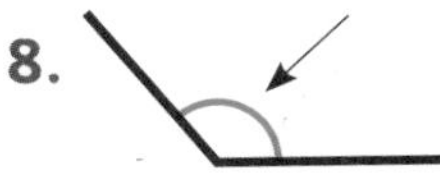 What sort of angle is shown? obtuse

9. Find the perimeter of the shape. 16

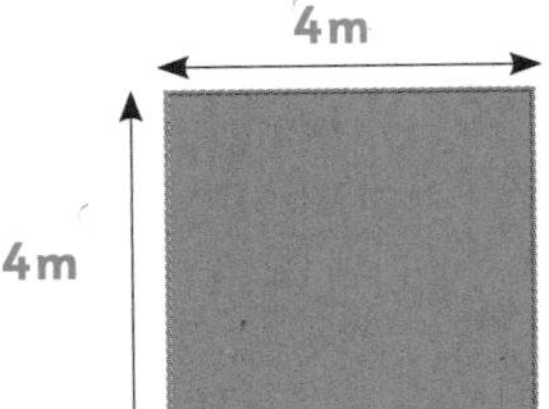


10. 
$$\begin{array}{r} 91\,450\text{ml} \\ \times \quad 5 \\ \hline 512\,250\text{ml} \end{array}$$

11. €2·02 = 202 c

12. Write $\frac{9}{100}$ as a decimal fraction. 0.09

13. 45 + 17 = 62

14. (8 × 8) + 11 = 75

15. Round 82,425 to the nearest 1,000. 82,000

16. How many hours and minutes are there from 2:25 to 5:10? 3h 25m

17. A bus journey from Athlone to Galway usually takes 2 hours 14 minutes. If the journey took 25 minutes extra due to traffic, how long did the journey take? 2h 39m

18. John spends 2 hours exercising every evening. If he spends $\frac{1}{4}$ of this time on the treadmill, how long does he spend on the treadmill? 30 mins

/18

## Thursday

1. Round 73,685 to the nearest 100. ______

2. (6 × 3) + ____ = 25

3. Complete the sequence.
   5,070, 5,080, 5,090, ______

4. 
$$\begin{array}{r} 52{,}493 \\ +\ 18{,}624 \\ \hline \end{array}$$

5. Tick ✓ the smaller number.
   ☐ 14,078 ☐ 14,780

6. Prisms cannot have curved faces.
   True or false? ______

7. Write $\frac{4}{5}$ as a decimal fraction. ____

8. Draw a line of symmetry through the letter: E

9. How likely is it that tomorrow is Monday? ______
   (likely, unlikely, certain, impossible)

10. 17·6 ÷ 8 = ____

11. Put these decimals in order of size, starting with the smallest: 0·45, 0·56, 0·4.
    ______, ______, ______

12. Measure the line. ____ cm

13. €4·05 + €3·22 + €6 = ______

14. What time will it be 25 minutes later than the time shown on the clock? [ : ]

15. $\frac{3}{4}$ = 0·70. True or false? ______

| Day | Temperature |
|---|---|
| Monday | 14°C |
| Tuesday | 16°C |
| Wednesday | 24°C |
| Thursday | 19°C |

16. Which day had the highest temperature? ______

17. What was the total temperature for Monday, Tuesday and Wednesday? ______

18. What was the average temperature of these three days?
    (Hint! Divide answer to Q17 by 3.) ______

/18

See page 69 for test.

## Monday

1. Complete the sequence.
6,150, 6,250, 6,350, ______

2. 47 ÷ 5 = ____ R ____

3. Put in order of size, starting with the smallest: 17,520, 16,344, 13,128, 19,421.
______, ______, ______, ______

4. 45,125
− 12,876
______

5. Round 63,568 to the nearest 100. ______

6. Find the average of the following weights: 4kg, 6kg, 9kg, 5kg. ______

7. 63,895 + 1,000 = ______

8. (6 × 8) + ____ = 58

9. Find the perimeter of the following shape. ______

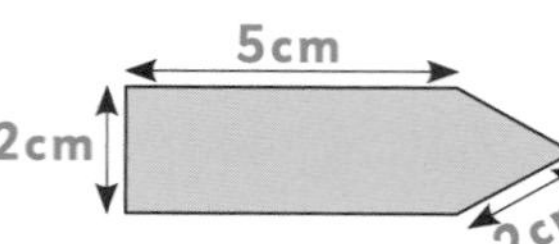


10. 29 × 10 = ______

11. Write $5\frac{1}{10}$ as a decimal fraction. ______

12. Name the shape. ______

13. Name the shape. ______

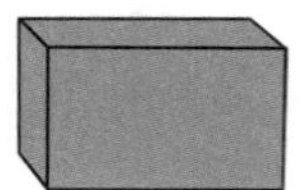

14. What time is 35 minutes later than the time shown on the clock? ___ : ___

15. 45 − ____ = 12

16. Mark wrote down the number 786 instead of 678. What was the difference between the number he wrote down and the correct number? ______

17. A farmer valued a cow at €1,650 and a sheep at €368. He sold the two animals for €2,200. How much more than expected did the farmer receive? ______

18. The temperature in Dublin was 25°C on Monday, 24°C on Tuesday and 20°C on Wednesday. What was the average temperature over the three days? ______

/18

## Tuesday

1. Which number is larger: 45,322 or 43,522? ______

2. (7 × 9) + ____ = 70

3. Complete the sequence.
1,000, 1,250, 1,500, ______

4. Round 29,645 to the nearest 1,000. ______

5. Find the average of the following amounts of money: €5, €8, €9, €10. ______

6. 73,429 ÷ 10 = ______

7. Measure the line. ____ cm

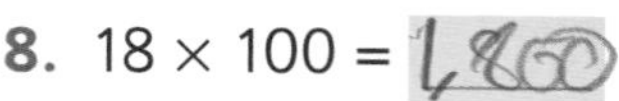

8. 18 × 100 = ______

9. Can circles tesselate? ______

10. Which letter has more than one line of symmetry: **A**, **B**, **X** or **W**? ______

11. Write $\frac{11}{100}$ as a decimal fraction. ______

12. If there are 3 blue cubes and 1 red cube in a bag, what are the chances of pulling out a red cube? ____ in ____

13. Find the perimeter of the following shape. ______

7cm
3cm
1cm

14. If one bucket holds 3·2l, how much would 3 buckets hold? ______

15. €1·08 = ______c

16. How many children voted altogether? ______

17. What was the average number of votes given to each food? ______

18. How many more votes than the average did pizza get? ______

/18

## Wednesday

1. Complete the sequence. 4,400, 4,600, 4,800, 5,000

2. 98,999 − 49,678 = 49,321

3. Round 68,999 to the nearest 1,000. 69,000

4. What is the value of the underlined digit: 38,3<u>4</u>5? 40

5. 6,450 ÷ 10 = 645

6. (7 × 2) + 8 = 22

7. How many sides has a pentagon? 5

8. Name the shape. cylinder

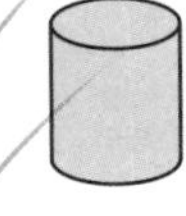

9. 36 × 20 = 720

10. Find the average of the following numbers: 7, 4, 8, 6, 5. 6

11. Find the perimeter of the shape. 18

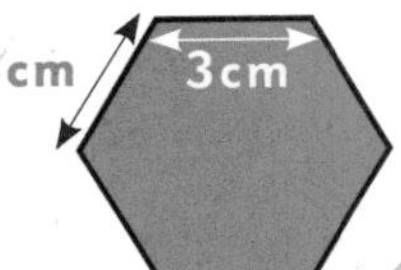


12. €4·05 + €3·26 + €9·14 = 16.45

13. What time is 35 minutes later than the time shown on the clock? 2:10

14. Name this angle. obtuse

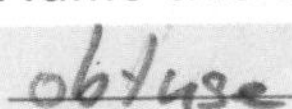

15. Write $6\frac{1}{10}$ as a decimal fraction. 6.1

16. The capacity of Croke Park is 82,300. The capacity of Old Trafford is 75,731. How many more spectators does Croke Park hold than Old Trafford? 6,569

17. 1,550 people went to the cinema in Mallow on Thursday. Twice as many went on Friday. How many went on Friday? 3,100

18. A gardener planted 456 roses. $\frac{1}{4}$ of them were red. How many were red? 114

18 /18

## Thursday

1. Complete the sequence. 1·2, 1·3, 1.4

2. 64,397 + 300 = 64,697

3. Put in order of size, starting with the smallest: 24,328, 25,816, 20,217, 23,562. 20,217, 23,562, 24,328, 25,816

4. Round 44,359 to the nearest 100. 44,400

5. (5 × 8) + 9 = 49

6. What time is 35 minutes later than the time shown on the clock? 4:55

7. 31 × 10 = 310

8. Find the perimeter of the shape. 16

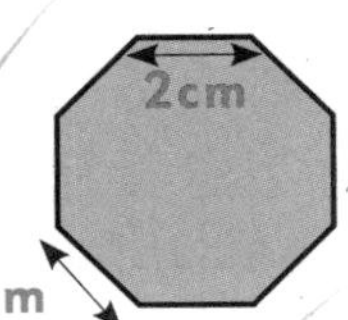


9. Name the shape. cone

10. 8kg 900g × 4 = 35kg 600g

11. Write $4\frac{1}{100}$ as a decimal fraction. 4.01

12. 36 × 100 = 3600

13. If there are 3 red cubes and 1 blue cube in a bag, what are the chances of picking a blue cube? 1 in 4

14. What is the value of the underlined digit: 83,4<u>2</u>0? 20

15. 9·52l ÷ 8 = 1.19

16. Ann bought three cups of tea and three scones. How much did she pay? €3.90

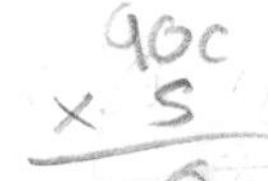


17. She gave the shopkeeper €10. How much change did she receive? €6.10

18. Paul had €20. He bought 5 cups of coffee, 3 buns and 2 scones. How much change did he get back? 13.30

18 /18

See page 70 for test.

## Monday

1. Complete the sequence.
   5,000, 5,750, 6,500, ______
2. Round 43,632 to the nearest 1,000. ______
3. The ages of three children are 7 years, 12 years and 8 years. What is their average age? ______
4. (9 × 8) + ______ = 90
5. Find the perimeter of the following shape. ______

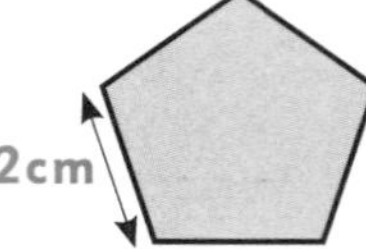


6. 21,435 + 10,000 = ______
7. 71,359
   + 22,463
   ______
8. Can this shape tesselate? ______

9. Write $8\frac{1}{10}$ as a decimal fraction. ______
10. 52 × 100 = ______
11. A straight angle has ______°.
12. €4·20 + €3·75 = ______
13. Measure the line. ______ cm
14. How many glasses that can hold 500ml could I fill from this bottle? ______

15. Write the time 40 minutes later than the time shown on the clock. ___ : ___

16. A box of chocolates weighed 1·7kg. When 800g of the chocolates were eaten, what weight of chocolates was left in the box? ______
17. If mince beef costs €5·65 per 500g, how much would 2kg cost? ______
18. When Jack had drank 100·6ml of a 2l bottle of water, how many more ml had he left to drink? ______

/18

## Tuesday

1. €6·23 = ______ c
2. Write $\frac{3}{4}$ as a decimal number. ______
3. Complete the sequence.
   7,135, 7,335, 7,535, ______
4. 4,250 ÷ 100 = ______
5. Round 62,445 to the nearest 100. ______

The children were asked to vote for their favourite activity at the school sports day.

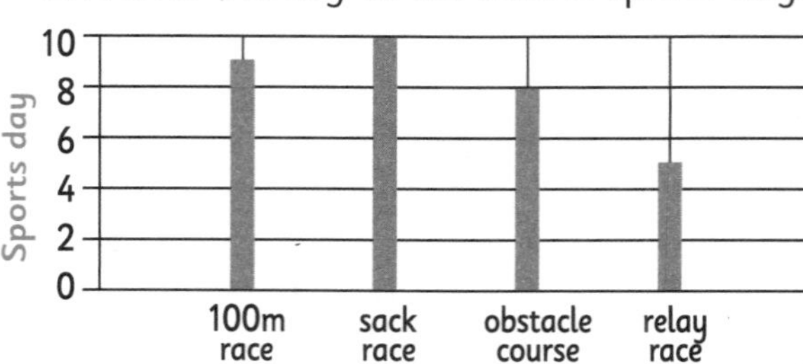


6. Which activity was the most popular?

7. How many children voted altogether? ______
8. What was the average number of votes given to each activity? ______
9. Name the 3-D shape. ______

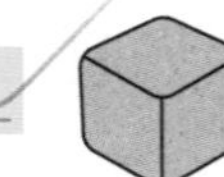

10. 6)656
    ______ R ______
11. Write $7\frac{1}{100}$ as a decimal fraction. ______
12. Write the time 40 minutes later than the time shown on the clock. ___ : ___

13. Find the perimeter of the shape. ______

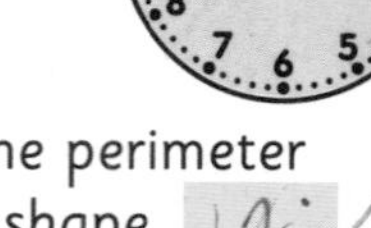


14. 52,385 + 10,000 = ______
15. 41 × 10 = ______

John is 1m 46cm tall. Jim is 45cm taller than John. Harry is 18cm smaller than John.

16. How tall is Harry? ______
17. What is the total height of the three boys? ______
18. What is the average height of the three boys? ______

/18

## Wednesday

1. Complete the sequence.
   3,250, 3,450, 3,650, ______
2. What is the value of the underlined digit: <u>5</u>2,336? ______
3. (6 ___ 3) + 12 = 30
4. 63 × 10 = ______
5. Write $4\frac{7}{100}$ as a decimal fraction. ______
6. 1·25 × 3 = ______
7. Write the time 40 minutes later than the time shown on the clock. [ ___ : ___ ]

8. 25,483 ÷ 10 = ______
9. 7km 250m × 4 = ______
10. Name the 2-D shape. ______
11. How many degrees in a right angle? ______
12. There are 3 **green** cubes and 1 **red** cube in a bag. What are the chances of picking a **red** cube? ___ in ___
13. €5 – €1·35 = ______
14. Tick ✓ the unit of measurement you would use to measure the amount of water in a bath. ☐ l ☐ ml
15. Which is heavier: 15g or 5kg? ______

16. There are 52 cards in a pack. How many cards are there in 12 packs? ______
17. There are 981 trees in a forest. $\frac{4}{9}$ of them are oak trees. How many are oak trees? ______
18. A driver left Sligo at [2:45]. He arrived in Galway 2 hours and 39 minutes later. At what time did he arrive in Galway? [ ___ : ___ ]

/18

## Thursday

1. 74 – ______ = 32
2. 
$$\begin{array}{r} 59{,}435 \\ +\ 18{,}176 \\ \hline \end{array}$$

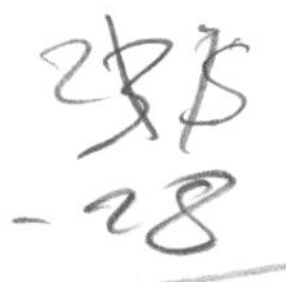

3. Complete the sequence.
   4,050, 4,100, 4,150, ______
4. Put in order of size, starting with the smallest: 17,145, 56,224, 9,030, 41,228.
   ______, ______, ______, ______
5. (7 × 4) + ______ = 35
6. Write the time 35 minutes later than the time shown on the clock. [ ___ : ___ ]

7. Name the 3-D shape. ______

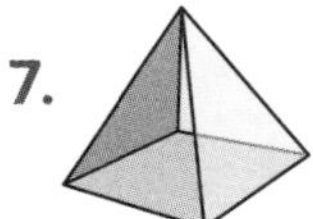

8. Show **A** turned 180°.

9. Write $5\frac{1}{10}$ as a decimal fraction. ______
10. The average of these four numbers is 7. What is the missing number? 7, 8, ______, 5
11. 22 × 20 = ______
12. How many sides has a rectangle? ______
13. How likely is it that next month will be November? ______
    (likely, unlikely, certain, impossible)
14. €4 – €1·45 = ______
15. What is the value of the underlined digit: 41,<u>3</u>69? ______

David had €50. He spent €17·95 in **Shop A** and €15·40 in **Shop B**. He put the rest of his money into the bank.

16. How much did David spend in **Shop A** and **Shop B** altogether? ______
17. How much did David put into the bank? ______
18. If he already had €76 in the bank, how much would he have in the bank now? ______

/18

See page 71 for test.

## Monday

1. What is the value of the underlined digit: 15,345? ______
2. (12 × 3) + 4 = ______
3. Complete the sequence. 98, 95, 92, ______
4. $2\frac{1}{2}$l = ______ ml
5. Find the average of the following amounts of money: €1·25, €4·30, €0·75. ______
6. 346 × 10 = ______
7. Write $\frac{1}{4}$ as a decimal fraction. ______
8. The factors of 4 are 1, ______ and 4.
9. Can this shape tesselate? ______
10.  What are the chances of throwing a 1 when rolling one die? ______ in ______
11. Name the angle. ______

12. Measure the line. ______ cm

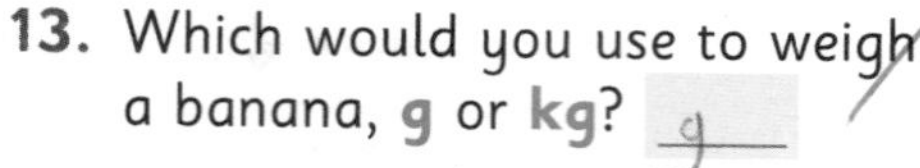

13. Which would you use to weigh a banana, **g** or **kg**? ______
14. Draw a line of symmetry in this triangle.

15. How many mugs measuring 500ml can be filled from a 3l kettle? ______
16. There are 165 straws in a box. How many straws are there in 10 boxes? ______
17. Ray had 60 oat bars. He gave 5 bars to each of his 6 children. How many bars has he left? ______
18. There are 34 cards in a packet. There are 12 packets in a box. How many cards are in the box? ______

/18

## Tuesday

1. Complete the sequence. 99, 92, 85, ______
2. Put in order of size, starting with the largest: 17,321, 17,523, 17,369, 17,850. ______, ______, ______, ______
3. (11 × 4) + 8 = ______
4. Write $\frac{1}{2}$ as a decimal fraction. ______
5. What type of triangle is this? ______

6. Measure the line. ______ cm
7. Would the distance from Cork to Dublin be measured in **cm**, **m** or **km**? ______
8. 136 ÷ 10 = ______
9. What are the chances of throwing a 3 when rolling one die? ______ in ______

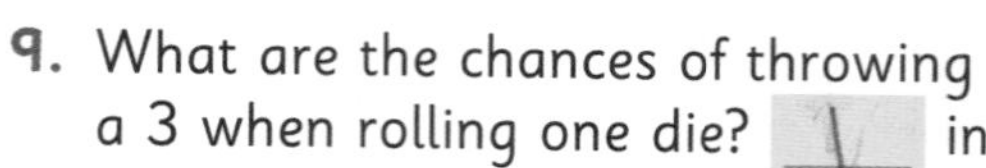

10. The factors of 8 are 1, 2, ______ and 8.

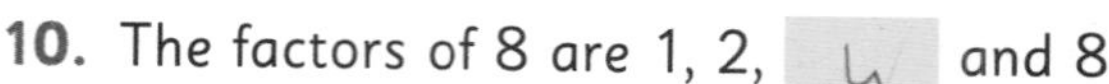

11. What time will it be in 15 minutes? ___ : ___

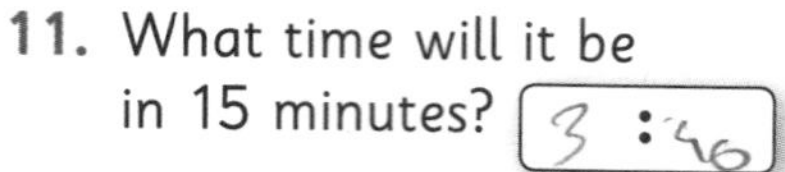

12. 3cm Find the perimeter of this shape. ______
13. €6·25 + €4·32 + €7·10 = ______

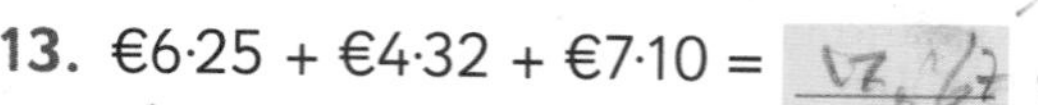

14. Find the average of the following weights: 12kg, 15kg, 17kg, 12kg. ______
15. How many faces has a cone? ______

16. If there was 20% off everything in the sale, how much would the jumper and trousers together cost in the sale? ______
17. How much would you save by buying the jacket and runners in the sale? ______
18. If there was 50% off the price of the jumper, how much would it cost? ______

/18

## Wednesday

1. Complete the sequence.
81, 74, 67, ____

2. What is the value of the underlined digit: 84,23<u>5</u>? ____

3. 72 ÷ ____ = 9

4. Name the 2-D shape. ____

5. 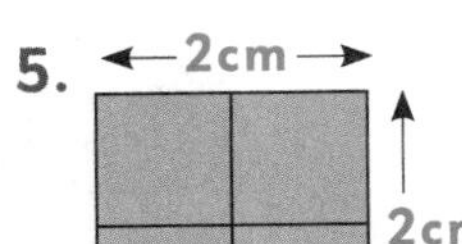

Find the area of this shape. ____

6. Write $\frac{3}{4}$ as a decimal fraction. ____

7. Round 5,256 to the nearest 1,000. ____

8. Write $\frac{27}{5}$ as a mixed number. ____

9. Name the angle. ____

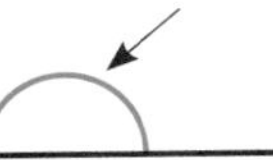

10. €8 – €2·25 = ____

11. 5)254
____ R ____

12. (7 × ____ ) + 4 = 46

13. What are the chances of throwing a 2 or a 6 when rolling one die? ____ in ____

14. What time will it be in 25 minutes? ____ : ____

15. 4l 650ml
× 8
____

16. One complete lap of the park is 1·5km. How many km will a person run if they complete four laps of the park? ____

17. $\frac{1}{2}$ of my money is €10·25. How much money do I have altogether? ____

18. How many minutes are there in $3\frac{1}{2}$ hours? ____

/18

## Thursday

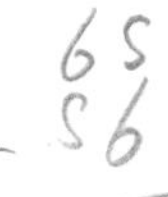

1. (9 × 8) – 14 = ____

2. The factors of 12 are 1, 2, 3, 4, ____ and 12.

3. Complete the sequence. 65, 56, 47, ____

4. What is the value of the underlined digit: 5<u>4</u>,125? ____

5. €8·52 – €2·21 = ____

6. Write $\frac{1}{100}$ as a decimal fraction. ____

7. What sort of angle is shown? ____

8. 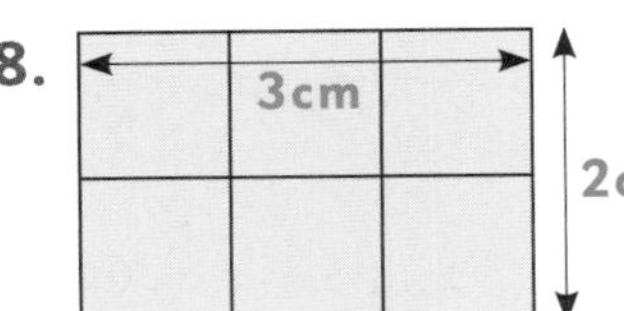

Find the area of this shape. ____

9. Find the perimeter of the above rectangle. ____

10. $0{\cdot}10 = \frac{1}{100}$. True or false? ____

11. This is the net of a ____

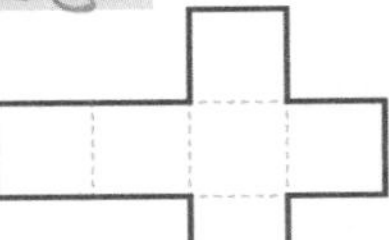

12. What are the chances of throwing a 4 when rolling one die? ____ in ____

13. There are ____ cm in a metre.

14. Find the average of the following amounts of money: €3·25, €2·40, €1·25. ____

15. 12·5 ÷ 10 = ____

This table shows the length of time spent at swimming each day for Conor and Claire.

| Days | Conor | Claire |
|---|---|---|
| Monday | 30 mins | 40 mins |
| Tuesday | 40 mins | 20 mins |
| Wednesday | 50 mins | 50 mins |
| Thursday | 25 mins | 30 mins |

16. How long did Conor spend swimming altogether? ____

17. How long did Claire spend swimming altogether? ____

18. What was the average time spent by Claire swimming over the four days? ____

/18

See page 72 for test.

Week 8

## Monday

1. Round 59,686 to the nearest 1,000. ______
2. Complete the sequence. 48, 39, 30, ______
3. 68 × 100 = ______
4. What is the value of the underlined digit: 54,0<u>7</u>5? ______
5. 

$$\begin{array}{r} 43{,}382 \\ -\ 28{,}396 \\ \hline \end{array}$$

6. How many degrees does the following angle measure?
☐ 0° ☐ 45° ☐ 90°

7. 2·45 × 2 = ______

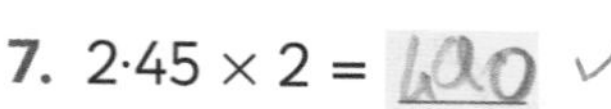

8. Find the average of the following weights: 63kg, 56kg, 44kg, 37kg. ______
9. (17 × 10) – 14 = ______
10. 643 ÷ 4 = ______ R ______
11. How many minutes in $\frac{2}{3}$ of an hour? ______
12. Name the 2-D shape. ______

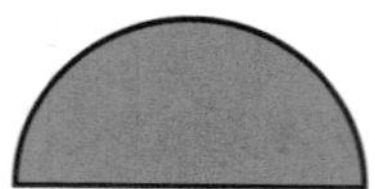

13. $\frac{1}{4}$ ______ $\frac{1}{2}$ (<, > or =)
14. €7 – €3·25 = ______
15. 5l 625ml ÷ 5 = ______
16. A biscuit factory produces 421 packets of biscuits every day. How many packets of biscuits will it produce in a week (5 days)? ______
17. A cinema has 258 seats. If the cinema was completely full for 9 showings of a film, how many less than 2,400 would this be? ______
18. Jason had a bar of chocolate. He ate 0·3 of it. What fraction of his chocolate bar had he left? ______

/18

## Tuesday

1. (6 × 8) + 12 = ______
2. Complete the sequence. 100, 88, 76, ______
3. What is the value of the underlined digit: <u>7</u>6,245? ______
4. How many minutes are there in $\frac{1}{4}$ of an hour? ______
5. How many degrees are there in a triangle? ______
6. 857 ÷ 7 = ______ R ______

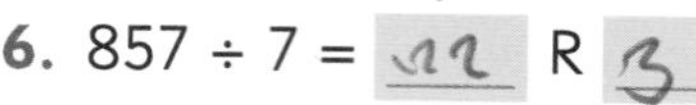

7. Write $\frac{1}{4}$ as a decimal fraction. ______
8. 1·56 × 10 = ______

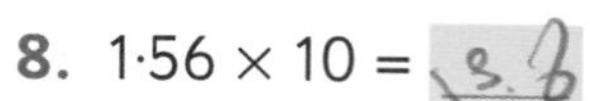

9. Name the angle. ______
10. Which would you use to measure the length of a maths book? ☐ cm ☐ m
11. What type of pyramid is shown? ______

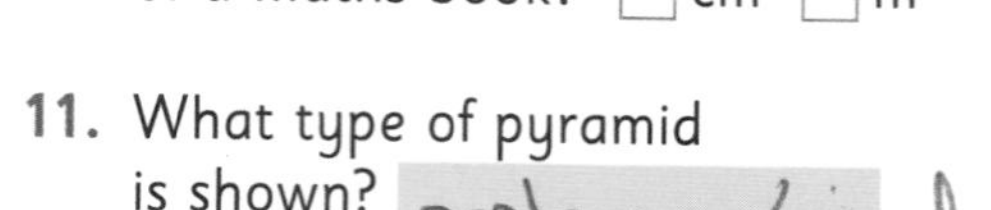

12. 52,386 + 10,000 = ______

13. Put in order of size, starting with the smallest: 52,428, 51,226, 52,963, 54,179.
______, ______, ______, ______
14. $\frac{3}{10}$ of 60 = ______

15. €8 – €2·65 = ______

16. How much do the jug and bucket hold altogether? ______ l ______ ml
17. How much more does the fish tank hold than the bucket? ______ l ______ ml
18. If the fish tank is only half full, how much more will it take to fill it? ______ l ______ ml

/18

## Wednesday

1. Complete the sequence. 71, 65, 59, ___
2. Which number is larger: (a) 51,225 or (b) 51,252? ___
3. Write the value of the missing angle. ___

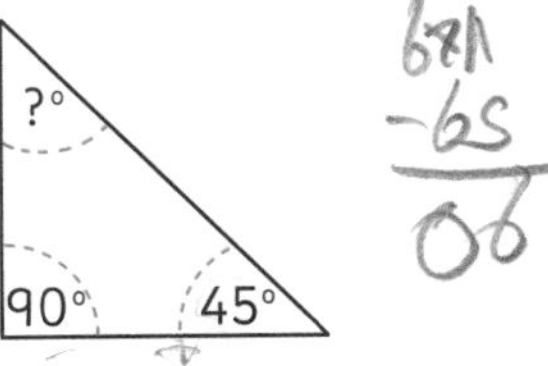


4. Round 65,428 to the nearest 1,000. ___
5. $\frac{1}{8}$ ___ $\frac{1}{2}$ (<, > or =)
6. 4 + 0·5 + 3·1 = ___
7. 11,463 + 10,000 = ___
8. How many minutes are there in $\frac{3}{4}$ of an hour? ___
9. €20 – €7·75 = ___
10. A rhombus has ___ line(s) of symmetry.
11. 786 ÷ 9 = ___ R ___
12. Find the average of the following temperatures: 17°, 20°, 23°, 22°, 13°. ___
13. Which would you use to measure the height of your principal?
    ☐ mm ☐ cm ☐ m
14. 14 × 20 = ___
15. Find the perimeter of the following shape. ___ 3cm
16. Patrick left home at 3:25. He arrived back at 6:10. How many hours and minutes was he away? ___
17. Maura had 200 stickers. Lisa had $\frac{1}{10}$ less than Maura. How many stickers had Lisa? ___
18. Five oranges cost €3·45. How much would 2 oranges cost? ___

/18

## Thursday

1. (7 × 8) – ___ = 42
2. Complete the sequence. 85, 76, 67, ___
3. What is the value of the underlined digit: 96,<u>3</u>28? ___
4. Put in order of size, starting with the smallest:
   81,225, 81,524, 81,325, 81,428.
   ___, ___, ___, ___
5. Measure the line. ___ cm
6. How many degrees are there in each angle of an equilateral triangle? ___

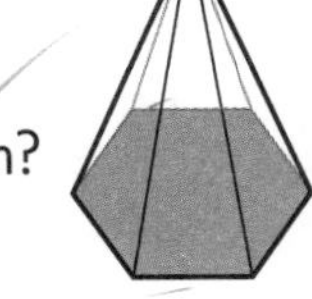

7. 8 + 1·2 + 0·1 = ___
8. What type of pyramid is shown? ___
9. How many minutes in $\frac{2}{5}$ of an hour? ___
10. $\frac{1}{10}$ ___ $\frac{1}{2}$ (>, < or =)
11. Round 40,555 to the nearest 1,000. ___
12. What are the chances of throwing a 2 or a 4 when rolling one die? ___ in ___

13. 453 ÷ 7 = ___ R ___
14. Write $\frac{7}{100}$ as a decimal fraction. ___
15. 5·326km × 8 = ___

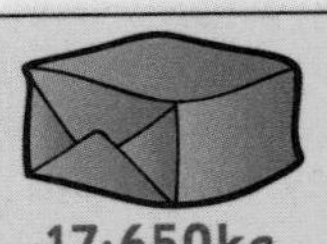

16. What is the total weight of the three boxes? ___
17. What is the average weight of each box? ___
18. If the trolley could only carry 50kg on it, by how much are the three boxes together overweight? ___

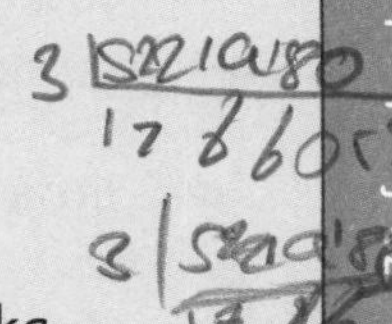

/18

See page 73 for test.

Week 9

## Monday

1. (14 – ____ ) × 2 = 20
2. Complete the sequence. 0·1, 0·2, 0·3, ____
3. The factors of 9 are ____, ____ and ____.
4. This is an ________ triangle.

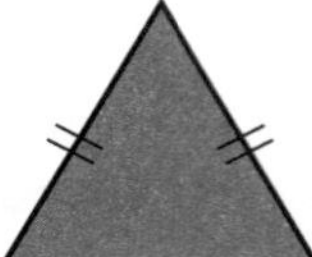

5. How many degrees are there in the above triangle? ____
6. Write these numbers from largest to smallest: 17,250, 1,725, 11,250.
   ____, ____, ____
7. 2·35 × 100 = ____
8. 4·36 + 1·49 = ____
9. How many surfaces has a triangular prism? ____
10. 430 ÷ 10 = ____

11. What are the chances of rolling an even number on a die? ____ in ____
12. Round 19,625 to the nearest 1,000. ____
13. Draw 8:30 on the clock.

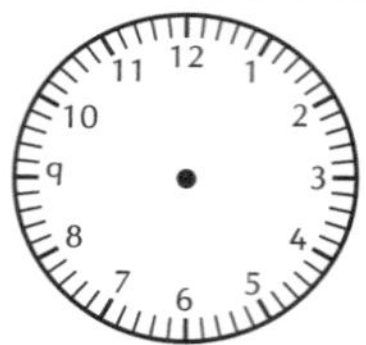


14. $\frac{3}{4}$ ____ $\frac{1}{8}$ (<, > or =)
15. Find the perimeter of the triangle. ____

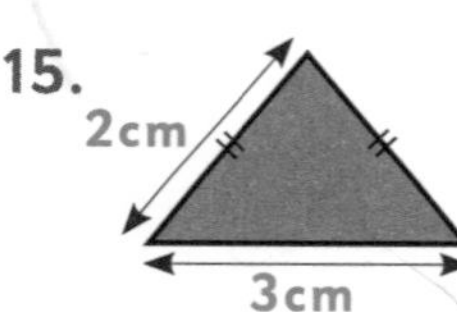


16. $\frac{1}{4}$ of Patricia's money is €7·75. How much money has Patricia? ____
17. Bernard watched a film on television from 4:15 to 5:55. He also watched a documentary that lasted for 45 minutes. How long did he spend watching television altogether? ____ hrs ____ mins
18. Mark was having a birthday party. There were eight people including himself at the party. He wanted to give each person 500ml of lemonade. How many litres would he have to buy in total? ____

/18

## Tuesday

1. Complete the sequence. 0·2, 0·4, 0·6, ____
2. What is the value of the underlined digit: 45,34<u>8</u>? ____
3. Which number is larger: (a) 3,450 or (b) 3,405? ____
4. 30% of 210 = ____
5. Turn this shape 90° clockwise and draw.

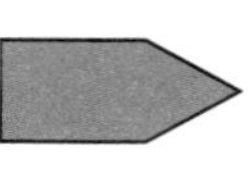

6. The factors of 8 are ____, ____, ____ and ____.
7. Find the value of the missing angle. ____

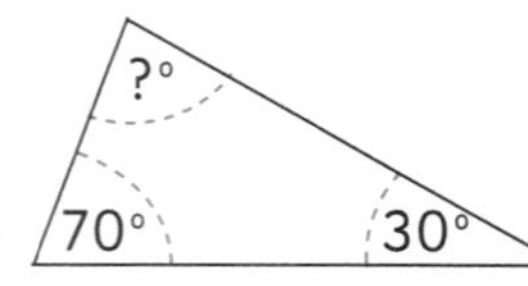


8. Round 45,235 to the nearest 100. ____
9. Which would you use to measure the weight of a feather, g or kg? ____
10. 750 ÷ 10 = ____
11. $\frac{3}{5} > \frac{4}{10}$. True or false? ____
12. 23·5 + 12·2 = ____
13. This is the net of a ________.

14. (4 × 5) + (3 × 3) = ____

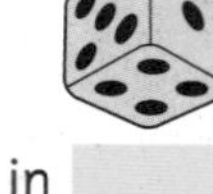

15. What are the chances of rolling an odd number on a die? ____ in ____

John rang a pizzeria to order a pizza. They offer five toppings for pizzas: ham, mushrooms, pineapples, tomatoes and peppers. John ordered a pizza with ham and mushrooms. Unfortunately, the server only wrote down that he wanted 2 toppings but didn't write down what they were.

16. How likely is it that John will get the two toppings he hoped for? ____ in ____
17. How likely is it that John will get two toppings he didn't ask for? ____ in ____
18. If John ordered two toppings out of five, what fraction is this? ____

/18

## Wednesday

1. Complete the sequence. 0·3, 0·6, 0·9, ____

2.
$$\begin{array}{r} 41{,}234 \\ +\ 21{,}113 \\ \hline \end{array}$$

3. Find the perimeter of the triangle. ____

3cm

4cm

4. Which is better value for money: (a) 5 bars at €2·90 or (b) 7 bars at €3·50? ____

5. €9·72 – €4·31 = ____

6. Find the missing angle in the triangle. ____

?°

60°

50°

7. 620 ÷ 10 = ____

8. 4·55 × 2 = ____

9. Draw 7:10 on the clock.

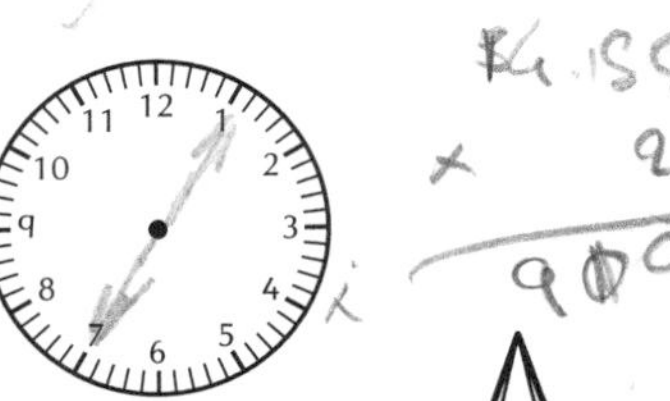

10. What is the value of the underlined digit: 85,<u>4</u>69? ____

11. A square pyramid has ____ faces.

12. The factors of 26 are ____, ____, ____ and ____.

13. 89,425 – 300 = ____

14. 5l 450ml = ____ml

15. Write $\frac{13}{100}$ as a decimal fraction. ____

16. Michaela eats 550g of vegetables every day. How many kilogrammes of vegetables does she eat in a full week? ____

17. A glass holds 450ml. If Ciara opens a litre carton of orange juice and pours a full glass, how much orange juice will be left in the carton? ____

18. A milkman delivers 5·845l of milk to a family every week. What is the average amount of milk the family uses per day? ____

/18

## Thursday

1. (22 + ____) – 11 = 17

2. 830 ÷ 10 = ____

3. 4,640 + 1,000 = ____

4. 7·36 + 2·1 = ____

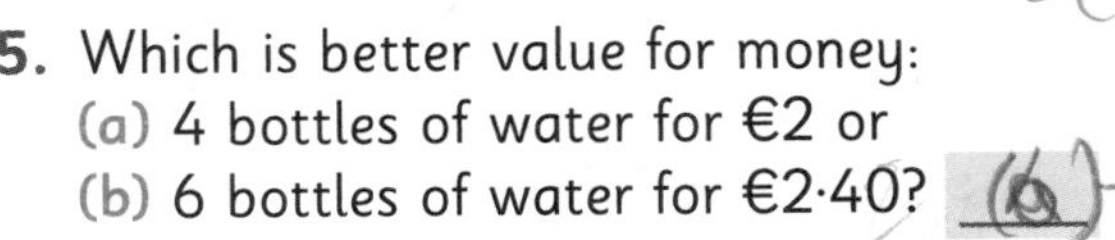

5. Which is better value for money: (a) 4 bottles of water for €2 or (b) 6 bottles of water for €2·40? ____

6. Which of the following is a multiple of 8: 12, 32 or 49? ____

7. Write these numbers from smallest to largest: 63,120, 6,312, 16,320.

____, ____, ____

8.
$$\begin{array}{r} 21{,}456 \\ -\ 19{,}679 \\ \hline \end{array}$$

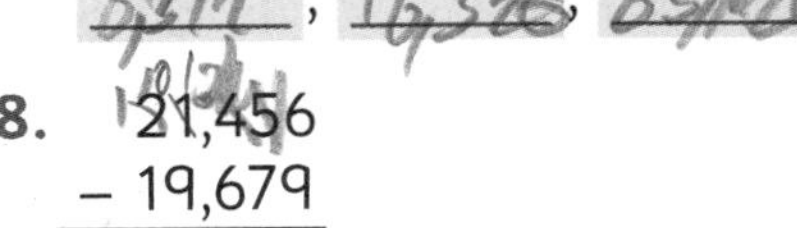

9. How many degrees are there in a square? ____

10. (7 × 6) – (4 × 5) = ____

11. How many edges has a cuboid? ____

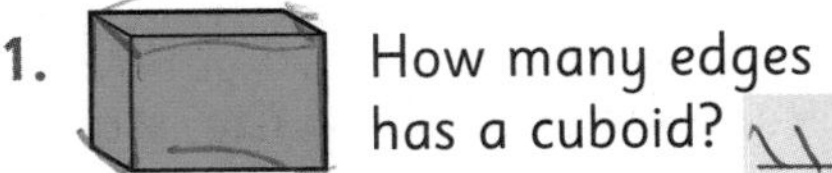

12. Write the time 25 minutes later than the time shown on the clock. ____

13. 3·5km = ____m

14. Write $\frac{19}{100}$ as a decimal fraction. ____

15. What are the chances of throwing a multiple of 2 on one die? ____ in ____

A car holds 63 litres of petrol when it is full. It had 49·5l of petrol in it when entering the petrol station.

16. How much petrol did it take to fill the car's tank? ____

17. If petrol costs 90c per litre, how much would 10l cost? ____

18. How much would it cost to put 63l of petrol into the car? ____

/18

See page 74 for test.

## Monday

1. 96 – 32 = ____
2. 710 ÷ 100 = ____

3. This is the net of a ____
4. Write the time 50 minutes later than the time shown on the clock. ____ : ____

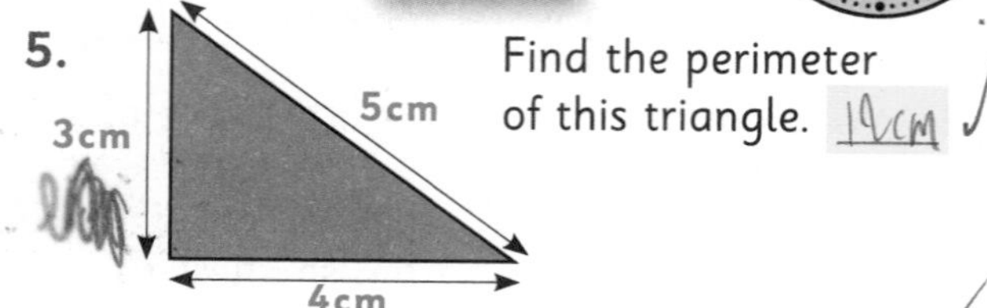


5. Find the perimeter of this triangle. ____
6. The triangle above is a ____ triangle.
7. Complete the sequence. 1·6, 1·8, 2·0, ____
8. What is the value of the underlined digits: <u>45</u>,825? ____
9. What are the chances of landing on heads when you toss one coin? ____ in ____
10. 10 pencils cost €4. How much would one pencil cost? ____
11. Put these fractions in order of size, starting with the largest: $\frac{3}{4}$, $\frac{1}{4}$, $\frac{1}{2}$. ____, ____, ____
12. Which of these angles is most likely to be 20°? ____

(a) (b) (c)

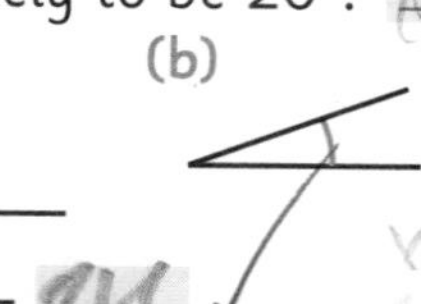

13. 12m × 7 = ____
14. What is the perimeter of a square with a side of 4cm? ____

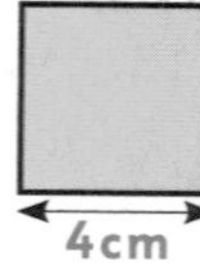


15. $\frac{3}{4} + \frac{1}{12} =$ ____
16. May had 16 boxes with 20 tissues in each box. How many tissues had May altogether? ____
17. It takes 26 biscuits to fill a box. How many boxes can be filled with 390 biscuits? ____
18. A gardener plants flowers with 35 flowers in each row. How many rows can he sow with 630 flowers? ____

/18

## Tuesday

1. Complete the sequence. 1·4, 1·6, 1·8, ____
2. What is the value of the underlined digits: 45,<u>320</u>? ____
3. 850 ÷ 100 = ____
4. How much would 1 orange cost if 7 oranges cost €3·85? ____
5. (9 × 6) – (4 × 8) = ____
6. How many faces has a pentagonal prism? ____

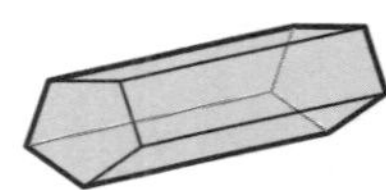

7. Can this shape tesselate? ____
8. Round 81,345 to the nearest 1,000. ____
9. What are the chances of landing on tails when you toss one coin? ____ in ____
10. Put these fractions in order of size, starting with the smallest: $\frac{1}{4}$, $\frac{1}{8}$, $\frac{5}{8}$, $\frac{1}{2}$. ____, ____, ____, ____
11. How many lines of symmetry has this shape? ____

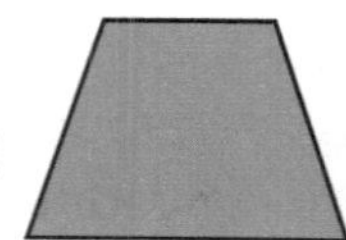

12. (4 × 5) + ____ = 28
13. Write the number fifty-six thousand three hundred and five. ____
14. If one glass holds 300ml of water, how much water would 9 glasses hold? ____ l

15. 3·25 + 1·6 = ____

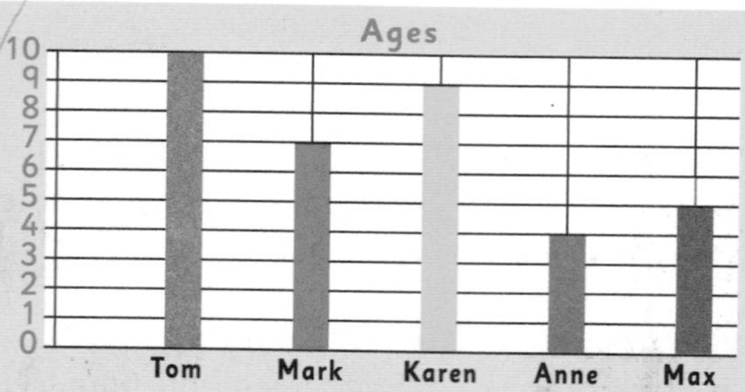


16. What is the average age of the children? ____
17. How many children are older than the average? ____
18. Which child has the same age as the average age? ____

/18

## Wednesday

1. Complete the sequence. 2·4, 2·2, 2·0, ____

2. 
$$\begin{array}{r} 82{,}105 \\ -\ 35{,}466 \\ \hline \end{array}$$

3. Find the perimeter of this shape. ____

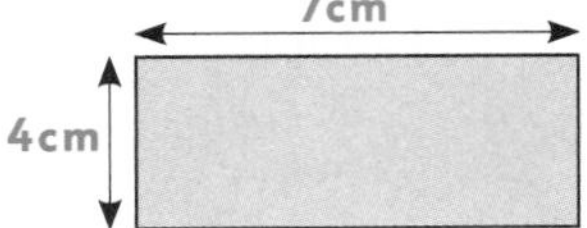


4. Put these fractions in order of size, starting with the largest: $\frac{3}{8}$, $\frac{1}{4}$, $\frac{1}{2}$, $\frac{3}{4}$.
____, ____, ____, ____

5. This is an ____ triangle.

6. What are the outcomes of tossing two coins?
(a) heads and ____; (b) heads and ____;
(c) tails and ____.

7. 962 ÷ 7 = ____ R ____

8. If 500ml of orange juice costs €1·10, how much would 2l of orange juice cost? ____

9. 17·3 + 22·8 = ____

10. 0·75kg + ____ = 2·25kg

11. $\frac{2}{5}$ of a number is 22.
Whole number = ____

12. A pentagonal prism has ____ edges.

13. Which would you use to measure the length of a rubber? ☐ mm ☐ m

14. There are ____ ° in a full rotation.

15. (7 × 6) – (4 × 3) = ____

16. 260 children and 20 adults were going on a school tour. If each bus holds 60 people, how many buses will they need to bring everyone on tour? ____

17. Mary had €765. She spent $\frac{3}{5}$ of it. How much had she left? ____

18. The sides of an equilateral triangle add up to 54cm. What is the length of each side? ____

/18

## Thursday

1. (6 × 7) – ____ = 34

2. To measure the capacity of a glass, would you use ml or l? ____

3. Complete the sequence. 3·5, 3·7, 3·9, ____

4. What is the value of the underlined digits: 8<u>5,6</u>35? ____

5. This is a ____ triangle.

6. If 9 bars of chocolate cost €1·08, how much would 6 bars cost? ____

| Mon | Tue | Wed | Thurs | Fri |
|---|---|---|---|---|
| 17°C | 18°C | 4°C | 16°C | 20°C |

7. How many days will be sunny? ____

8. How likely is it that you will get wet on Thursday? ____
(likely, unlikely, certain, impossible)

9. What is the average temperature of the two hottest days? ____ °C

10. Find the average temperature of the five days. ____ °C

11. A straight angle is ____ °.

12. How many faces has a cylinder? ____

13. This is a ____.

14. 4·22 × 10 = ____

15. $\frac{1}{2}$ of 1·256kg = ____

John F. Kennedy was born in May 1917 and died in November 1963. He became president in January 1961.

16. How old was John when he died? ____

17. How old was he when he became president? (Be careful of the months!) ____

18. If he had lived until December 2002, at what age would he have died? ____

/18

See page 75 for test.

## Monday

1. Complete the sequence. $\frac{1}{4}$, $\frac{1}{2}$, $\frac{3}{4}$, ____
2. Write $\frac{19}{6}$ as a mixed number. ____
3. Put in order of size, starting with the smallest: 0·45, 0·1, 1·3, 0·5.
   ____, ____, ____, ____
4. If 9 copybooks cost €5·85, how much would one copybook cost? ____
5. 58,548 + 10,000 = ____
6. Name the 3-D shape. ____

7. Find the value of the missing angle. ____

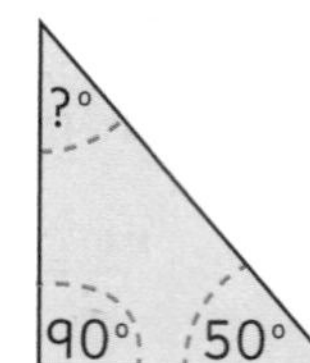

8. $\frac{3}{9}$ of 27 = ____
9. Which angle is likely to be 60°? ____
   (a) (b) (c)

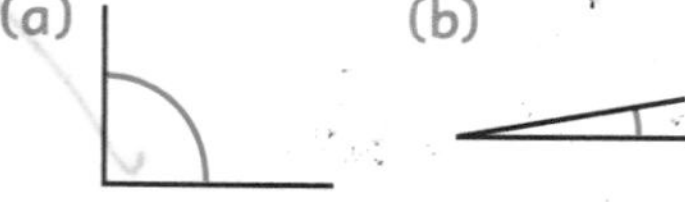

10. Is 1·41 nearer to 1 or 2? ____
11. The angles in an equilateral triangle are all ____ (equal/unequal).
12. Round 251 to the nearest 100. ____

13. Write $\frac{27}{100}$ as a decimal fraction. ____
14. Which number is a multiple of 7: 12, 27 or 35? ____
15. Write the time 55 minutes later than the time shown on the clock. ____

16. Jane had €10. She spent €3. What fraction of her money did she spend? ____
17. Sarah had 12 stickers. She gave 5 of them to Kevin. What fraction of her stickers had she left? ____
18. Molly had 24 apples. She had to throw $\frac{1}{3}$ of them away as they were rotten. How many had she left? ____

/18

## Tuesday

1. Is 4·55 nearer to 4 or 5? ____

2. 2,640 – 110 = ____
3. 25·3 + 58·2 = ____
4. Complete the sequence. $\frac{1}{8}$, $\frac{3}{8}$, $\frac{5}{8}$, ____
5. Write $\frac{24}{5}$ as a mixed number. ____
6. Draw 10:05 on the clock.

7. Find the perimeter of the triangle. ____

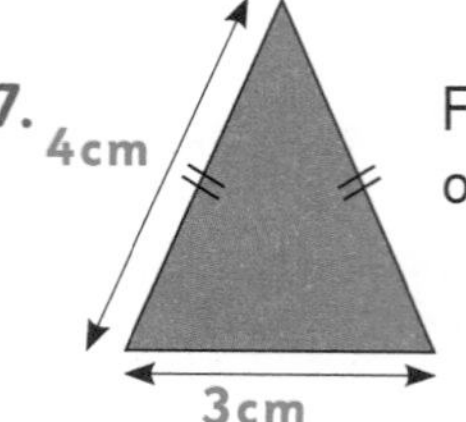

8. Turn this shape 180° and draw.

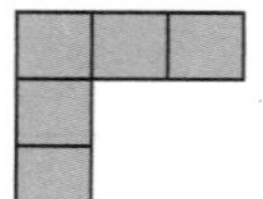

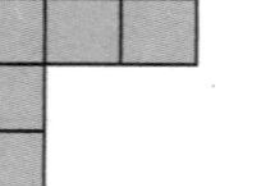

9. $\frac{2}{10} = \frac{\square}{100}$

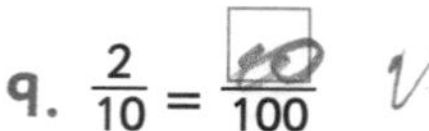

10. A hexagonal prism has ____ faces.
11. $\frac{3}{8}$ of 32 = ____
12. Round 45,638 to the nearest 100. ____
13. What are the chances of picking a heart card from a deck of cards (52 cards)? ____ in ____

14. $\frac{2}{3}$ ____ $\frac{1}{2}$ (>, < or =)

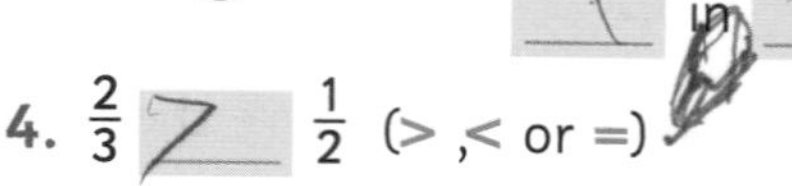

15. A rhombus has ____ sides.

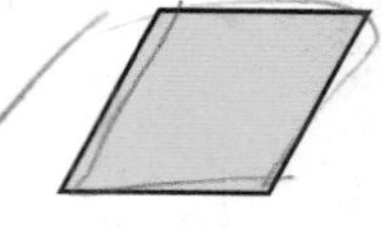

Henry is 1·25m tall.
Mark is 0·05m taller than Henry.
Jack is 0·23m taller than Henry.
If Tina were 0·20m taller, she would be 0·10m taller than Henry.

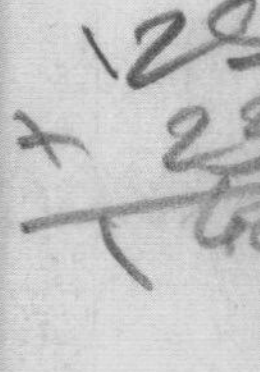

Write the correct height under each child's name.

| 16. Mark | 17. Jack | 18. Tina |
|---|---|---|
| | | |

/18

## Wednesday

1. Complete the sequence. $\frac{1}{8}$, $\frac{1}{4}$, $\frac{3}{8}$, $\frac{1}{2}$, ____
2. Write $\frac{17}{8}$ as a mixed number. ____
3. Find $\frac{2}{3}$ of 42. ____
4. Name the 2-D shape. ____

5. How many hours and minutes from 4:32 to 6:45?
   ____ hours ____ minutes
6. Put in order of size, starting with the largest: 0·3, 1·8, 0·45, 0·9.
   ____, ____, ____, ____.
7. Name the angle. ____
8. Find the value of the missing angle. ____

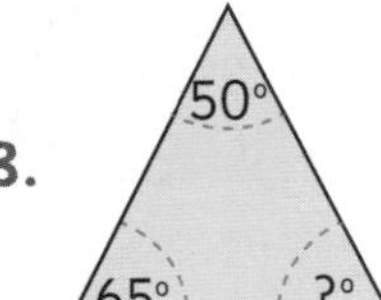


9. 1·305kg = ____ g
10. Find the average of the following amounts: €3·65, €2·50, €1·80, €2, €3·10. ____
11. What are the chances of picking a club card from a pack of cards (52 cards)?
    ____ in ____
12. $\frac{7}{8}$ ____ $\frac{1}{2}$ (>, < or =)
13. 48·9 + 17·6 = ____
14. Which is better value for money? ____
    (a) 7 pens for €1·68 or (b) 9 pens for €2·25
15. Is 1·65 nearer to 1 or 2? ____
16. $\frac{5}{8}$ of the pupils in a school are girls. If there are 96 pupils in the school, how many are girls? ____
17. A bus can carry 30 passengers. How many buses are needed to carry 270 passengers? ____
18. James has 7 bags with 8 plums in each bag. He also has 10 loose plums. How many plums has he altogether? ____

/18

## Thursday

1. $\frac{3}{4}$ of 28 = ____
2. Complete the sequence. $\frac{1}{10}$, $\frac{1}{5}$, $\frac{3}{10}$, ____
3. Round 45,269 to the nearest 10. ____

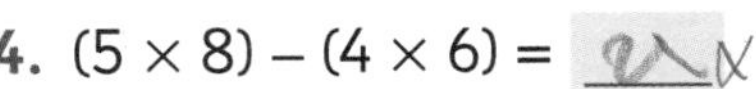

4. (5 × 8) – (4 × 6) = ____
5. Write $\frac{30}{7}$ as a mixed number. ____
6. What are the chances of picking a spade from a pack of cards (52 cards)? ____ in ____

7. $\frac{1}{4} = \frac{\square}{8}$
8. $\frac{5}{8}$ of 56 = ____
9. The factors of 15 are ____, ____, ____ and ____.
10. How many faces has a hexagonal pyramid? ____

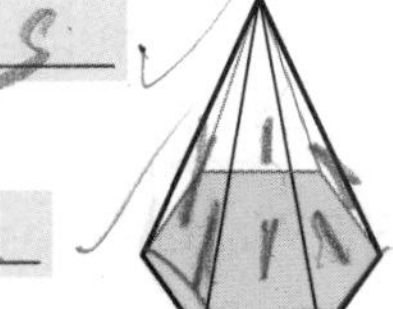

11. How many containers that can hold 500g could I fill from a bag of sugar weighing 3kg? ____
12. €20 – €4·45 = ____
13. Rotate the shape 270° clockwise and draw.

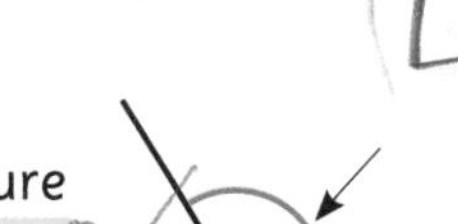

14. Does this angle measure 20°, 90° or 120°? ____
15. 8:35 = ____ minutes to ____

Andrew can cycle 6km in 15 minutes.
Shane can cycle 11km in 30 minutes.

16. How far will Andrew cycle in an hour? ____
17. How far will Shane cycle in an hour? ____
18. How long would it take Shane to cycle 33km?
    ____ hour(s) ____ minute(s)

/18

See page 76 for test.

## Monday

1. 85 + ____ = 120
2. Complete the sequence.
   14, 16, 19, 23, ____
3. 5:50 = ____ minutes to ____
4. This is the net of a ____________.
5. 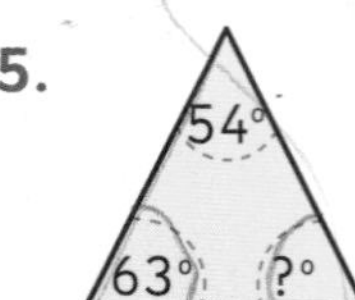
   
   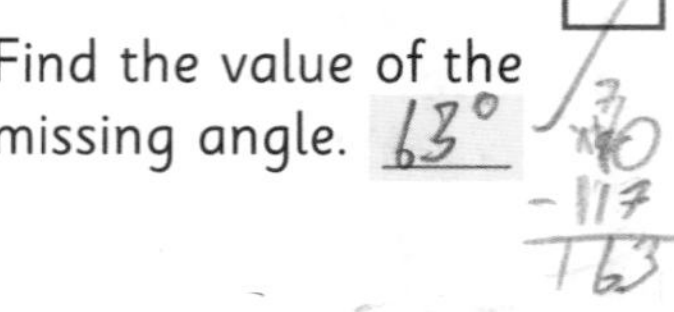
   Find the value of the missing angle. ____
6. Name the triangle above. ____________
7. $(7 \times 6) + (4 \times 2) =$ ____
8. In the number 42,360, what does the 4 represent? ____
9. Write $2\frac{1}{2}$ as an improper fraction. ____
10. 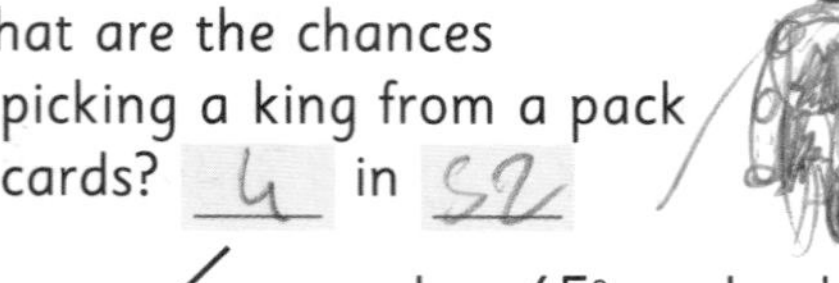
    What are the chances of picking a king from a pack of cards? ____ in ____
11. 

    Is a 45° angle obtuse or acute? ____
12. Find the whole amount if $\frac{1}{4}$ = €3. ____
13. $\frac{2}{3} - \frac{1}{9} =$ ____
14. Name the shape.
    ____________
15. 40% = 0·45.
    True or false? ____
    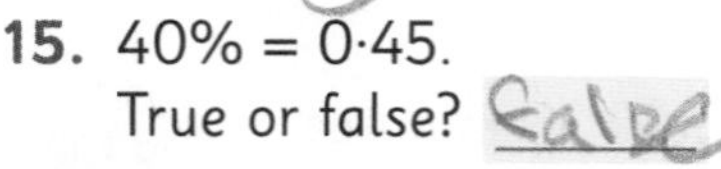
16. There are 500 pupils in a school. 0·57 of them are boys. What fraction of the pupils are girls? ____
17. 0·7 of the flowers in a garden are roses. If there are 686 roses in the garden, how many flowers are there in the garden altogether? ____
18. The sum of two numbers is 245. If one of the numbers is 137, what is the second number? ____

/18

## Tuesday

1. Complete the sequence. 1, 3, 7, 13, ____
2. Name the 2-D shape.
   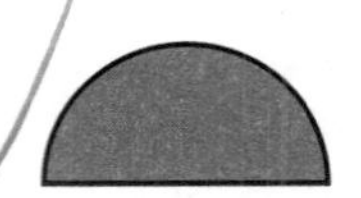
   ____________
3. Round 5,612 to the nearest 10. ____
4. What are the chances of picking a queen from a pack of cards? ____ in ____
5. Write $2\frac{3}{100}$ as a decimal number. ____
6. 1:20 = ____ minutes past ____
7. 7·35kg – 1·23kg = ____
8. The average of four numbers is 22. If three of the numbers are 17, 25 and 20, what is the fourth number? ____
   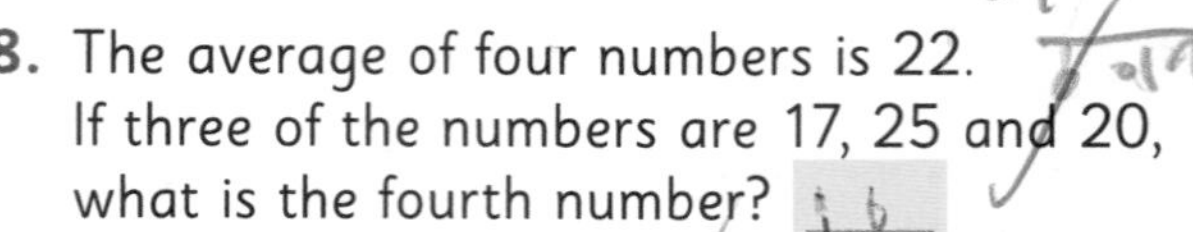
9. The angles in a trapezium add up to ____°.
10. $530 \times 20 =$ ____
    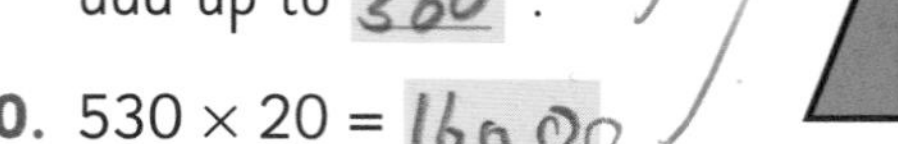
11. The factors of 18 are ____, ____, ____, ____, ____ and ____.
    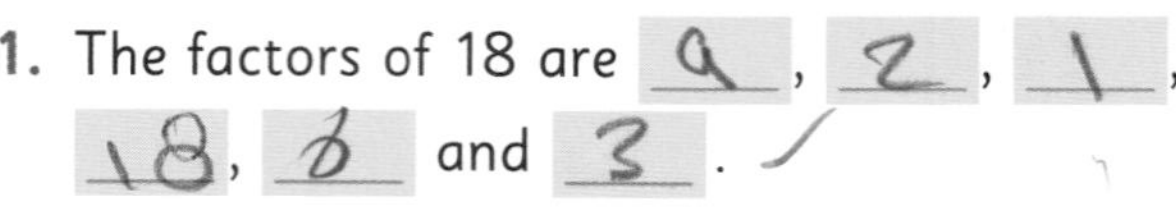
12. $\frac{3}{5}$ of 45 = ____
13. If one side of a square measures 5cm, what is the perimeter of the square? ____
    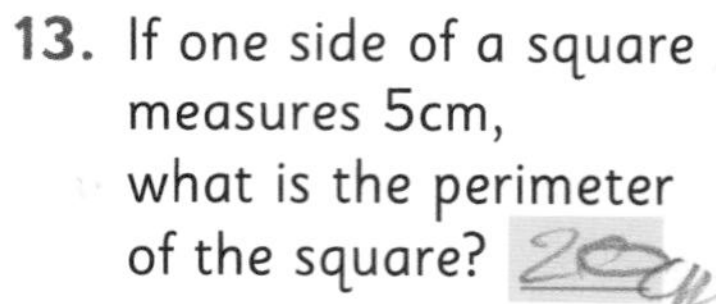
    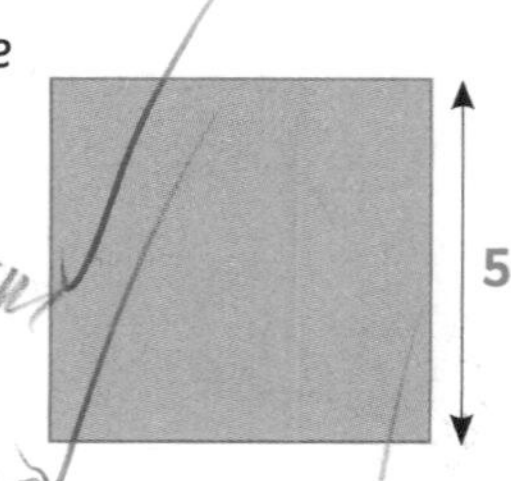
    
14. What is the area of the square? ____
15. $\frac{1}{2}$ = 50%. True or false? ____

Jack had 10 litres of petrol in his lawnmower. He used 3 litres mowing the lawn.

16. What fraction of the petrol did he use mowing the lawn? ____
17. Write the decimal amount that was left in the lawnmower. ____
18. If he used 3·5l more petrol, how many litres would have been left in the tank then? ____

/18

## Wednesday

1. 2,000 + 420 + 9 = ____
2. 12 × 8 = ____
3. 1·386l ÷ 6 = ____
4. 
$$\begin{array}{r} 21{,}129 \\ +\ 16{,}492 \\ \hline \end{array}$$
5. $\frac{1}{2} + \frac{3}{8} =$ ____
6. 3)61
   ____ R ____
7. 25 past 2 = ____ : ____
8. Complete the sequence. 2, 3, 6, 11, ____
9. Draw a right angle.

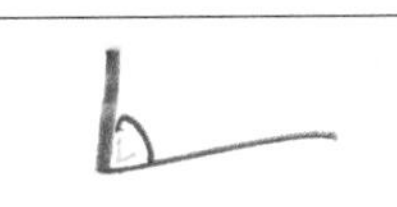

10.  What are the chances of picking a jack from a pack of cards? ____ in ____
11. Draw the line(s) of symmetry on this trapezium.

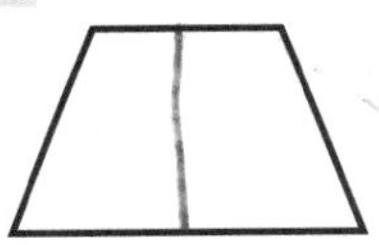

12. Find the whole number if $\frac{1}{8} = 7$. ____
13. €21 – €4·45 = ____
14. 0·2 = 25%. True or false? ____
15. This is the net of a ____ ____.

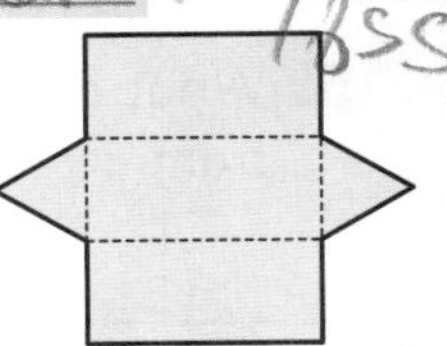

16. Jason lives 6km from the school. His friend Alan lives 1·36km nearer than that to the school. How far does Alan live from the school? ____
17. A field has 47 rows of turnips with 125 turnips in each row. How many turnips altogether are in the field? ____
18. One piece of wood is $3\frac{1}{2}$m long. Another piece of wood is 1·20m long. What is the total length of the two pieces of wood? ____

/18

## Thursday

1. Complete the sequence. 63, 61, 58, 54, ____
2. 45 ÷ ____ = 9
3. What is the value of the 2 in 42,345? ____

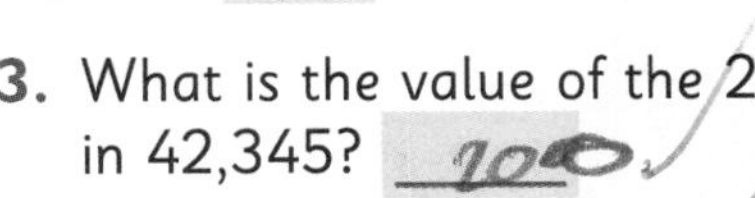

4. Find $\frac{2}{3}$ of 123. ____

5. What are the chances of picking a pentagon from the jar? ____ in ____

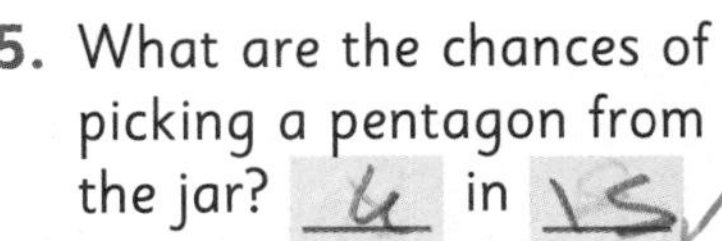

6. What are the chances of picking a triangle from the jar? ____ in ____
7. What are the chances of picking a trapezium from the jar? ____ in ____

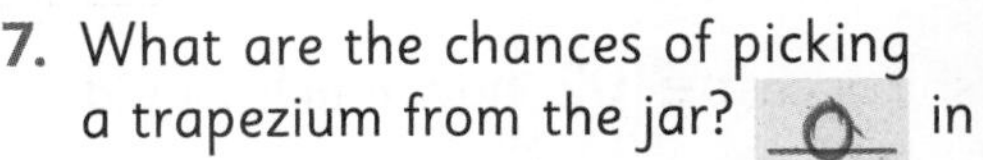

8. Which shape has the best chance of being picked? ____

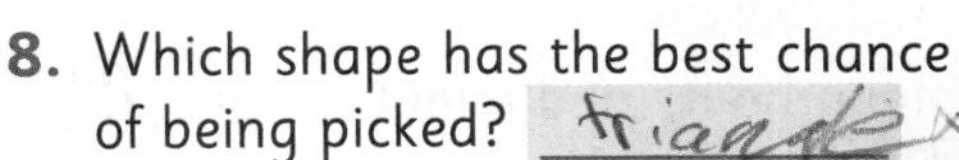

9. 10 minutes to 7 = ____ : ____

10. Write 25% as a decimal fraction. ____
11. 4 × ____ → 10 + 10

12. Which unit of measurement would be better to measure the weight of a bicycle: (a) grammes or (b) kilogrammes? ____
13. The first five multiples of 6 are 6, 12, 18, ____ and ____.

14. 680 ÷ 100 = ____
15. This is the net of a ____.

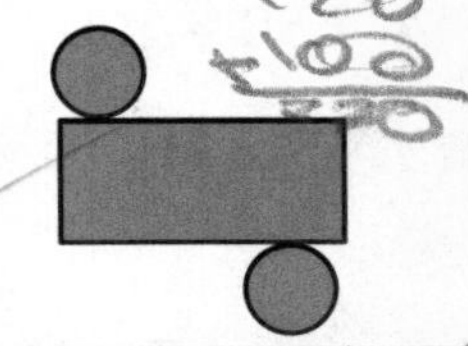

A cake shop sold 120 buns on Monday, 100 buns on Tuesday and 150 buns on Wednesday.

16. How many buns did they sell altogether over the three days? ____
17. If they had made 175 buns on Wednesday, how many buns did they not sell? ____
18. The amount of buns they sold on Wednesday was $\frac{2}{3}$ of the amount they sold on Thursday. How many did they sell on Thursday? ____

/18

See page 77 for test.

## Monday

1. Complete the sequence.
   1·1, 1·15, 1·2, 1·25, ____
2. Would a square and a rectangle together tessellate? ____
3. $\frac{3}{8} + \frac{1}{8} =$ ____
4. This is the net of a ____.
5. 1,200 × 3 = ____
6. What are the chances of picking a face card (jack, queen or king) from a pack of cards? ____ in ____
7. Is this shape symmetrical? ____
8. If 8 shirts cost €102, how much would one shirt cost? ____
9. How many hours and minutes from 2:45 to 5:05? ____ hours ____ minutes
10. The factors of 30 are ____, ____, ____, ____, ____, ____, ____ and ____.
11. Each angle of a square is ____°.
12. Find the value of the missing angle. ____
    52° 71° ?°
13. If one bag of flour holds 450g, how much will 7 bags hold? ____
14. 550 ÷ 100 = ____
15. (7 × 7) – (9 × 3) = ____

16. A baker had 60 cupcakes. She sold 0·3 of them. How many cupcakes did she sell? ____
17. Fiona has €29·70. Joe has 0·8 of that amount. How much money has Joe? ____
18. Two children each ate $\frac{1}{4}$ of a pizza. What fraction of the pizza did they eat altogether? ____

/18

## Tuesday

1. Find $\frac{2}{5}$ of 45. ____
2. Find the perimeter of the octagon with 2cm sides. ____

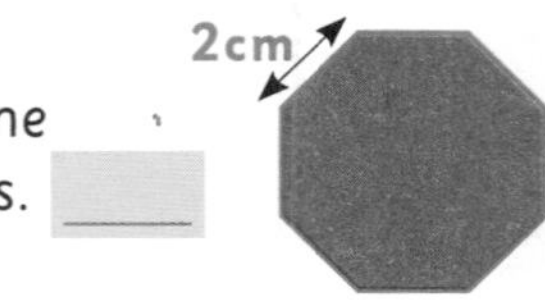


3. 35 + ____ = 105
4. How much liquid must be added to 670ml to make 1 litre? ____
5. What is the value of the 7 in 735? ____
6. Complete the sequence.
   2, 2·05, 2·1, 2·15, ____
7. $\frac{1}{3} + \frac{2}{9} =$ ____
8. 1,850 ÷ 100 = ____

9. Write the time 22 minutes later than the time shown on the clock. ____ : ____

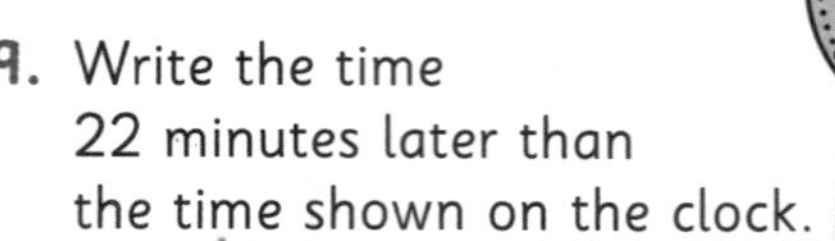

10. This is the net of a ____ ____.

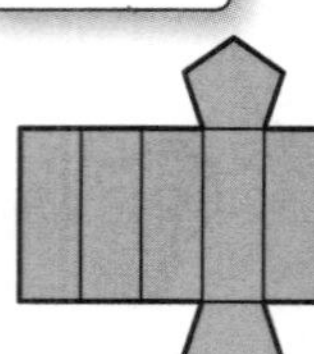

11. The angles in this quadrilateral add up to ____°.
    quadrilateral
12. 0·6 = ____%
13. 17 + ____ = 40
14. 5 × ____ → 62 – 7
15. What are the chances of picking a 10 from a pack of cards? ____ in ____

A square running track has a perimeter of 400m.

16. What length is each side? ____
17. James ran 7 laps of the track. How far did he run? ____
18. How many times would a runner have to run around the track to complete 1km? ____

/18

## Wednesday

1. Complete the sequence.
   0·2, 0·25, 0·3, 0·35, ____

2. Find the third angle in a triangle if the other two angles are 70° and 50°. ____°

3. This is the net of a ____________

4. Round 8,456 to the nearest 100. ____

5. Which of the following numbers is a factor of 36: 7, 14 or 18? ____

6. If one t-shirt costs €7·85, how much would 5 t-shirts cost? ____

7. 5:30 = ____ past ____

8. 780 ÷ 100 = ____

9. 550g + 650g = ____ kg
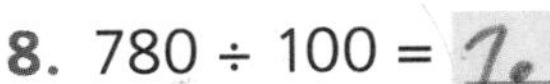

10. 1·345l = ____ ml
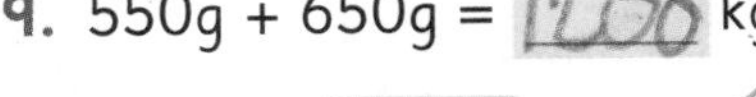

11.  What are the chances of picking a 3 from a pack of cards?
    ____ in ____

12. What is the value of $x$? ____

13. Name the type of triangle above.
    ____________

14. $\frac{3}{10} + \frac{2}{5} =$ ____
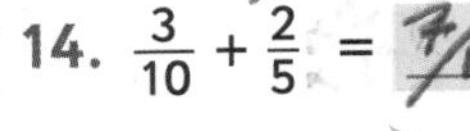

15. 0·9 = ____ %

16. A room is 6m long and 4m wide. How much will it cost to carpet the room at €10 per square metre? (Hint! Find the area.) ____

17. The cost of rope is €1·40 per 500cm. How much would 2·5m of rope cost? ____

18. John drank 16·1l of water in a week. What was the average amount he drank per day? ____

/18

## Thursday

1. 2·05l = ____ ml

2. 43 – ____ = 28

3. $\frac{1}{3} + \frac{1}{6} =$ ____
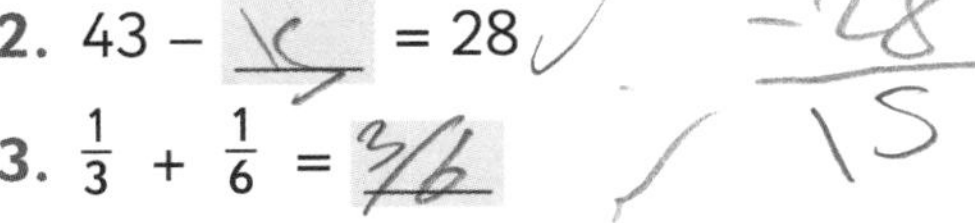

4. Complete the sequence.
   5·1, 5·3, 5·5, 5·7, ____

5. What fraction of this shape is shaded? ____
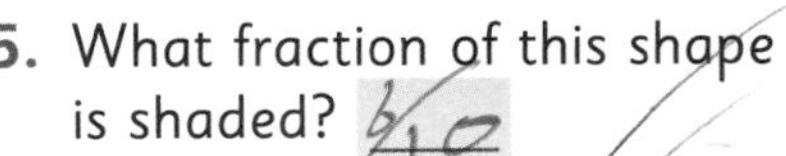
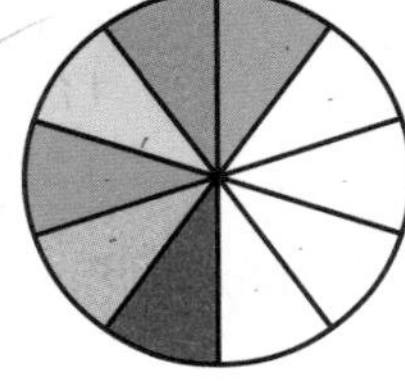

6. $\frac{3}{7}$ of 42 = ____
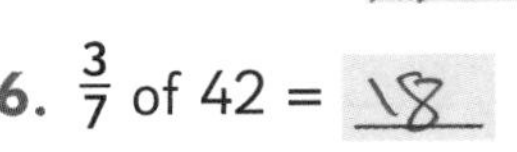

7. $\frac{1}{3} = \frac{\square}{6}$

8. Will a square and a triangle together tessellate? ____

9. How many faces has a sphere? ____

10. Round 7,856 to the nearest 100. ____

11. 2:35 = ____ to ____

12. Write 35% as a decimal fraction. ____

13. What are the chances of picking an even number from a pack of cards?
    ____ in ____

14. This is the net of a ____________

15. Write $\frac{25}{9}$ as a mixed number. ____

William drives to and from work at a factory five days a week.

16. If he travels 82·5km driving to and from work every week, how far is it from his house to the factory? ____

17. He works an eight-hour day. How many hours does he work in a week? ____

18. If he earns €9 an hour, how much does he earn in a week? ____

/18

See page 78 for test.

## Monday

1. Complete the sequence.
95·45, 92·95, 90·45, ______

2. Write the time 15 minutes later than the time shown on the clock. [ : ]

3. Draw the net of a cylinder.

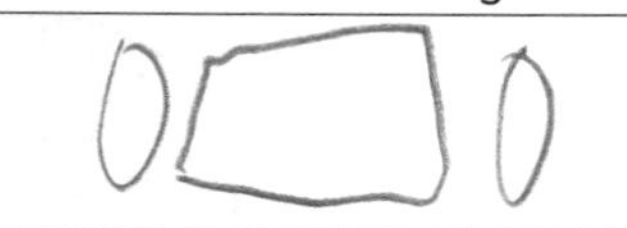

4. Name the angle.

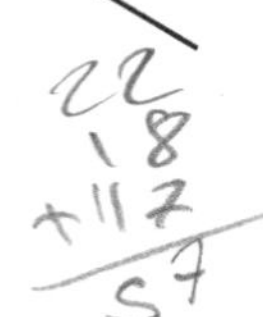

5. (22 + 18 + 17) ÷ 3 = ______

6. Which is nearer to 40,000: 39,000 or 42,000? ______

7. If there are 3 red cubes, 5 blue cubes and 2 green cubes in a bag, what are the chances of picking a green cube?
______ in ______

8. 330ml × 10 = ______l

9. 942 ÷ 7 = ______ R ______

10. $2\frac{1}{4} + 1\frac{1}{4} =$ ______

11. Find the whole number if $\frac{3}{4}$ = 798. ______

12. Write the composite numbers between 0 and 10 (not including 0 or 10).
______, ______, ______ and ______

13. 74 × 20 = ______

14. 55·8 – 4·9 = ______

15.
$$\begin{array}{r} 34{,}561 \\ -\ 12{,}982 \\ \hline \end{array}$$
______

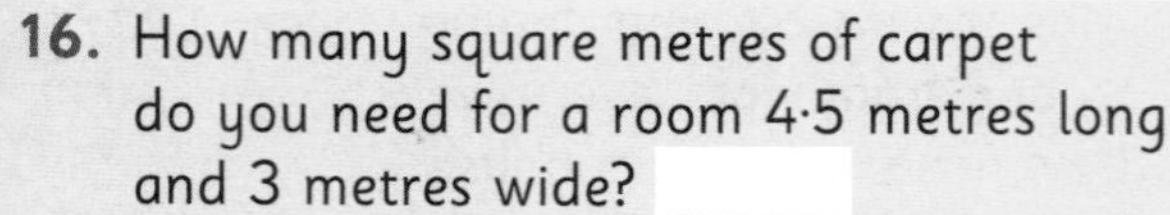

16. How many square metres of carpet do you need for a room 4·5 metres long and 3 metres wide? ______

17. There are 204 sweets in a jar. How many sweets would there be in 20 jars? ______

18. A concert started at 2:25 and finished at 6:10. How many hours and minutes did the concert last?
______ hours ______ minutes

/18

## Tuesday

1. $\frac{1}{6}$ of 306 = ______

2. Complete the sequence.
70·75, 69·50, 68·25, ______

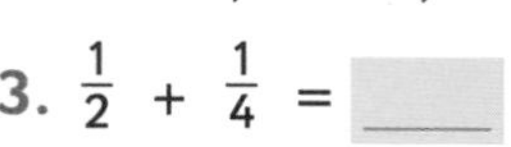

3. $\frac{1}{2} + \frac{1}{4} =$ ______

4. Double 48. ______

5. Draw the net of a cube.

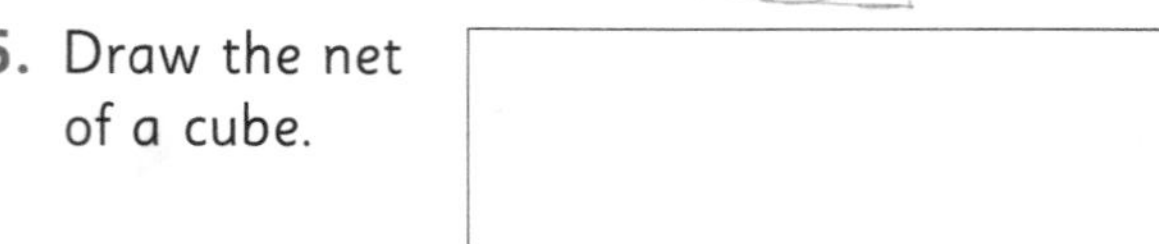

6. 749 ÷ 9 = ______ R ______

7. Write the composite numbers between 10 and 20 (not including 10 or 20).
______, ______, ______, ______ and ______

8. 920 ÷ 10 – 37 = ______

9. Round 59,450 to the nearest 1,000. ______

10. How many hours and minutes from 3:25 to 7:56? ______ hours ______ minutes

11. A straight angle is ______°.

12. Find the perimeter of the hexagon. ______

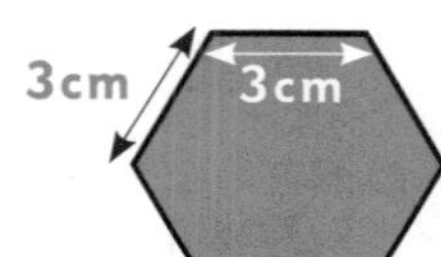


13. 76 × 100 = ______

14. If one bucket weighs 8kg, how much would 25 buckets weigh? ______

15. Write 9% as a decimal fraction. ______

A = 1·675kg | B = 2·325kg | C = 0·824kg

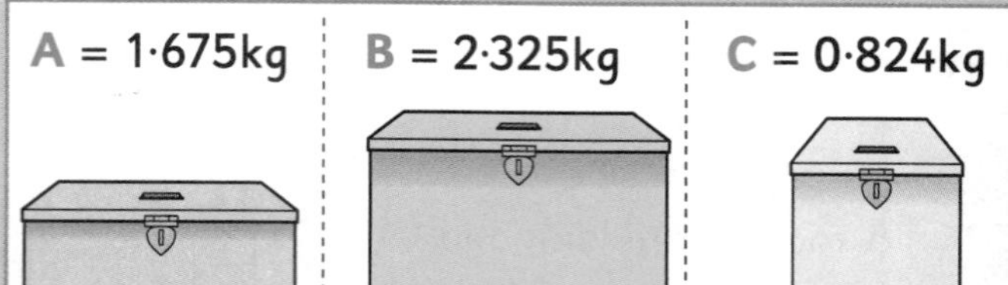

16. What is the total weight of the three boxes? ______

17. How many grammes need to be added to Box A to make it 2kg? ______

18. If 1·3kg was added to Box C, what weight would it be then? ______

/18

## Wednesday

1. $3 \times (5 + 7) =$ ____
2. $\frac{3}{5} + \frac{3}{10} =$ ____
3. Find the whole number if $\frac{7}{8} = 49$. ____
4. $56{\cdot}8 + 12{\cdot}9 =$ ____
5. This is a ____.

6. Draw a right angle.
7. How many sides has a trapezium? ____
8. Which is nearer to 51,000: 49,000 or 53,500? ____
9. Write the time 25 minutes later than the time shown on the clock. ____

10. $658 \div 8 =$ ____ R ____
11. 2·2kg = ____ g
12. 2,000 + 240 + 35 = ____
13. Write the prime numbers between 0 and 10. ____, ____, ____ and ____

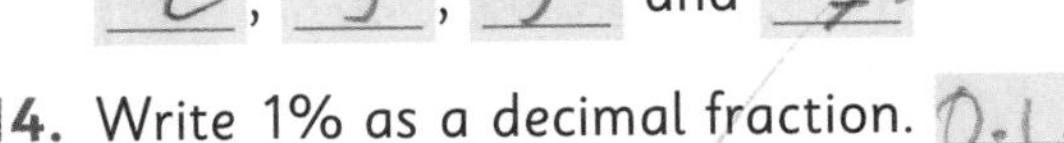

14. Write 1% as a decimal fraction. ____
15. Find the perimeter of a rectangle 6m by 7m. ____

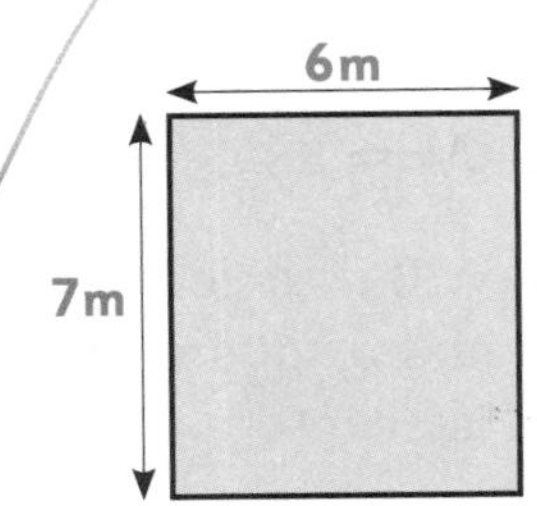


16. How much would 1kg of sugar cost if 250g of sugar cost €1·25? ____
17. A pencil is 45mm long. Another pencil is 5cm long. What is the total length of the two pencils in centimetres? ____
18. Jack cycled 12·55km one day and $9\frac{3}{4}$km the next day. How far did he cycle over the two days? ____

/18

## Thursday

1. Complete the sequence. 7·58, 7·38, 7·18, ____

2. $8 + (6 \times 4) =$ ____
3. $549 \div 7 =$ ____ R ____
4. Draw the net of a cuboid.

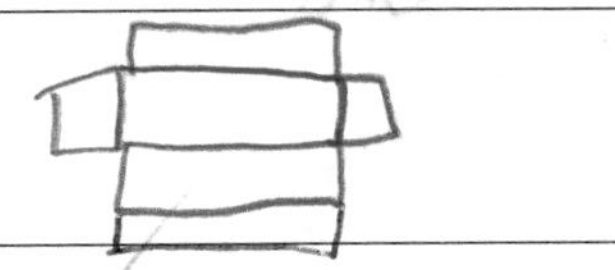

5. Find the average of these numbers: 7, 9, 6, 10. ____
6. Write 15% as a decimal fraction. ____
7. $\frac{5}{6}$ of 660 = ____

8. $73{\cdot}1 - 42{\cdot}9 =$ ____

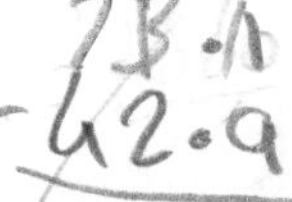

9. Which is nearer to 62,000: 60,500 or 64,500? ____
10. What fraction of this shape is shaded? ____

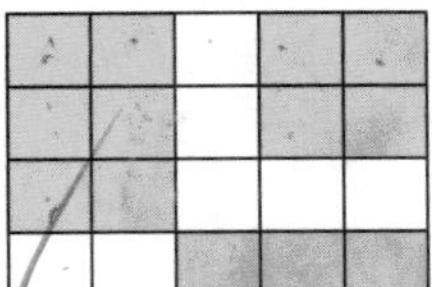

11. $81 \times 20 =$ ____
12. 2·45l = ____ ml
13. $2\frac{1}{8} + 1\frac{1}{4} =$ ____
14. Write the prime numbers between 10 and 20. ____, ____, ____ and ____
15. How certain are you that tomorrow is Sunday: 100%, 50% or 0%? ____

Colm — 31·480kg

16. Which child is the heaviest? ____
17. What is the difference in weight between the heaviest and lightest? ____
18. Find the average weight of the three children. ____

/16

See page 79 for test.

## Monday

1. Complete the sequence. $\frac{1}{4}$, $\frac{3}{4}$, $1\frac{1}{4}$, ____
2. Which is nearer to 25,500: 24,000 or 26,500? ____
3. (39 ÷ 3) + 7 = ____
4. 581 ÷ 6 = ____ R ____
5. $5\frac{1}{5} - 2\frac{1}{10}$ = ____
6. How many hours and minutes are there from 12:24 to 3:45? ____ hours ____ minutes
7. Which number is composite: 7, 6, 5 or 11? ____
8. $\frac{2}{5}$ = ____ %
9. This is the net of a ____________.

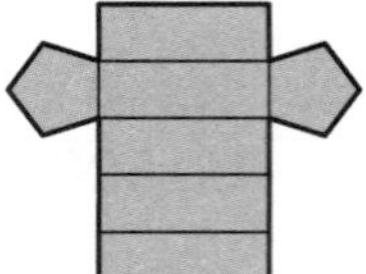

10. 3)624 ____
11. 1·35 × 2 = ____
12. Find the perimeter of this shape. ____

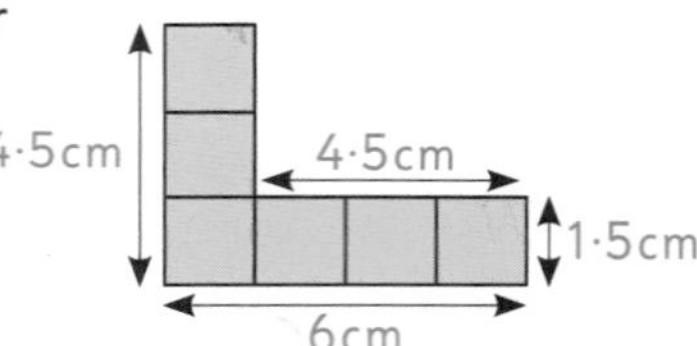


13. €44·65 × 3 ____
14. $\frac{9}{10}$ of 540 = ____
15. 6·5kg = ____ g
16. 868 chocolates are divided into boxes that can each hold 31 chocolates. How many boxes are needed to hold the chocolates? ____
17. A length of rope was 8·35m long. Two lengths measuring 1·85m and 2·44m were cut off. How much rope was left? ____
18. The product of two numbers is 756. If one of the numbers is 27, what is the other number? ____

/18

## Tuesday

1. (14 × 3) + ____ = 58
2. The factors of 16 are ____, ____, ____, ____ and ____.
3. Complete the sequence. $\frac{1}{8}$, $\frac{5}{8}$, $1\frac{1}{8}$, ____
4. $6\frac{5}{6} - \frac{1}{12}$ = ____
5. Write the prime numbers from 20 to 30. ____ and ____
6. What is the value of the 7 in 24,873? ____
7. 71 – (5 × 8) = ____
8. Name this shape. ____________

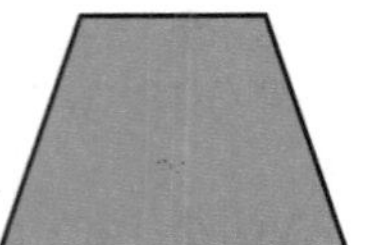

9. 5 jumpers cost €203·75. How much would one jumper cost? ____
10. Which would you use to measure the length of a room: **cm**, **m** or **km**? ____
11. One apple tart weighs 800g. How much would ten apple tarts weigh? ____ kg

12. How likely is it that the outcome will be a head when I toss a coin: 0%, 50% or 100%? ____
13. $\frac{2}{3}$ × 8 = ____
14. 0·1 = ____ %
15. Will a circle and a square together tessellate? ____

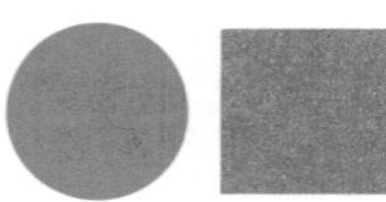

Four children shared a 2-litre bottle of water equally.

16. How many millilitres did each get? ____
17. What fraction of a litre did each get? ____
18. Write the amount each got in percentage form. ____

/18

## Wednesday

1. Complete the sequence. $\frac{1}{2}$, 1, $1\frac{1}{2}$, ____
2. $7 \times \frac{1}{2}$ = ____
3. Find the whole amount if $\frac{7}{9}$ = €140. ____
4. 18 + (9 × 4) = ____
5. 780 ÷ 100 = ____
6. This is a ____ triangle.
7. 45mm = ____ cm
8. $\frac{1}{5}$ = ____%
9. $2\frac{5}{6} + 1\frac{1}{12}$ = ____
10. Write the first five multiples of 8.

11. Round 8,395 to the nearest 10. ____
12. Write the time 55 minutes later than the time shown on the clock. ____

13. 2m 29cm – 1m 6cm = ____
14. 7 × ____ → 83 – 13
15. How likely is it that you will leave school early today? ____ (likely, unlikely, certain, impossible)
16. Mary poured 2·654l, $1\frac{1}{2}$l and 3l 65ml down the sink. How much water did she pour down the sink altogether? ____
17. How much would it cost to fence a garden 10m long and 9m wide if fencing costs €22 per square metre? ____
18. Ciara left her house at 4:23. She arrived at work 1 hour 14 minutes later. At what time did she arrive at work? ____

/18

## Thursday

1. 90 – (7 × 9) = ____
2. How many hours and minutes are there from 10:30 to 2:23?

____ hours ____ minutes

3. Complete the sequence. $\frac{1}{2}$, 2, $3\frac{1}{2}$, ____
4. $8 \times \frac{1}{3}$ = ____
5. $\frac{6}{7} \times \frac{3}{14}$ = ____
6. 9 + ____ → 4 × 8
7. Will a square and a rectangle together tessellate? ____

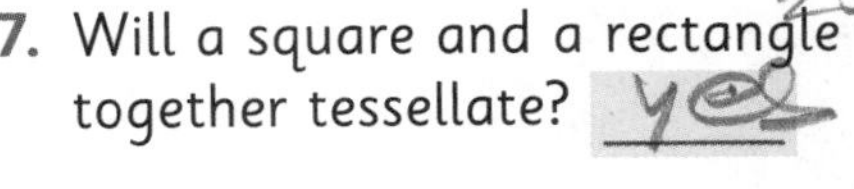

8. Find the value of the missing angle. ____



9. What percentage of this hundred square is shaded? ____

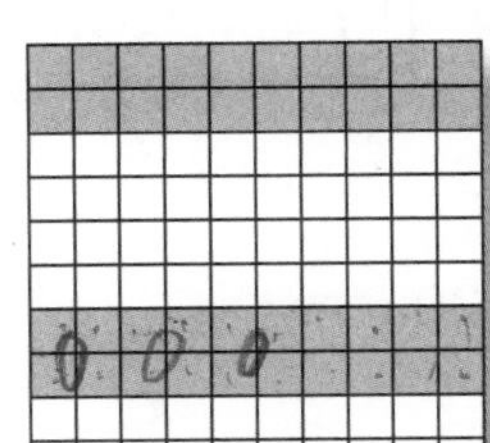

10. Circle the odd number.

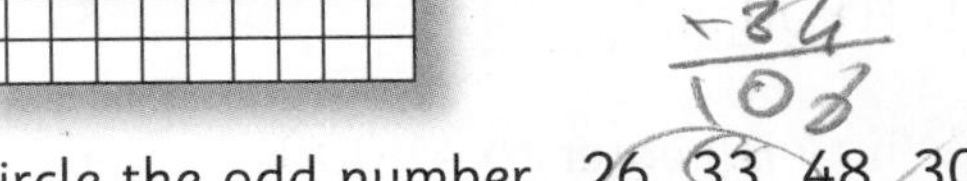

26 33 48 30

11. 7l 25ml = ____ ml
12. Which is nearer to 61,000: 59,000 or 62,500? ____

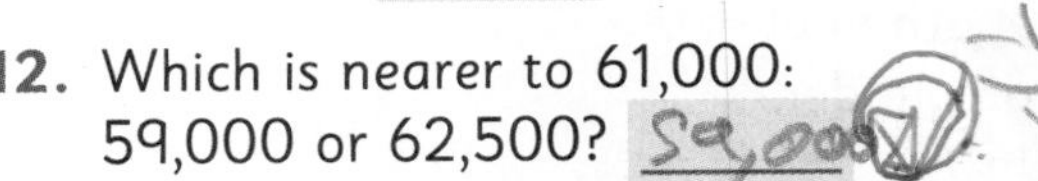

13. Write $\frac{3}{5}$ as a decimal fraction. ____
14. Draw the net of a cone.

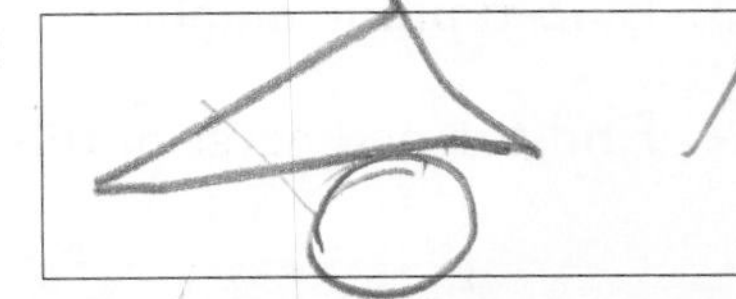

15. Each angle of an equilateral triangle measures ____°.

Write the following word problems as equations.

16. Jasmine had thirty-nine stickers. She gave thirteen of them to her brother. How many had she left? ____
17. There are twelve apples in a bag. Linda sold eight bags. How many apples did she sell? ____
18. A trainer made teams of six from a group of forty-two children. How many teams did she make? ____

/18

See page 80 for test.

## Monday

1. Complete the sequence.
   0·1, 0·15, 0·2, ____
2. Write $2\frac{1}{5}$ as a decimal fraction. ____
3. Can 216 be divided evenly by 3? ____
4. (6 × 8) – (2 × 9) = ____
5. Will a circle and a rectangle together tessellate? ____

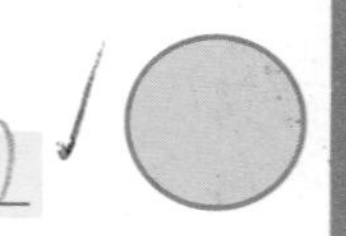

6. $\frac{5}{9} - \frac{1}{3} =$ ____
7. $7 \times \frac{1}{2} =$ ____
8. Name the triangle.
   ____

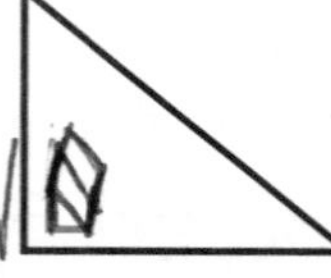

9. $\frac{1}{100}$ = ____ %
10. Is 23:00 = (a) 11.00am or (b)11.00pm? ____
11. Which is nearer to 41,000: 39,500 or 42,000? ____
12. Draw the net of a cylinder.

13. Is 15 a prime number? ____
14. Find the perimeter of this shape. ____

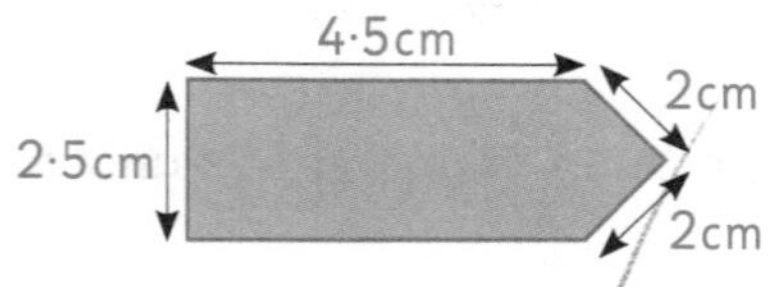


15. 2·07kg = ____ g

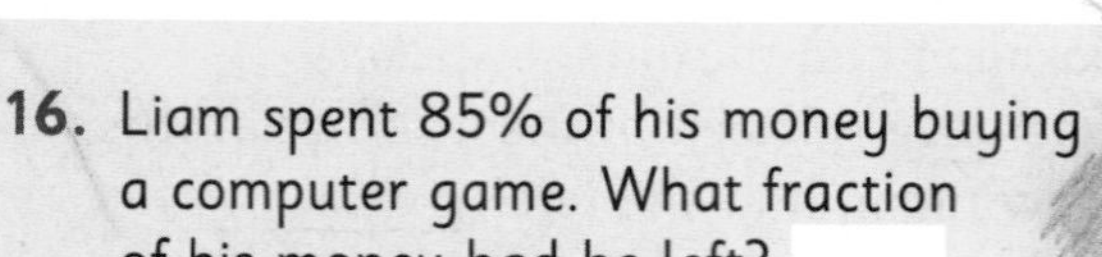

16. Liam spent 85% of his money buying a computer game. What fraction of his money had he left? ____
17. 9 of the 20 children in a group are girls. What percentage of them are girls? ____
18. There are 840 people living in Castletown. If 0·4 of them are adults, how many children live there? ____

/18

## Tuesday

1. $4\frac{1}{3} + 3\frac{2}{9} =$ ____
2. Which is nearer to 40,500: 39,500 or 41,000? ____
3. Is 7 a composite number? ____
4. (7 × 6) – (4 × ____ ) = 30
5. $8 \times \frac{1}{3} =$ ____
6. Complete the sequence.
   2·3, 2·32, 2·34, ____
7. Write $\frac{3}{100}$ as a decimal fraction. ____
8. What are the chances of picking a red ball from a bag with 5 red balls, 3 blue balls and 2 green balls?
   ____ in ____

9. 104cm = ____ m

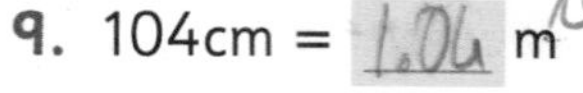

10. 1·67 × 10 = ____

11. What is the perimeter of this equilateral triangle? ____

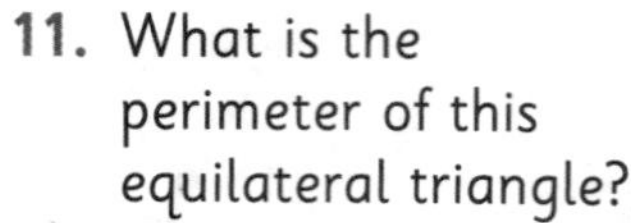


12. How many litres are there in 8 glasses if each glass holds 330ml? ____

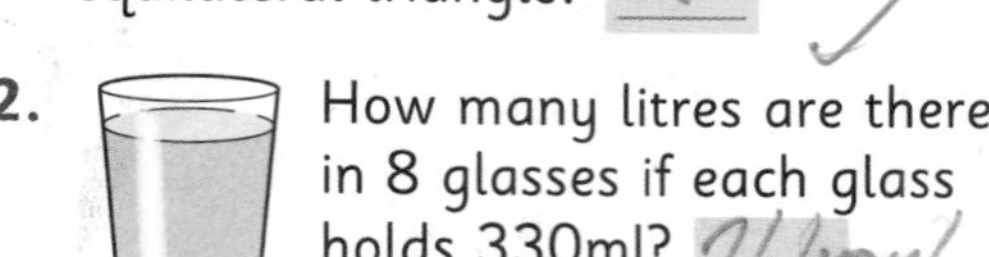

13. If $\frac{2}{7} = 542$, find the whole number. ____

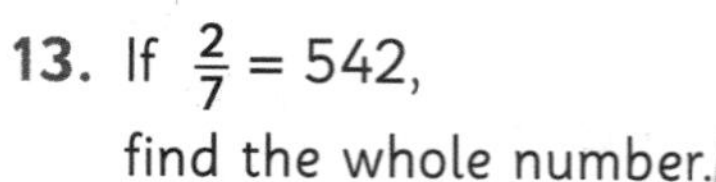

14. $\frac{11}{100}$ = ____ %

15. 6·35 + 2·59 = ____

Packets of crackers are sold in multipacks, with ten in each multipack.

16. How many full multipacks can be made from 55 packets of crackers? ____
17. If each of these multipacks were sold for €2·50, what would be the average price of each packet of crackers? ____
18. How much would four multipacks cost? ____

/18

# Wednesday

1. Complete the sequence.
   1·1, 1·25, 1·4, ____
2. Write $\frac{1}{1000}$ as a decimal fraction. ____
3. $\frac{3}{8}$ of 320 = ____
4. Is 08:00 = (a) 8.00am or (b) 8.00pm? ____
5. 33 × 3 = ____
6. Write the prime numbers between 30 and 40.
   ____ and ____
7. Double 270. ____
8. How many degrees in a straight angle? ____
9. 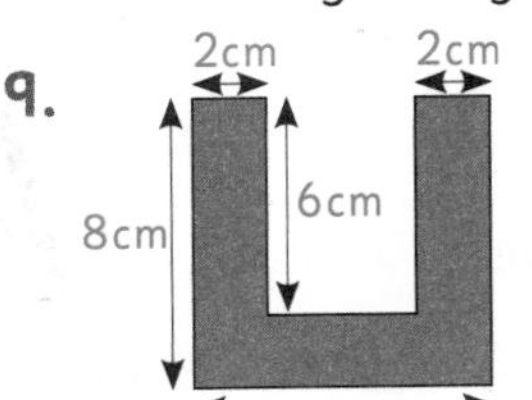

   Find the perimeter of this shape. ____
10. (6 × ____) + 7 = 61
11. Name the shape.

12. €12·81 ÷ 7 = ____
13. 2·8l = ____ml
14. 
   Every time I roll a die, I have an equal chance of landing on each of the six numbers. True or false?
   ____
15. How many hours and minutes are there from 04:25 to 05:45?
   ____ hour(s) ____ minutes
16. Mary spent $\frac{1}{2}$ her money buying a tennis racquet. She had €22·45 left.
   How much money had she at first? ____
17. Two angles in a triangle are 72° and 49°.
   What is the third angle? ____°
18. Fiona had a box full of stamps. She gave $\frac{1}{8}$ of them to her friend. She had 35 stamps left. How many had she at first? ____

/18

# Thursday

1. Round 5,247 to the nearest 100. ____
2. 86,429 – 1,000 = ____
3. Complete the sequence.
   $2\frac{1}{8}$, $2\frac{5}{8}$, $3\frac{1}{8}$, ____
4. Write 0·003 in fraction form. ____
5. (7 × 8) + (8 × 2) = ____
   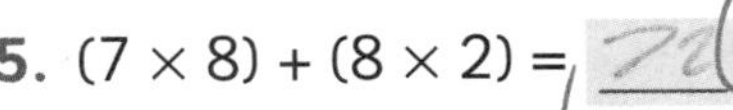
6. 3·2l × 4 = ____
   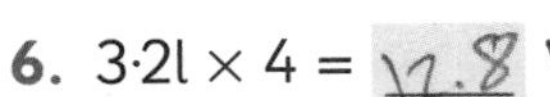
7. 07:30 = ____am
8. The factors of 18 are ____, ____, ____, ____, ____ and ____.
9. These are the favourite colours of a group of children. What fraction like red? ____
   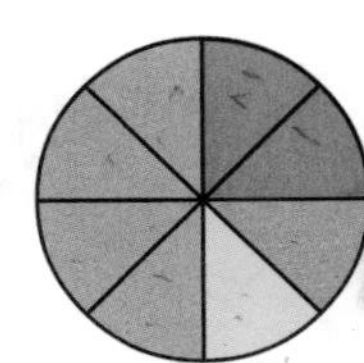
10. What percentage like green? ____
11. If 6 children voted for red, how many children voted for green? ____
12. How many children voted altogether? ____
13. 487 ÷ 9 = ____ R ____
   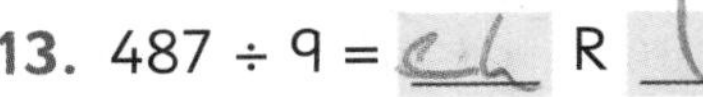
14. Name the angle.
   ____
15. 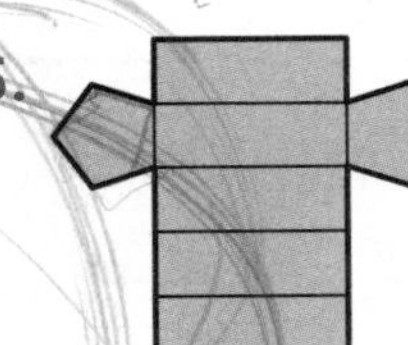
   This is the net of a
   ____

A group of 40 children were brought to their local restaurant. 17 of the children chose a meal costing €4·99.

16. How much did the 17 meals cost? ____
17. If the remaining children chose a meal costing €4·50, how much did their meals cost? ____
18. How much did the meals cost for the 40 children altogether? ____

/18

See page 81 for test.

Week 17

## Monday

1. Complete the sequence. 3,000, 300, 30, ____
2. Write the prime numbers between 1 and 10.
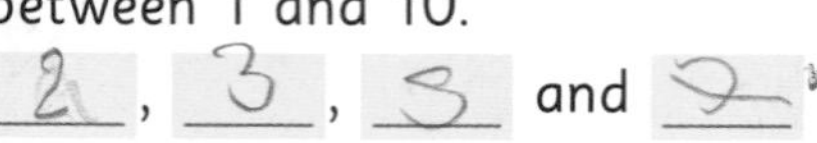
____, ____, ____ and ____
3. Write $\frac{8}{1000}$ as a decimal fraction. ____
4. 76 × 10 = ____
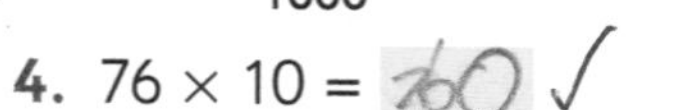
5. What are the chances of picking a king from a pack of cards? ____ in ____
6. Draw a line of symmetry on the trapezium.
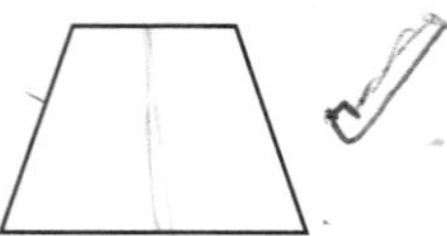
7. How many cups measuring 250ml can be filled from a bottle holding $2\frac{1}{2}$l? ____

8. $6\frac{5}{8} - 2\frac{1}{4} =$ ____
9. 36 × 20 = ____
10. Find the whole number if $\frac{3}{7}$ = 39. ____
11. 763 ÷ 8 = ____ R ____
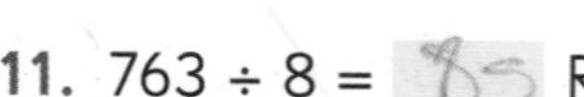

12. 14:30 = ____ pm
13. (7 × 4) + (8 × 2) = ____
14. Name the angle. ____

15. Find the perimeter of the octagon. ____

4cm

16. Peter's step is 1m 4cm. Ciaran's step is 14cm longer. How long is Ciaran's step? ____
17. $\frac{1}{4}$ of Lisa's money is €4·85. How much money has Lisa altogether? ____
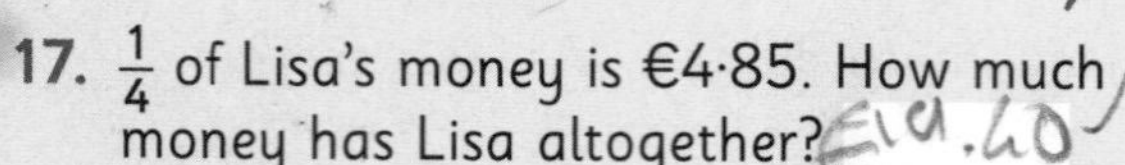
18. Jim left Dublin at 15:20. He arrived in New York 6 hours 35 minutes later. At what time did he arrive in New York (Dublin time)? ____ : ____
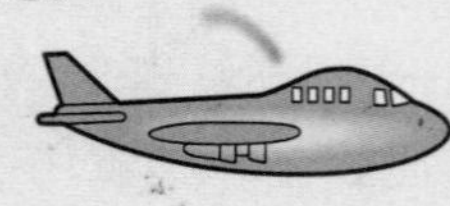

/18

## Tuesday

1. Round 48,250 to the nearest 100. ____
2. Complete the sequence. 400, 40, 4, ____
3. 68,422 + 5,000 = ____
4. €5·86 × 100 = ____
5. How many vertices has a cone? ____
6. Find the perimeter of this shape. ____
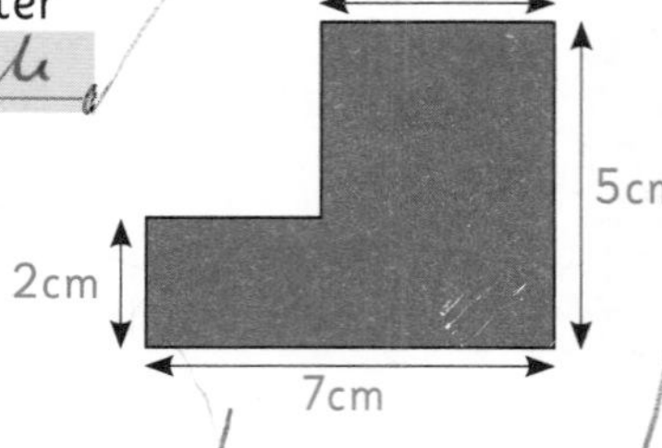

7. How many minutes in $\frac{1}{5}$ of an hour? ____
8. 6.15pm = ____ : ____
9. Circle the prime number. 16 9 23 30
10. What are the chances of picking an odd numbered card from a pack of cards? ____ in ____
11. (8 × ____) – (4 × 4) = 40
12. Write $\frac{7}{100}$ as a decimal fraction. ____
13. $4\frac{1}{8} + 2\frac{1}{4} =$ ____
14. The factors of 9 are ____, ____ and ____
15. 6·2kg = ____ g

**Adventure Land Theme Park**

**Entrance fees:**

| Single tickets: | Special offer: |
|---|---|
| **Adult** = €15·60 | **Family ticket** – |
| **Child** = €7·85 | 2 adults and |
| | 2 children = €40 |

16. How much would it cost to buy single tickets for 2 adults and 2 children? ____
17. How much would the family save by purchasing the family ticket? ____
18. If there was a further 20% reduction on the family ticket, how much would the family pay then? ____

/18

## Wednesday

1. Complete the sequence.
   0·75, 0·69, 0·63, ____
2. $8\frac{11}{12} - 3\frac{1}{4} =$ ____
3. 15·3 × 10 = ____
4. How many edges has a cube? ____

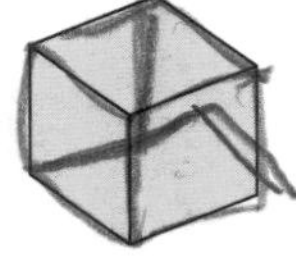

5. $\frac{3}{4}$ of 84 = ____
6. Which is nearer to 52,500: 51,000 or 53,000? ____
7. 5)435
8. Will a triangle and a square together tessellate? ____

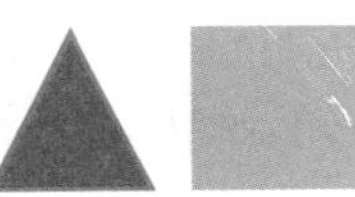

9. What are the chances of landing on heads when tossing one coin? ____ in ____
10. 9.15pm = [ : ]
11. 1,040ml = ____ l
12. If 8 footballs cost €50·80, how much would 3 footballs cost? ____
13. Name the triangle. ____

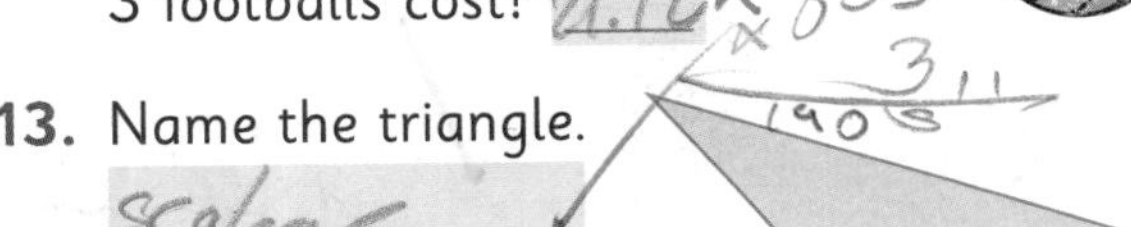

14. How many degrees are there in a square? ____
15. (7 × ____ ) + 8 = 50
16. A baker had 400 cakes. She sold 9% of them. How many did she sell? ____
17. There were 5 cubes in a bag. 2 of them were green. What percentage were green? ____
18. Joan had €32·40. She spent $\frac{3}{8}$ of her money buying a t-shirt. How much was the t-shirt? ____

/18

## Thursday

1. 7·8 × 100 = ____

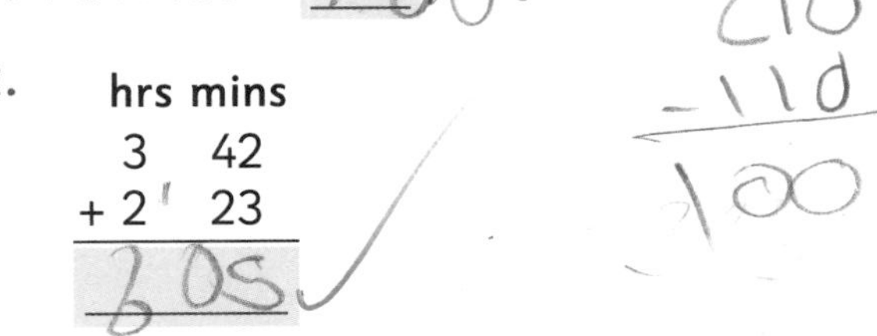

2. 

| | hrs | mins |
|---|---|---|
| | 3 | 42 |
| + | 2 | 23 |

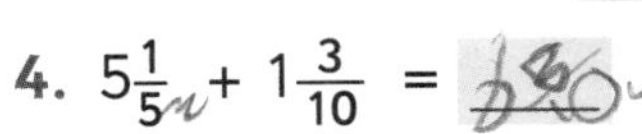

3. Complete the sequence.
   4·35, 3·25, 2·15, ____
4. $5\frac{1}{5} + 1\frac{3}{10} =$ ____
5. How many faces has a cylinder? ____

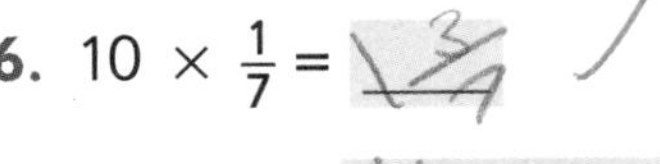

6. $10 \times \frac{1}{7} =$ ____

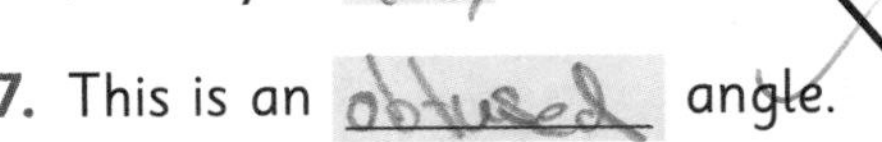

7. This is an ____ angle.
8. Two angles in a triangle measure 68° and 47°. What is the measurement of the third angle? ____

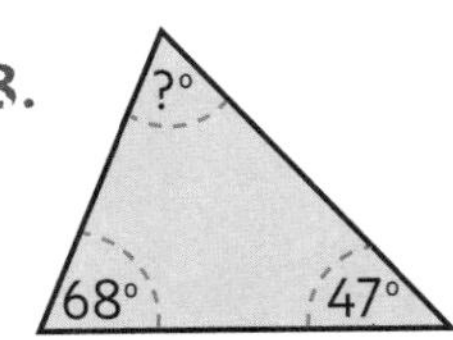


9. The first five multiples of 7 are ____, ____, ____, ____ and ____.
10. Write $\frac{23}{8}$ as a mixed number. ____
11. Find the average weight: 5·85kg, 4·967kg, 6·19kg. ____
12. 4.45am = [ : ]

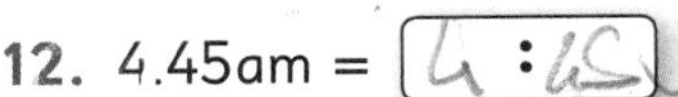

13. Decrease €55 by 11%. ____
14. Write 2·45km in metres. ____

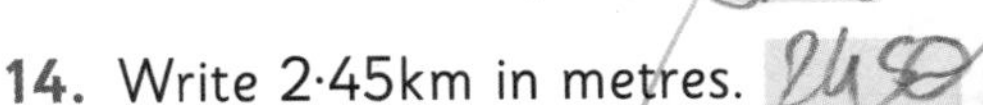

15. €2·34 = ____ c
16. How much would two teas and two waters cost? ____

**Menu**
**Tea €1·20**
**Coffee €1·50**
**Hot chocolate €1·10**
**Water €0·95**
**Soup €3·45**

17. How much dearer would one water and one soup be together than two hot chocolates? ____
18. How much cheaper would two coffees be than one soup? ____

/18

See page 82 for test.

## Monday

1. Complete the sequence. $\frac{1}{8}$, $\frac{1}{4}$, $\frac{3}{8}$, ____
2. $1{\cdot}76 \times 10 =$ ____
3. 29·415km ÷ 5 = ____
4. $3 \div \frac{1}{2} =$ ____
5. A cuboid has ____ vertices.
6. Draw an acute angle.
7. Find the perimeter of this shape. ____

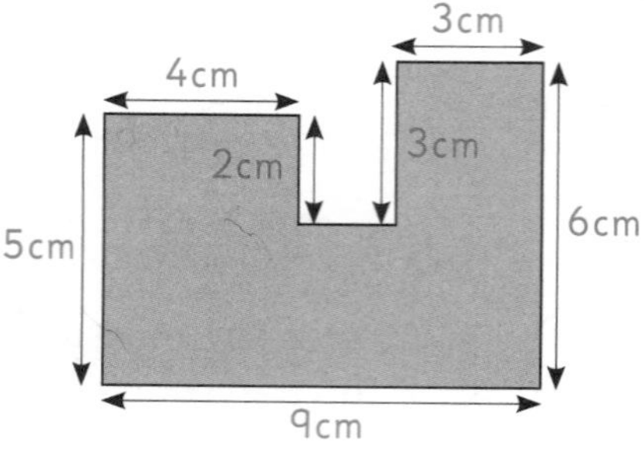


8. Can this shape tesselate? ____
9. The possible outcomes when you toss two coins are: heads and ____; tails and ____; ____ and ____.

10. 8cm 6mm + $7\frac{1}{2}$cm = ____
11. 750 – 220 = ____
12. 450 × 3 = ____
13. Increase €8 by 50%. ____
14. Write $\frac{19}{4}$ as a mixed number. ____
15. 5)624 ____ R ____
16. Maura can run 500m in two minutes. How far will she run in 10 minutes? ____
17. A box weighs $2\frac{1}{4}$kg. How many grammes does it weigh? ____
18. The total capacity of four buckets is 9·376l. What is the average capacity per bucket? ____

/18

## Tuesday

1. $\frac{1}{4} = \frac{\square}{12}$
2. 1·4km × 6 = ____
3. $4 \div \frac{1}{3} =$ ____
4. This is the net of a ____
5. Decrease €4 by 25% ____

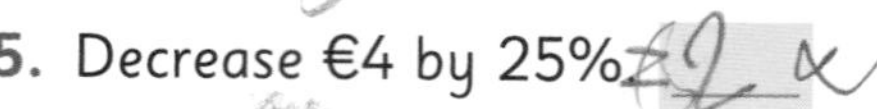

6. 1,356g + $3\frac{1}{2}$kg = ____ kg
7. A regular pentagon has ____ lines of symmetry.

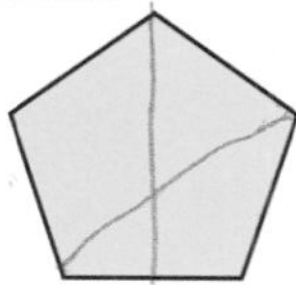

8. Write $3\frac{9}{100}$ as a decimal fraction. ____
9. 1·58 × 10 = ____
10. Round 42,628 to the nearest 1,000. ____
11. Which is better value for money:
    (a) 3 apples at €1·30 or
    (b) 5 apples at €2·10? ____
12. Is 9 a composite number? ____
13. 1.15pm = ____

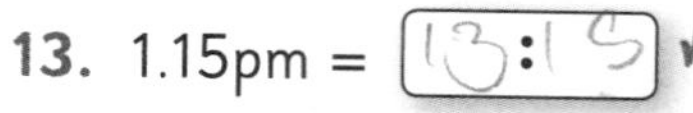

14. 76 – (5 × 9) = ____
15. Is this angle approximately 30°, 80° or 120°? ____

This jug holds 1 litre of juice.
Each glass can hold $\frac{1}{8}$ of a litre.

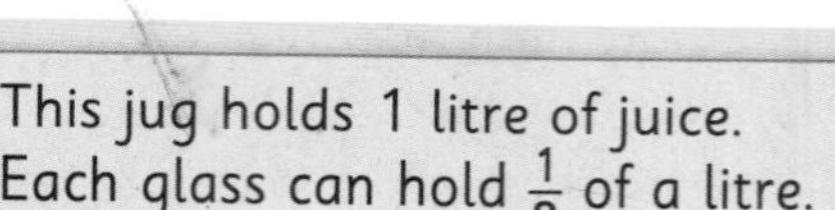

16. James drank two glasses of juice and Peter drank three glasses. What fraction of the juice did they drink? ____
17. How many millilitres of juice did they drink altogether? ____
18. What percentage was left in the jug? ____

/18

## Wednesday

1. 0·2 ____ $\frac{1}{5}$ (<, > or =)
2. $\frac{2}{3}$ = $\frac{\square}{6}$
3. 73,296 – 6,000 = ____

4. What percentage of the hundred square is shaded? ____

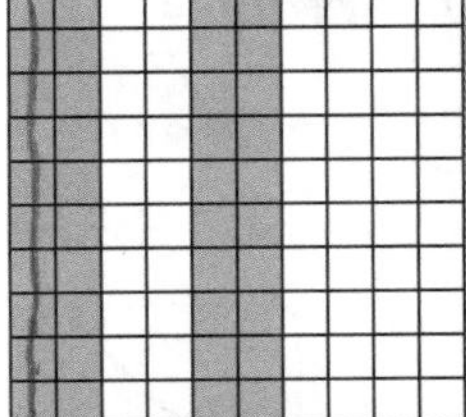

5. Draw the net of a cone.

6. An equilateral triangle has ____ lines of symmetry.

7. What is the perimeter of a hexagon with 2cm sides? ____

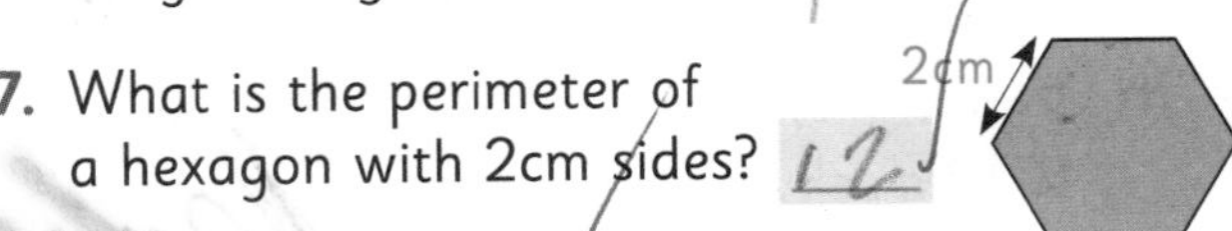


8. $8\frac{7}{9} - 3\frac{2}{3}$ = ____

9. 540ml × 8 = ____

10. Which would you use to measure the height of a room: mm, cm or m? ____
11. A straight angle has ____ °.
12. 2.30am = ____

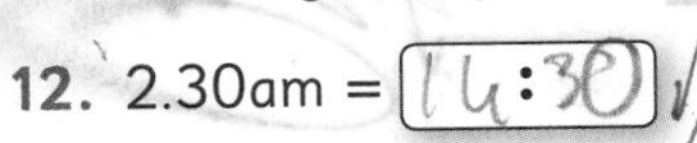

13. $\frac{1}{4}$ of 1,296 = ____
14. 5,897 ÷ 7 = ____ R ____
15. Write $9\frac{3}{100}$ as a decimal fraction. ____

16. An oil tank holds 800 litres of oil. What would it cost to fill the tank at 50c per litre? ____

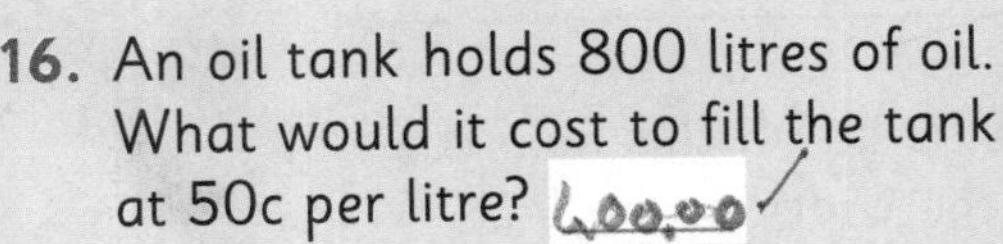

17. A cinema ticket costs €12·15. How much are 5 tickets? ____
18. If 1kg of oranges cost €3·90, how much would $\frac{1}{2}$kg cost? ____

€3·90

/18

## Thursday

1. $\frac{3}{5}$ = $\frac{\square}{10}$
2. 6·315 + 1·032 = ____
3. 6·57 × 10 = ____
4. $4\frac{1}{2} + 3\frac{1}{8}$ = ____
5. Find the whole number if $\frac{2}{5}$ = 26. ____
6. Draw the net of a cylinder.

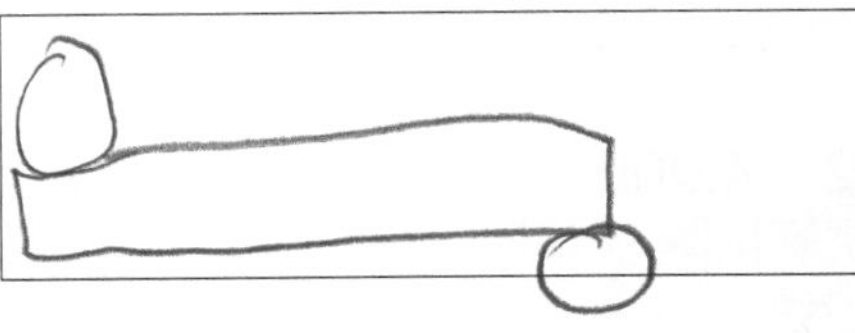

7. Which is better value for money?
   - ☐ 7 pens at €4·90
   - ☐ 9 pens at €6·39

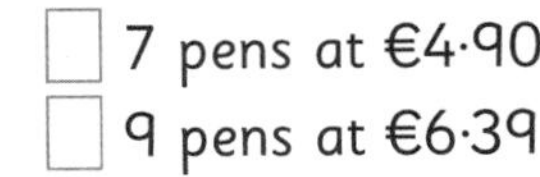

8. 6·545km ÷ 7 = ____
9. Is this angle approximately 10°, 70° or 110°? ____ °

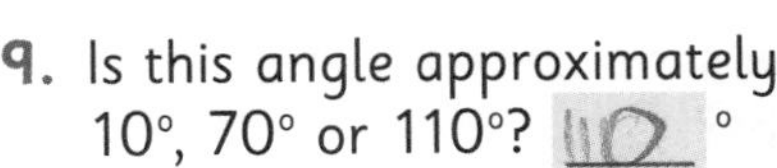

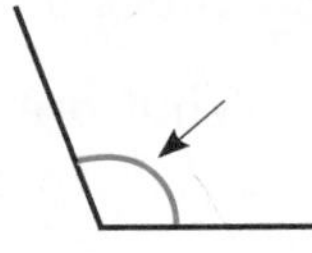

10. 35% ____ $\frac{3}{5}$ (<, > or =)
11. Write $4\frac{3}{100}$ as a decimal fraction. ____
12. Round 36,945 to the nearest 100. ____
13. Increase €15 by 20%. ____

14. Find the perimeter of the pentagon. ____

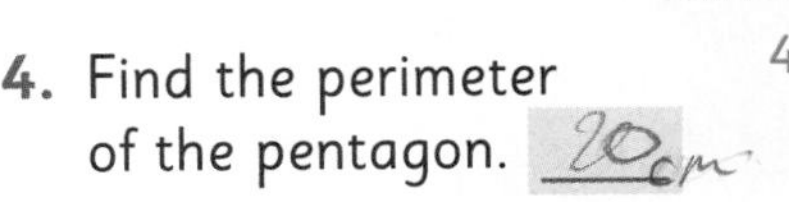

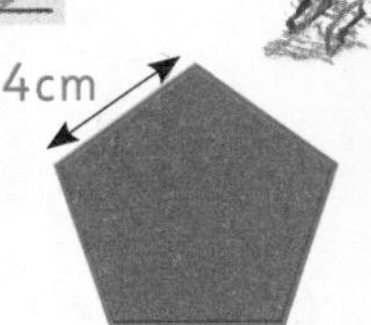


15. 65 – (9 × 3) = ____

Grace spent $\frac{1}{8}$ of her money on popcorn and $\frac{1}{4}$ of her money on a drink.

16. If the drink cost €1·32, how much money had she altogether? ____
17. What fraction of her money did she spend? ____
18. How much money had she left? ____

/18

See page 83 for test.

## Monday

1. $17 + 3 \times 6 =$ ____

2. Find the perimeter of this shape. ____

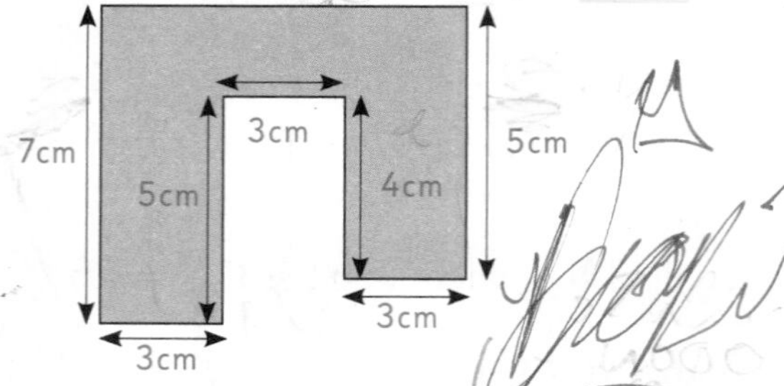


3. 25% of 4,064 = ____

4. 67,422 – 4,000 = ____

5. $\frac{3}{10} = \frac{\square}{20}$

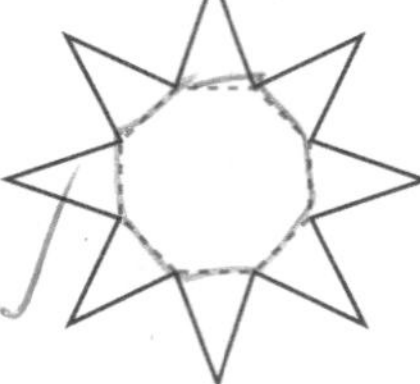

6. This is the net of a ____.

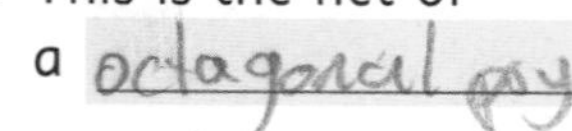

In a bag, there are 4 **green** cubes, 3 **blue** cubes, 2 **red** cubes and 1 **yellow** cube.

7. What are the chances of picking a **yellow** cube? ____ in ____

8. What are the chances of picking a **green** cube? ____ in ____

9. What are the chances of picking a **blue** or **red** cube? ____ in ____

10. What are the chances of picking an **orange** cube? ____ in ____

11. $123 \div 5 =$ ____ R ____

12. $6\frac{3}{8} + 1\frac{3}{4} =$ ____

13. $1{\cdot}23 \times 10 =$ ____

14. Write $\frac{27}{6}$ as a mixed number. ____

15. 12am = ____ : ____

16. There were 55 cakes on a tray. The baker sold 40% of them. How many did she sell? ____

17. What is the perimeter of a room 40m long and 20m wide? ____

18. One bag weighs 8·63kg. Another bag weighs $5\frac{1}{4}$kg. What is the difference in weight between the two bags? ____

/18

## Tuesday

1. $\frac{3}{5} = \frac{\square}{15}$

2. Write 2·05 as a fraction. ____

3. $6{\cdot}02 \times 10 =$ ____

4. 7·6l = ____ ml

5. Name the 2-D shape. ____

6. Draw the axes of symmetry on the square.

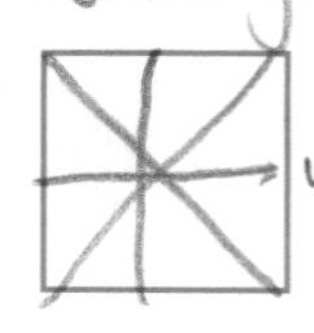

7. Write the composite numbers between 11 and 19.
____, ____, ____, ____ and ____

8. $22 \times 5 =$ ____

9. How many 400g are there in 2kg? ____

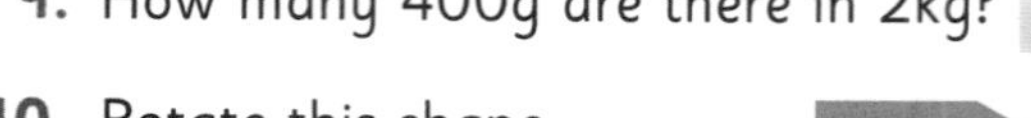

10. Rotate this shape 270° clockwise and draw.

11. Circle the composite number. 13 31 47 22

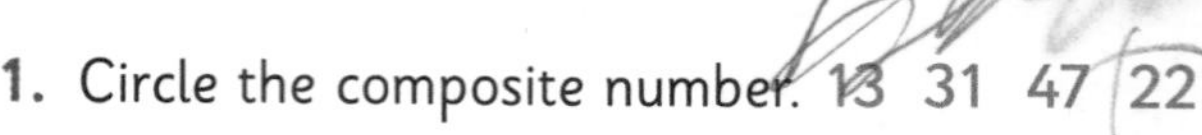

12. $(6 \times \_\_\_\_) + (9 \times 6) = 90$

13. Round 86,525 to the nearest 1,000. ____

14. Find the whole number if 25% = 276. ____

15. Write the number that is 7 less than 5,000. ____

The area of this field is 450m².

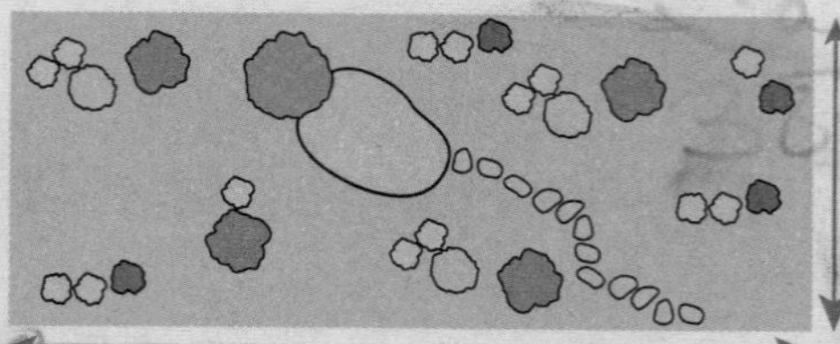

16. If the length of this field is 25m, find the width of the field. ____

17. What is the perimeter of this field? ____

18. If a farmer wanted to put a fence around the field and fencing cost €4·50 per metre, how much would it cost him to fence the field? ____

/18

## Wednesday

1. $\frac{6}{10} = \frac{\square}{5}$

2. Write the prime numbers between 10 and 20. ____, ____, ____ and ____

3. $7\frac{3}{5} - 2\frac{7}{15} =$ ____

4. Write 5·001 as a fraction. ____

5. 30% of 640 = ____

6. 3·4 × 100 = ____

7. Which is nearer to 62,200: 61,500 or 63,000? ____

8. This is the net of a ____.

9. 4m 24cm + 8·35m + $6\frac{1}{4}$m = ____

10. 0·54 = ____ %

11. y = ____ °

y 77°

12. $\frac{2}{5} \times 7 =$ ____

13. 5)978 ____ R ____

14. Increase €50 by 20%. ____

15. How many hours and minutes are there from 03:15 to 05:30? ____ hours ____ minutes

16. Karen decided to complete a 5km race. She ran 1,200m and then walked a further 1km 70m. How much further had she to go? ____ km

17. Martin spent 50% of his money in one shop and 30% in another shop. He then had €14 left. How much money had he at first? ____

18. There are 26 stamps in a book. If George bought 8 books, how many less than 250 stamps is that? ____

/18

## Thursday

1. 7·35 × 10 = ____

2. What decimal fraction of this shape is shaded? ____

3. Round 71,863 to the nearest 1,000. ____

4. $\frac{8}{10} = \frac{4}{\square}$

5. $8\frac{4}{5} - 3\frac{9}{10} =$ ____

6. $\frac{38}{100} =$ ____ %

7. 40% of 520 = ____

8. 75 – 72 ÷ 8 = ____

9. How many lines of symmetry are there in a rhombus? ____

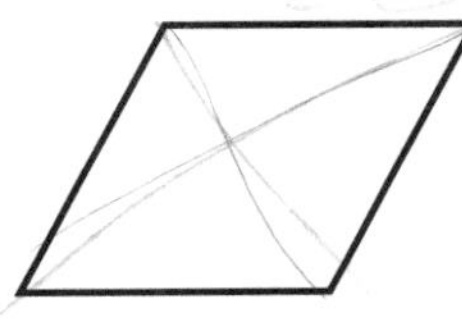

10. Draw the net of a tetrahedron.

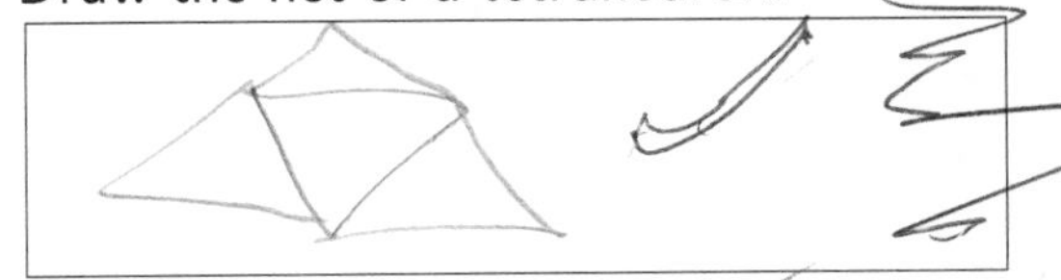

11. 00:25 = ____ am

12. 4·09km + 3,658m = ____ km

13. Draw an acute angle.

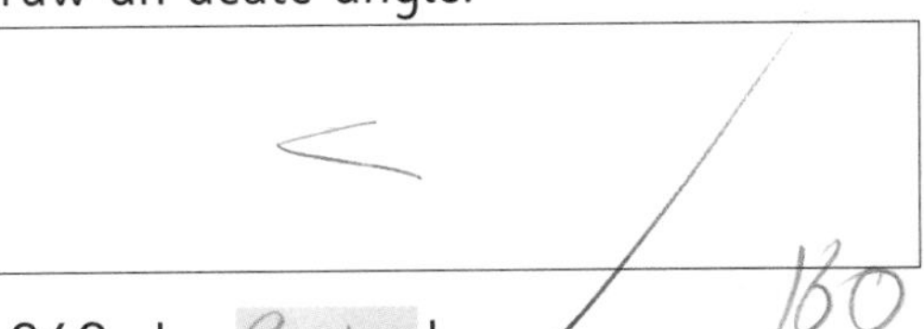

14. 2,040ml = ____ l

15. (3 × 10) ÷ (2 × 3) = ____

A family with six people used 3l of milk each day from Monday to Friday. However, they used $3\frac{3}{4}$ l each day at the weekend.

16. How many litres of milk did the family use in 7 days? ____

17. What was the average amount of milk used per family member? ____

18. If milk costs 80c a litre, how much would the family have to pay every week? ____

/18

See page 84 for test.

## Monday

1. Write $8\frac{3}{5}$ as an improper fraction. ____
2. $6\frac{2}{3} + 2\frac{5}{12}$ = ____
3. 1,247 × 10 = ____
4. Colour 0·2 of this shape.

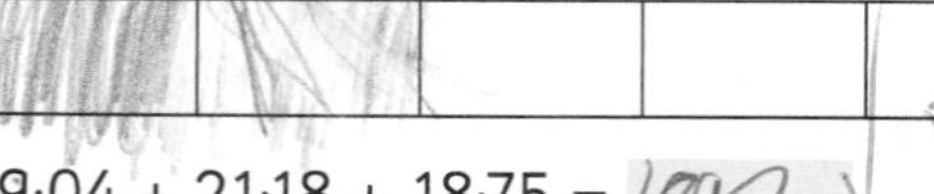

5. 29·04 + 21·18 + 18·75 = ____

| News | 13:00 |
|---|---|
| Film | 13:35 |
| Nature Programme | 15:05 |
| Cartoon | 15:50 |

6. How long did the News last? ____
7. If the Nature Programme was 5 minutes late starting, at what time did it start? ___ : ___
8. If someone watched the Film and the Nature Programme, how long would they be watching television? ____
9. If the Cartoon lasted for 20 minutes, at what time did it end? ___ : ___
10. Which of the following is a prime number: 7, 8 or 9? ____
11. $\frac{8}{10}$ = ____ %
12. 5% of 40 = ____
13. How many edges has a sphere? ____
14. 4·5m = ____ cm
15. 6kg 543g
   – 4kg 433g
   ____
16. $\frac{3}{4}$ of the animals on a farm are cattle. If there are 153 cattle, how many animals are on the farm? ____
17. Orange juice costs 75c per 500ml. How much would 2·5l of orange juice cost? ____
18. During a sale, a jacket was reduced by 20%. If the original price of the jacket was €255, what was the sale price? ____

/18

## Tuesday

1. How many minutes in $\frac{2}{5}$ of an hour? ____
2. Round 8,976 to the nearest 100. ____
3. Write $7\frac{4}{5}$ as an improper fraction. ____
4. 1·675 + 3·019 = ____
5. What is the value of the underlined digit: 86,2<u>3</u>9? ____
6. Each angle in a rectangle measures ____

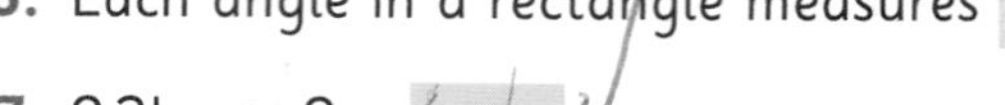

7. 2·3km × 2 = ____
8. How many edges has a cylinder? ____

9. 6% of 500 = ____

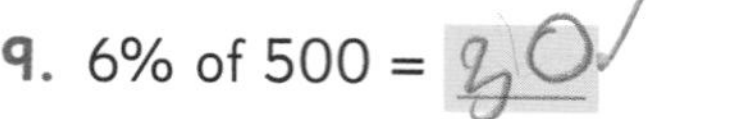

10. Colour 0·4 of the shape.
11. $5\frac{1}{2}$kg – $2\frac{1}{4}$kg = ____

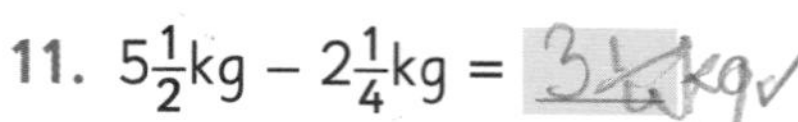

12. Which of the following is a composite number: 29, 30 or 31? ____
13. $\frac{7}{100}$ = ____ %
14. 6·42 × 10 = ____
15. 18:25

What time will it be 25 minutes later than the time shown? ___ : ___

This drawing is the plan of a room.

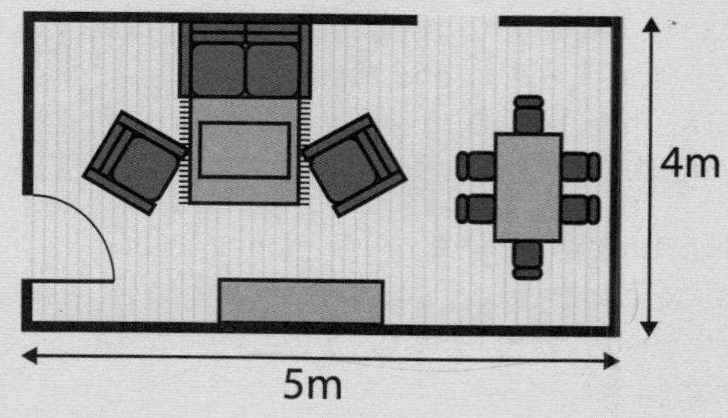


16. What is the area of this room? ____
17. How much will it cost to carpet the room at €35 per square metre? ____
18. How much change would you receive from €1,000? ____

/18

## Wednesday

1. Write $\frac{34}{8}$ as a mixed number. ____
2. €4·85 ÷ 5 = ____
3. Find the whole number if 0·4 = 2,420. ____
4. 

| | hrs | mins |
|---|---|---|
| | 6 | 35 |
| + | 2 | 40 |
| | ____ | |

5. 21:15 = ____ pm
6. 3,250ml – 1l 150ml = ____
7. List the first five prime numbers.
   ____, ____, ____, ____, ____
8. 7·639 × 100 = ____
9. A tetrahedron has ____ edges.

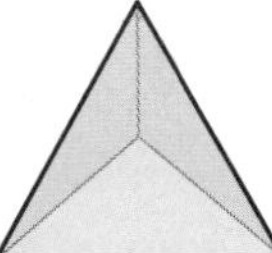

10. 18 + 5 × 7 = ____
11. Turn this shape 90° anticlockwise and draw.

12. Write 38% as a decimal. ____
13. Find the area of a square with a side of 5cm. ____

5cm

14. What are the chances of throwing a 6 on one die? ____ in ____

15. The value of 8 in 2,418 is ____.
16. Coffee costs €3·75 per 250g. How much change will I get back from €20 if I buy $1\frac{1}{4}$kg of coffee? ____
17. A dishwasher that cost €560 last year costs 10% more this year. How much does it cost this year? ____
18. A box of sweets weighs 1·582kg. How much would 7 boxes weigh? ____

/18

## Thursday

1. 12·5 ÷ 10 = ____
2. 63 – 4 × 9 = ____
3. Write $\frac{39}{7}$ as a mixed number. ____
4. 1·24 + 3·56 = ____
5. 

| | hrs | mins |
|---|---|---|
| | 2 | 25 |
| × | | 5 |
| | ____ | |

6. Write 7% as a decimal. ____
7. Round 1,076 to the nearest 100. ____
8. 60% of 4,525 = ____
9. A hemisphere has ____ faces.
10. 6·291 × 10 = ____
11. Is 64 evenly divisible by 12? ____
12. Find the average of 6, 9, 4, 3 and 8. ____
13. The perimeter of a square is 36cm. What is the length of each side? ____
14. $6\frac{1}{8} - 1\frac{3}{4}$ = ____
15. Name the shape.
    ____

| Air Travel | Supersun |
|---|---|
| Dublin to Paris return | Dublin to Paris one way |
| Adults €240 | Adults €150 |
| Children €125 | Children €80 |

16. How much would a return trip to Paris with Air Travel cost a family of 2 adults and 2 children? ____
17. How much would a return trip to Paris with Supersun cost a family of 2 adults and 2 children? ____
18. How much would they save by travelling with Air Travel? ____

/18

See page 85 for test.

**Week 21**

## Monday

1. $\frac{4}{5}$ = ____%

2. Put in order of size, starting with the smallest: $\frac{1}{5}$, 18%, 0·21.

____, ____, ____

3. A triangular prism has ____ vertices.

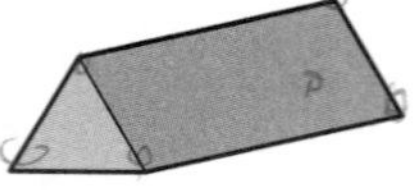

4. How many hours and minutes are there from 10:30 to 13:00?

____ hours ____ minutes

5. Find the area of the following shape. ____

perimeter = 20cm

6cm

6. The three angles in a triangle add up to ____°.

7. 60% of €25 = ____

8. 4·8cm – 85mm = ____

9. Find the average of 14, 13 and 9. ____

10. $4\frac{3}{4}$kg = ____ g

11. 2·45 × 10 = ____

12. How many degrees hotter is $^{+}5°$ that $^{-}7°$? ____

13. **c** – 36 = 9, so **c** = ____

14. 10,000 + 8,000 + 500 + 60 + 7 = ____

15. Write $6\frac{7}{9}$ as an improper fraction. ____

16. A room is 5 metres long and 6 metres wide. How much will it cost to carpet the room at €10 per square metre? ____

17. A bus can carry 45 passengers. How many buses will it take to carry 810 passengers? ____

18. Jack had €64. He spent 75% on a new jersey. How much did he spend? ____

/18

## Tuesday

1. 75,840 – 7,000 = ____

2. Circle negative one on the number line.

$^{-}3$ $^{-}2$ $^{-}1$ 0 $^{+}1$ $^{+}2$ $^{+}3$

3. Find the perimeter of a rectangle with a width of 4cm and area of 28cm². ____

4. 240 ÷ 20 = ____

5. Write $\frac{37}{8}$ as a mixed number. ____

6. $\frac{2}{3}$ – $\frac{2}{9}$ = ____

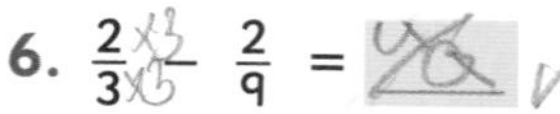

7. What is the value of 7 in 3·75? ____

8. Write 2·038 as a fraction. ____

9. Which of the following is a square number: 25, 26 or 27? ____

10. Put in order of size, starting with the smallest: 77%, $\frac{3}{4}$, 0·8.

____, ____, ____

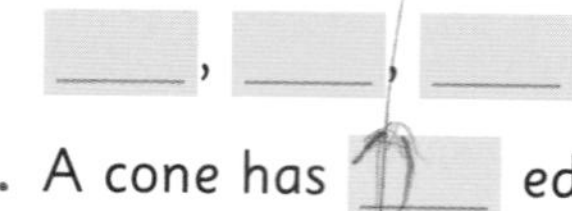

11. A cone has ____ edges.

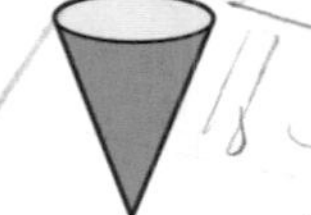

12. Write as am or pm: $\frac{1}{4}$ past 8 in the evening. ____

13. 3km 78m = ____ m

14. 2,250ml + $1\frac{3}{4}$l = ____

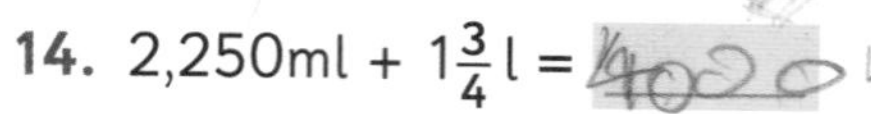

15. What are the chances of throwing a multiple of 2 on one die?

____ in ____

**CAR SALES**

Garage **A** sold 5,438.

Garage **B** sold 4,375.

Garage **C** sold 6,518.

16. How many cars did the three garages sell altogether? ____

17. What was the difference in car sales between Garage **A** and Garage **C**? ____

18. How many less than 5,000 cars did Garage **B** sell? ____

/18

## Wednesday

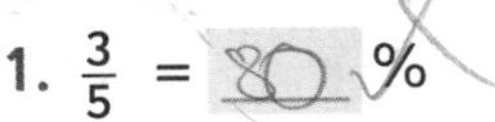

1. $\frac{3}{5}$ = ____ %

2. 8 + 35 ÷ 5 = ____

3. Fill in the missing number on the number line.

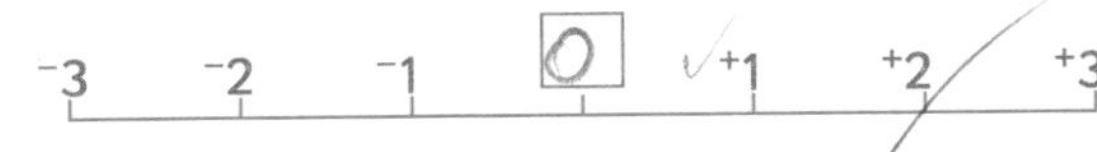


4. 2,786g + 1,100g = ____ kg

5. 7·296km ÷ 4 = ____

6. Increase 240 by 25%. ____

7. What is the area of a rectangle 7cm by 6cm? ____

8.

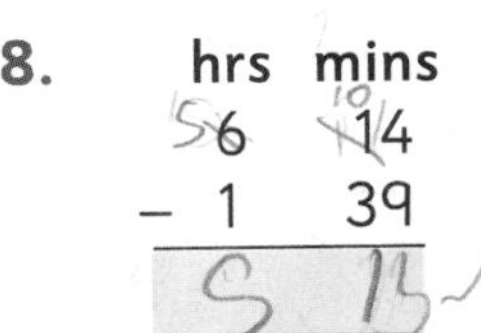
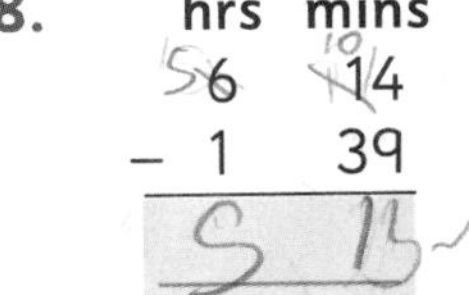

| | hrs | mins |
|---|---|---|
| | 6 | 14 |
| – | 1 | 39 |

9. A cuboid has ____ faces.

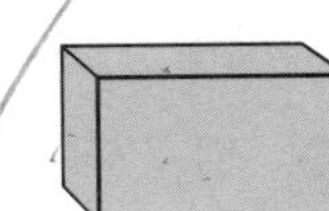

10. 0·3 of 280 = ____

11. $\frac{3}{20} = \frac{?}{100}$ = ____ %

12. Put these in order of size, starting with the largest: 0·45, 50%, $\frac{2}{5}$.

____, ____, ____

13. What is the value of **B**? ____ °

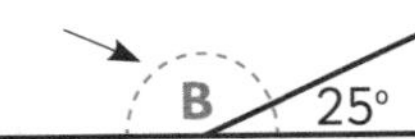


14. Write $8\frac{3}{5}$ as an improper fraction. ____

15. (7 × 2) – (6 × 2) = ____

16. There were 85 stickers in a box. 7 children each took 8 stickers from the box. How many stickers were left? ____

17. Jim has €4 and Sarah has €8. Express Jim's money as a fraction of Sarah's money in its lowest terms. ____

18. The distance from Cian's house to the nearest town is 6km. If he walked $\frac{1}{4}$ of the way and ran the rest of it, how far did he walk? ____

/18

## Thursday

1. 16 + 42 ÷ 7 = ____

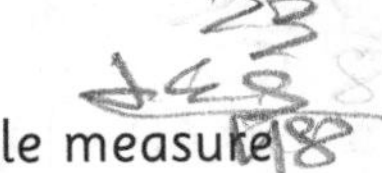

2. If two angles in a triangle measure 73° and 45°, what is the measurement of the third angle? ____ °

3. How likely is it that tomorrow is Friday? ____
(likely, unlikely, certain, impossible)

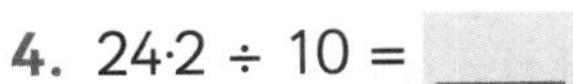

4. 24·2 ÷ 10 = ____

5. 56,425 – 5,000 = ____

6. $\frac{7}{8} - \frac{3}{4}$ = ____

7. Write $\frac{79}{9}$ as a mixed number. ____

8. 4kg 8g = ____ g

9. What is the value of the underlined digit: 18·6<u>4</u>? ____

10. Which of the following is a composite number: 19, 21 or 23? ____

11. Put these in order of size, starting with the largest: 0·2, $\frac{1}{4}$, 17%.

____, ____, ____

12. Find the area of a rectangle 11m by 4m. ____

13. 2·125km × 3 = ____

14. Circle positive 2 on the number line.

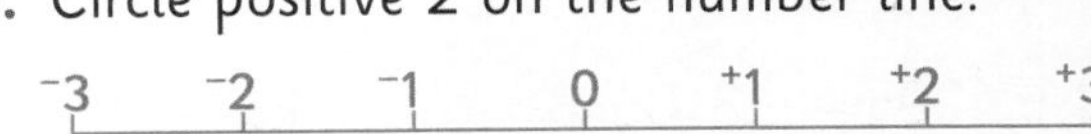


15. Write 2·004 as a fraction. ____

The boys and girls of Fifth Class were asked to select their favourite sport.

| Sport | Hurling | Basketball | Football | Swimming |
|---|---|---|---|---|
| Boys | 2 | 5 | 8 | 1 |
| Girls | 1 | 7 | 5 | 3 |

16. How many boys were surveyed? ____

17. Which sport was the most popular overall? ____

18. How many children completed the survey? ____

/18

See page 86 for test.

Week 22

## Monday

1. $\frac{1}{20}$ = ____ %
2. 5% of 40 = ____
3. Find the area of this shape. ____

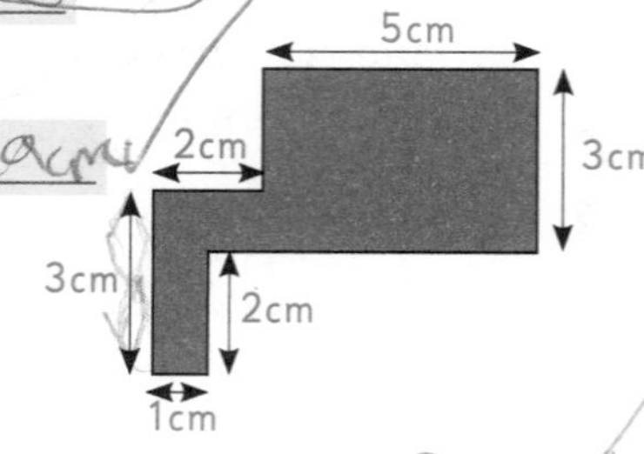


4. Find the perimeter of the shape. ____
5. Which of these is a square number: 34, 35 or 36? ____
6. Calculate the missing angle. ____ °

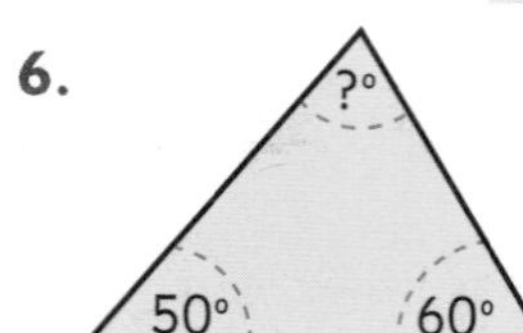

7. Turn this shape 180° and draw.

8. Write $9\frac{3}{4}$ as an improper fraction. ____
9. 935 ÷ 3 = ____ R ____
10. Draw the lines of symmetry on the rhombus.
11. 234 ÷ 10 = ____

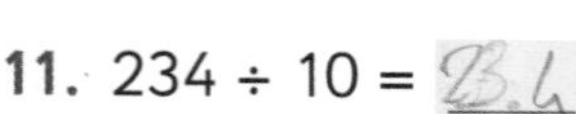

12. 23,003 + 10,635 = ____

13. 6,420g – 2,310g = ____ kg
14. 3·150km × 5 = ____
15. Which is nearer to 60,000: 71,200 or 53,800? ____

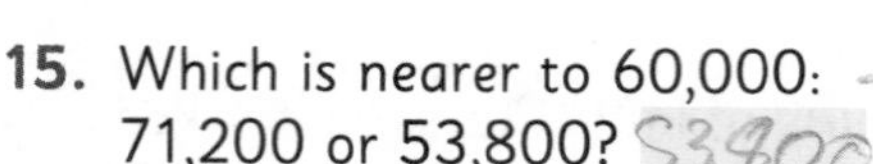

16. A car can travel 25km on one litre of diesel. What is the cost of diesel for a 250km journey at €1·45 per litre? ____
17. If a lotto prize of €15,000 was shared equally among ten people, how much did each get? ____
18. If a family ate $\frac{5}{8}$ of a shepherd's pie every day, how much would they eat in a week? ____

/18

## Tuesday

1. Increase €440 by 30%. ____
2. Put these in order of size, starting with the smallest: 0·6, $\frac{3}{4}$, 55%. ____, ____, ____
3. Write 0·048 as a fraction. ____

4. 6) 0·954
5. 34 × 20 = ____
6. $\frac{4}{9} \times 6$ = ____
7. $6\frac{1}{4} - 2\frac{7}{12}$ = ____
8. A parallelogram has ____ lines of symmetry.
9. $\frac{7}{20}$ = ____ %

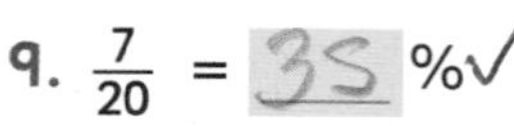

10. 61,735 – 8,000 = ____

11. 63 – 28 ÷ 4 = ____
12. A sphere has ____ face(s).
13. Double 9·3. ____

14.

| | hrs | mins |
|---|---|---|
| | 5 | 26 |
| – | 1 | 48 |

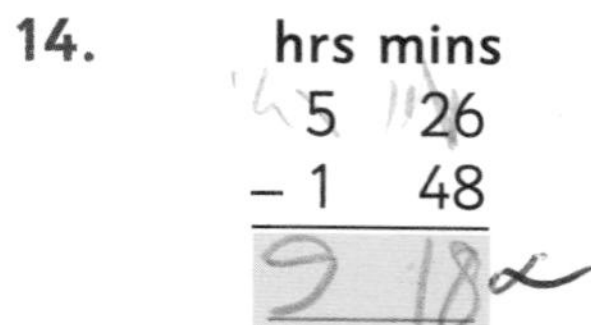

15. $\frac{8}{10} = \frac{?}{100}$ = ____ %

| Boy A = 30kg | Boy B = 35kg |
|---|---|
| Boy C = 45kg | Boy D = ?kg |

16. If the average weight of the four boys is 40kg, what is their total weight? ____
17. What is the weight of Boy D? ____
18. If Boy D weighed 34kg, what would the average weight of the four boys be then? ____

/18

## Wednesday

1. Turn this shape 90° anticlockwise and draw.
2. $86{,}402 - 57{,}315$ = ____
3. Write the number negative 2. ____

4. Name the triangle. ____

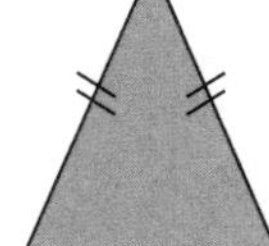

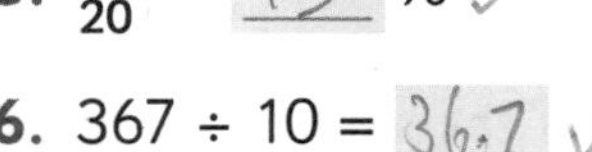

5. $\frac{3}{20}$ = ____ %
6. 367 ÷ 10 = ____

7. Write $\frac{35}{12}$ as a mixed number. ____
8. $6\frac{2}{3} - 2\frac{2}{9}$ = ____

9. $\frac{7}{8} \times 4$ = ____
10. What is the value of 6 in 5·62? ____

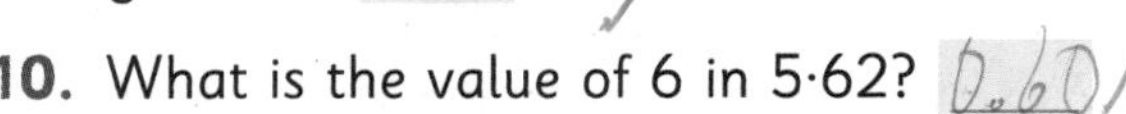

11. Write 3·259 as a fraction. ____
12. Write the time 20 minutes later than the time shown. ____

13. Is 15 a composite number? ____

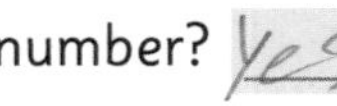

14. What is the area of this shape? ____

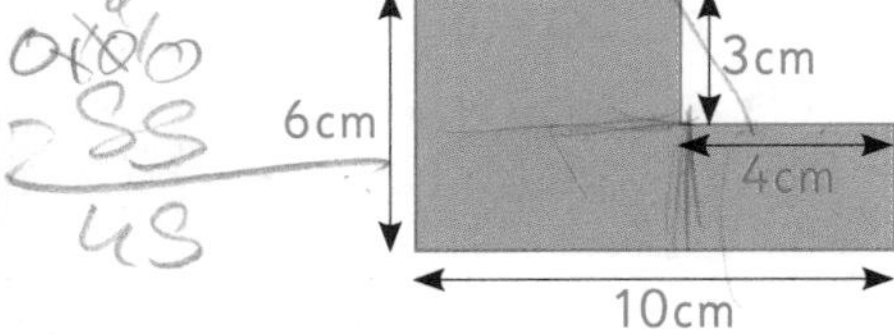



15. What is the perimeter of the square? ____
16. How many bags of sugar weighing 500g can be filled from a box that holds 3·5kg? ____

17. A jug holds 1·345 litres. What is the total capacity of five jugs? ____

1·345l

18. If I spent 0·15 of my money in one shop and $\frac{2}{5}$ of it in another shop, what percentage of my money had I left? ____

/18

## Thursday

1. $\frac{9}{20}$ = ____ %

There are 6 red marbles, 4 green marbles, 2 blue marbles and 3 yellow marbles in a bag.

2. What are the chances of picking a green marble? ____ in ____
3. What are the chances of picking a red or blue marble? ____ in ____
4. What are the chances of picking an orange marble? ____ in ____
5. Complete the sequence. 84, 77, 70, 63, ____
6. c + 28 = 48, so c = ____

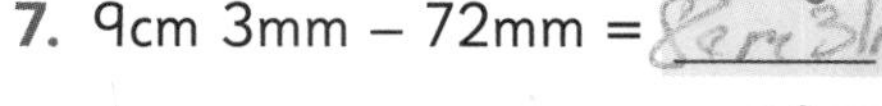

7. 9cm 3mm – 72mm = ____
8. Decrease €970 by 40%. ____
9. $5\frac{7}{10}$km = ____ m

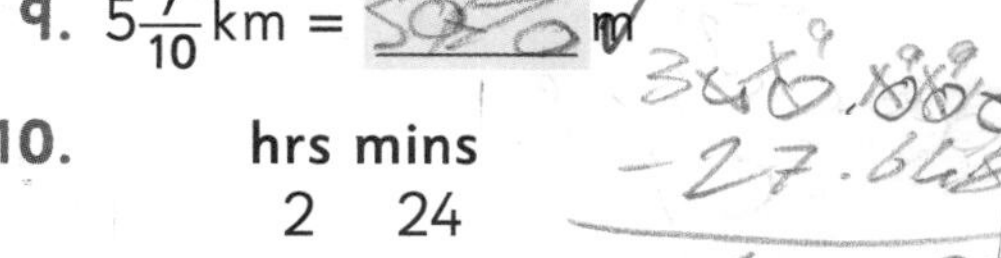

10.

| | hrs | mins |
|---|---|---|
| | 2 | 24 |
| × | | 6 |

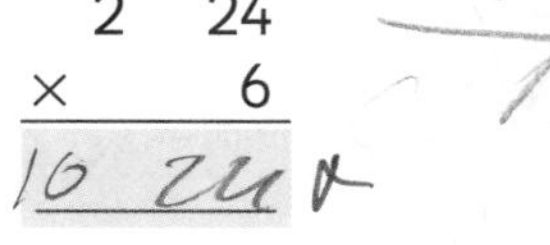

11. Put in order of size, starting with the smallest: $\frac{4}{10}$, $\frac{3}{5}$, 0·5. ____, ____, ____
12. 1·250 × 3 = ____
13. Write 0·076 as a fraction. ____
14. $5\frac{7}{10} - 1\frac{1}{5}$ = ____
15. 2·87 × 10 = ____

The Kelly family are going on holidays abroad and have a baggage allowance of 40kg.

16. If they have two bags packed weighing 15·6kg and 12kg 48g, how much more are they allowed to bring? ____
17. If they decided to bring this remaining amount in two bags of equal weight, how much would each bag weigh? ____
18. The family are bringing four bags. If they had divided the weight evenly between the four bags, how much would have been in each bag? ____

/18

See page 87 for test.

## Monday

1. 9,591 ÷ 7 = ____

2. 12,645 × 4

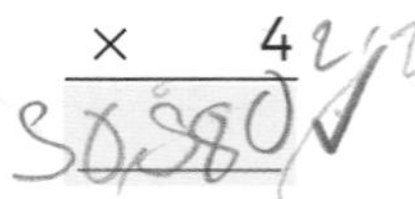

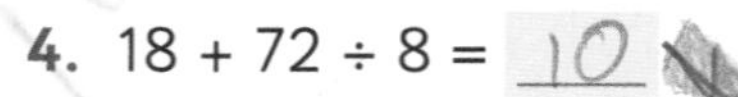

3. Write the number negative 1. ____

4. 18 + 72 ÷ 8 = ____

5. All the angles in a scalene triangle are ____. (equal/unequal)

6. Find the measurement of angle **A**. ____ °

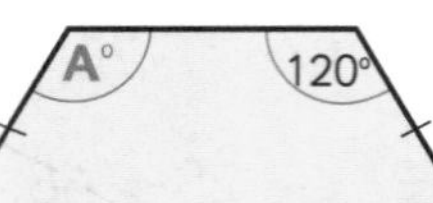


7. 380 ÷ 20 = ____

8. Write $2\frac{5}{12}$ as an improper fraction. ____

9. $\frac{9}{10} \times 5 =$ ____

10. $5\frac{7}{10} - 1\frac{2}{5} =$ ____

11. Put in order of size, starting with the smallest: 0·385, 37%, $\frac{2}{5}$.
____, ____, ____

12. What time is 35 minutes later than 17:35? ____ : ____

13. What angle is made by the hands of a clock showing 3 o'clock? ____

14. 1kg 100g – 1,063g = ____

15. A triangular prism has ____ faces.

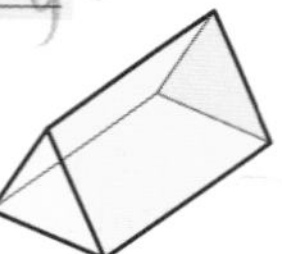

16. A bench is 4·06m long. Another bench is 25cm longer. What is the length of the second bench? ____

17. If one ice-cream costs 95c, how much change would I get from €5 if I buy 4 ice-creams? ____

18. Liam finished watching a film at 22:45. If the film lasted for 1 hour and 38 minutes, at what time did the film begin? ____ : ____

/18

## Tuesday

1. 9,563 + 16 = ____

2. $\frac{1}{5} = \frac{?}{100} =$ ____ %

3. Draw an acute angle.

4. Find the area of this shape. ____

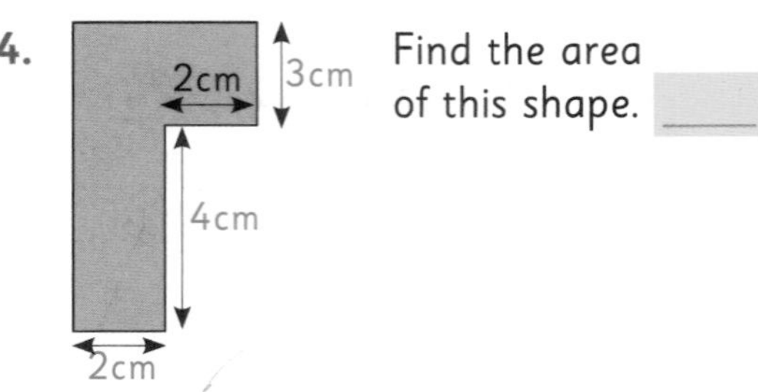


5. Find the perimeter of the shape. ____

6. If this month is February, what are the chances of next month being July: 0%, 50%, 100%? ____

7. $x =$ ____ °

x°
135°

8. Write the number negative 2. ____

9. 485 ÷ 10 = ____

10. 24 + 56 ÷ 8 = ____

11. $6^2 =$ ____

12. 0·2 of 170 = ____

13. Write $3\frac{5}{12}$ as an improper fraction. ____

14.

| hrs | mins |
|---|---|
| 5 | 19 |
| – 2 | 48 |
| ____ | |

15. Round 7,658 to the nearest 100. ____

Lorna went to the garage to buy a new car. The car she wanted to buy was priced at €32,000. The salesman said he would give her a 10% discount.

16. How much of a discount would she get off the price of the car? ____

17. What would be the new price of the car? ____

18. If she got a further reduction of €500, what would the car cost then? ____

/18

## Wednesday

1. $73 - 9 \times 6 =$ ____

2. $7{,}386 - 29 =$ ____

3. $1{\cdot}24 \times 100 =$ ____

4. $3\frac{1}{8} + 2\frac{3}{4} =$ ____

5. This is a ____ triangle.

6. $3^2 =$ ____

7. $2{\cdot}85 \div 10 =$ ____

8. If a boy can cycle 10km in 30 minutes, how far can he cycle in an hour? ____

9. Write $\frac{62}{7}$ as a mixed number. ____

10. If the temperature is $^{-}1$°C in London and it is 16°C hotter in Amsterdam, what temperature is it in Amsterdam? ____ °C

11. $2\frac{3}{5}$km = ____ m

12. $10^2 =$ ____

13. A pentagonal prism has ____ edges.

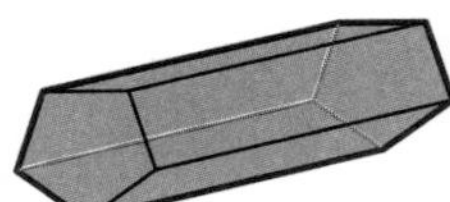

14. What time is 45 minutes later than 17:30 ? ____ : ____

15. Increase €70 by 50%. ____

16. Keith bought a car for €5,000. He sold it again and made a 10% profit. How much did he sell the car for? ____

17. $\frac{3}{4}$ of the children were present at school last Friday. If there were 90 children present, how many children were absent? ____

18. Jonathan spends 1 hour 10 minutes doing his homework every evening. How long does he spend every week doing his homework if he has homework four nights of the week? ____

/18

## Thursday

1. $16{,}482 - 200 =$ ____

2. What is the value of 2 in 6·32? ____

3. $\frac{1}{4} \times 9 =$ ____

4. $4\frac{5}{12} - 2\frac{3}{4} =$ ____

5. Write 5·097 in fraction form. ____

6. $845 \div 9 =$ ____ R ____

7. $5{\cdot}25 + 7\frac{3}{4} =$ ____

8. The angle made by the hands of a clock showing 6 o'clock is ____°.

9. A tetrahedron has ____ faces.

10. The square root of 49 is ____ .

11. 40% of 250 = ____

12. $4\overline{)9{\cdot}372\text{kg}}$ ____

13. How many steps from $^{-}2$ to $^{+}4$? ____

14. 
$$\begin{array}{r} 85{\cdot}62 \\ \times \quad 7 \\ \hline \end{array}$$
____

15. $68 - 4 \times 7 =$ ____

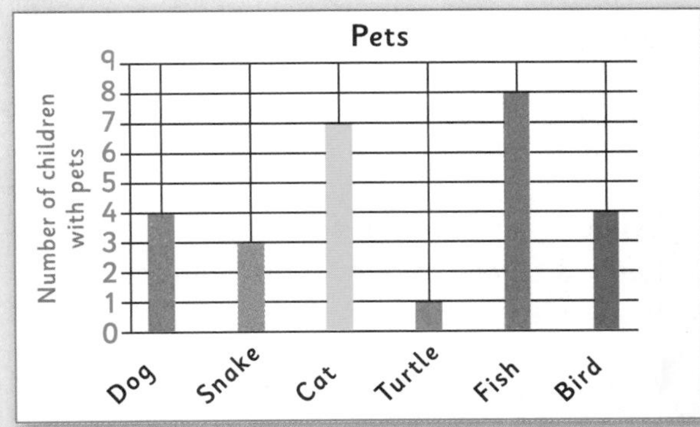


16. How many children have fish? ____

17. How many more children have cats than turtles? ____

18. Which two animals do the same number of children have? ____ and ____

/18

See page 88 for test.

## Monday

1. Draw the line of symmetry through this shape.

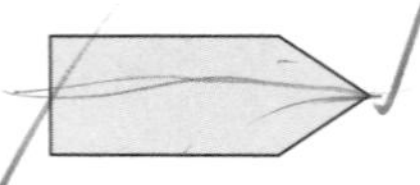

2. 12,583 + 17 = ____
3. What is the third composite number? ____
4. What fraction of the circle is shaded? ____

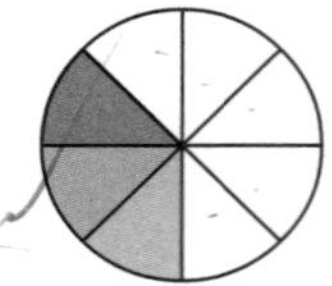

5. By how many degrees is 12°C warmer than ⁻2°C? ____
6.  Grace can cycle 2km in 5 minutes. How far can she travel in an hour? ____
7. Find the whole number if 30% = 36. ____
8. Draw the net of a cube.

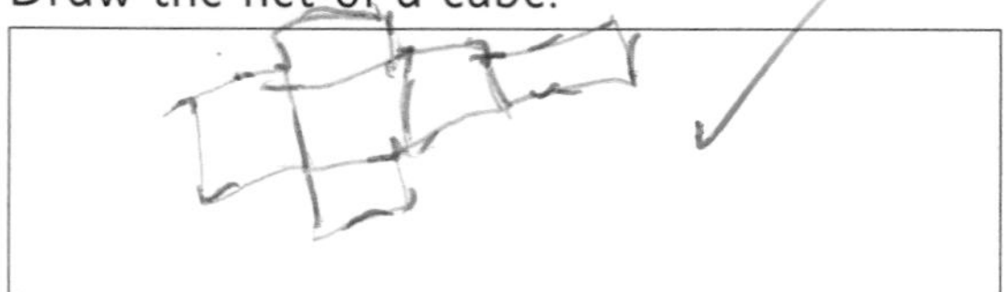

9. What is 40% of €300? ____
10. What is the value of angle **Y**? ____°

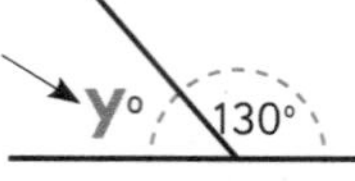


11. Write $\frac{11}{20}$ as a decimal fraction. ____
12. 80 × 20 = ____
13. Write $\frac{38}{9}$ as a mixed number. ____
14. 780 ÷ 10 = ____
15. $11^2$ = ____

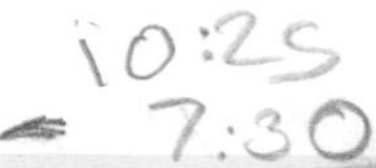

16. William is 1m 45cm tall. Leah is 50cm smaller than William. How tall is Leah? ____
17. A meeting started at 7.30pm. It lasted for 2 hours 45 minutes. At what time did the meeting end? ____
18. Sharon was asked to multiply 2·43 by 23. Instead she multiplied 2·43 by 32. By how much was her answer too big? ____

## Tuesday

1. 45,386 − 4,000 = ____
2. 4·56 × 10 = ____
3. Round 4·2 to the nearest whole number. ____
4. Which of these is a multiple of 7: 16, 20, 28, 34? ____
5. Name the 2-D shape. ____
6. Circle negative 5 on the number line.

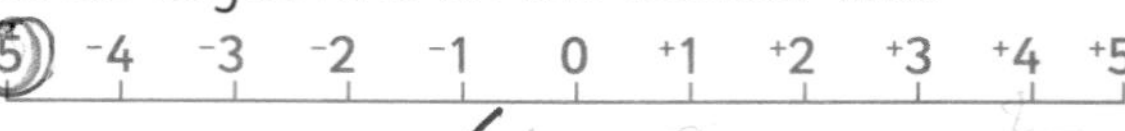


7. $4 \times \frac{2}{9}$ = ____
8. This is the net of a ____

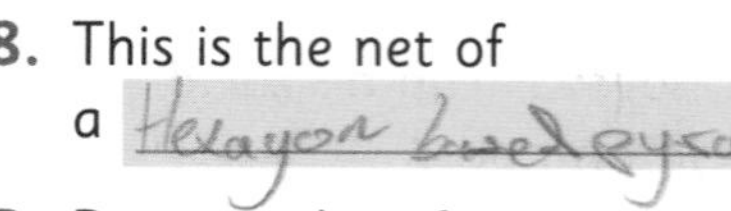

9. Put in order of size, starting with the smallest: $4\frac{1}{10}$, 4·23, $4\frac{1}{4}$.
____, ____, ____
10. If I face north and turn 90° clockwise, I am now facing ____.

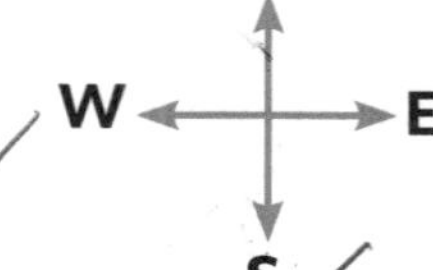


11. How many degrees are there between north and south? ____
12. From south, I go 90° anticlockwise. I land on ____.
13. 75% of 352 = ____

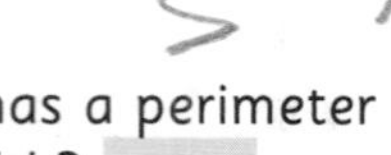

14. A rectangle 32cm long has a perimeter of 98cm. What is its width? ____
15. What is the area of the rectangle? ____

This is the plan of a sitting room in a house.

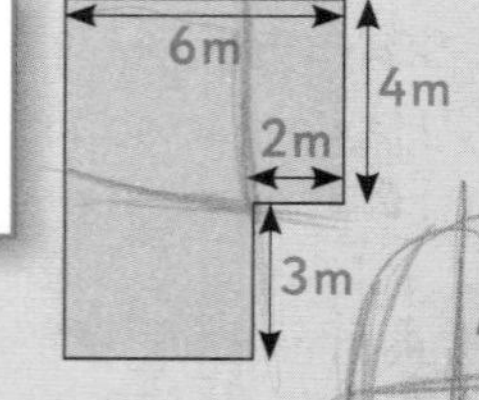


16. What is the area of this room? ____
17. If carpet cost €35 per square metre, how much would it cost to carpet the room? ____
18. The owner decided to put coving right around the ceiling of the room. If it costs €10 per metre, how much would it cost for the room? ____

/18

## Wednesday

1. $\frac{1}{3} + \frac{2}{9}$ = ___

2. Write $2\frac{5}{6}$ as an improper fraction. ___

3. 81,735 + 9,000 = ___

4. $5\overline{)8{\cdot}395}$km
___

5. 20% off a €240 jacket.
New price = ___

6. Write 2·035 as a fraction. ___

7. What type of angle is made by the hands of a clock pointing at 10 o'clock? ___

8. 1·6 + 0·39 = ___

9. Round 6·8 to the nearest whole number. ___

10. What is the radius of a circle if its diameter is 6cm? ___

11.

| | hrs | mins |
|---|---|---|
| | 8 | 12 |
| – | 3 | 46 |
| | ___ | |

12. This is the net of a ___

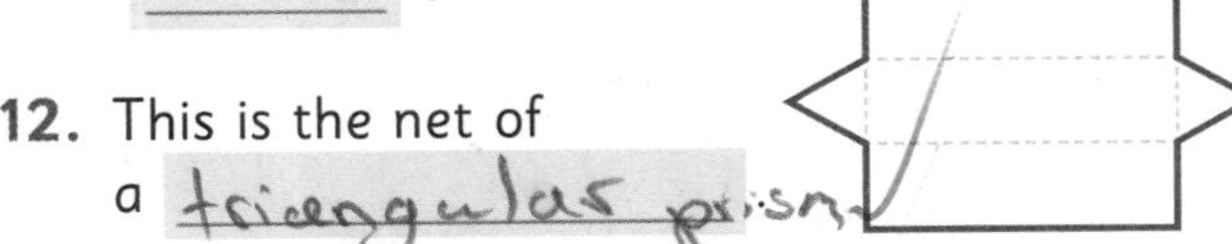

13. The first five multiples of 9 are ___, ___, ___, ___ and ___

14. Two angles in a triangle are 65° and 49°.
What is the third angle? ___°

15. 97 ÷ 10 = ___

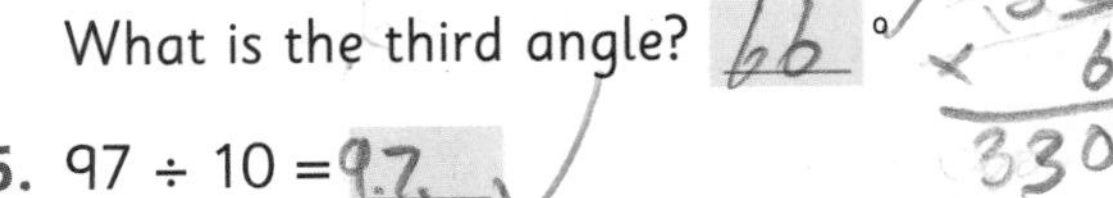

16. 45% of the children in a school are boys. If there are 600 children in the school, how many are girls? ___

17. A programme started at 17:40.
It lasted for $1\frac{1}{2}$ hours.
At what time did it end? ___

18. In a container of 1,000 apples, 48 of them were bad.
What decimal of them were bad? ___

/18

## Thursday

1. 645 ÷ 9 = ___ R ___

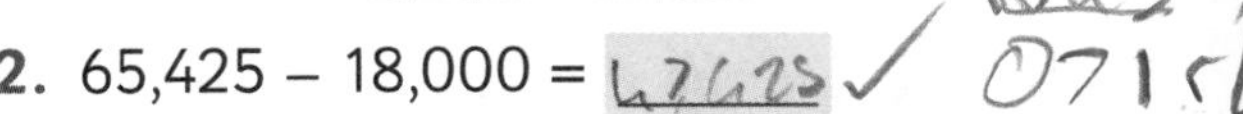

2. 65,425 – 18,000 = ___

3. Write $\frac{68}{7}$ as a mixed number. ___

4. Circle positive 4 on the number line.

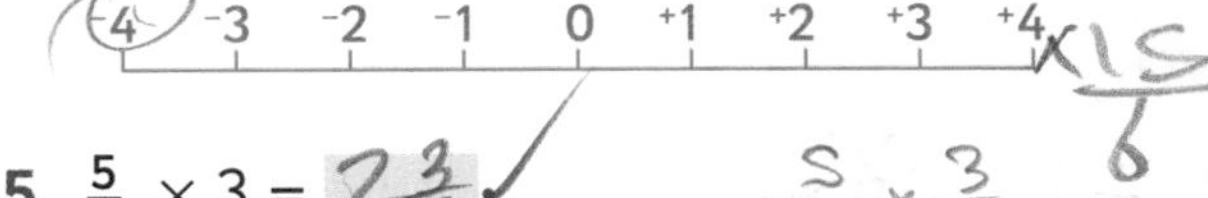


5. $\frac{5}{6} \times 3$ = ___

6. $4\frac{3}{4}$ $2\frac{7}{12}$ = ___

7. Name the 2-D shape. ___

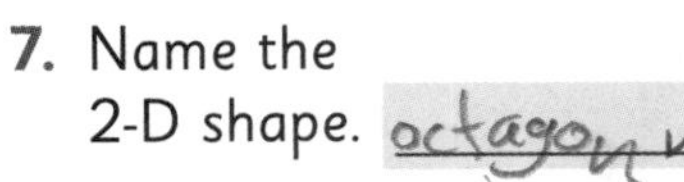

8. €9·42 ÷ 6 = ___

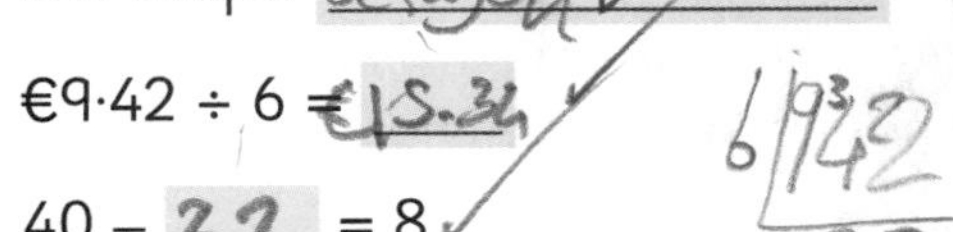

9. 40 – ___ = 8

10. Write as am or pm:
10 to 8 in the evening. ___

11. A tetrahedron has ___ vertices.

12. If the diameter of a circle is 16cm, what is the radius? ___

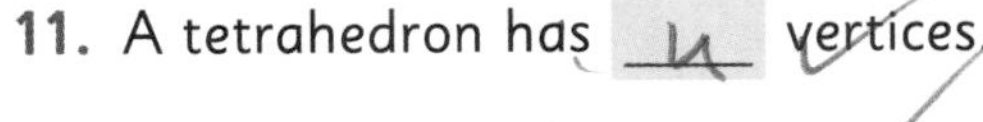

13. 5km 384m + 4·200km = ___

14. Find the average of these numbers: 10, 11, 9, 12, 8. ___

15. How many degrees is ⁻3° hotter than ⁻8°? ___

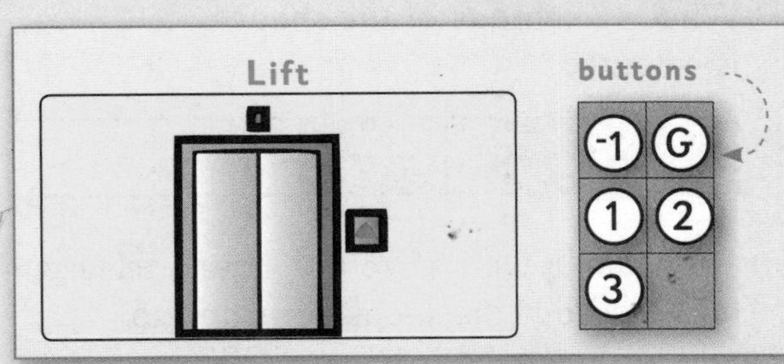


16. What number do you think could represent the letter **G**? ___

17. If Michael entered the lift on level 3 and went down two levels, then back up one, which floor would he be on? ___

18. How many floors are there from ⁻1 to ⁺3? ___

/18

See page 89 for test.

Week 25

## Monday

1. $12{\cdot}45 \times 100 =$ ____
2. Write $2\frac{3}{10}$ as an improper fraction. ____
3. $56{,}524 + 18{,}000 =$ ____
4. 

| | hrs | mins |
|---|---|---|
| | 4 | 25 |
| × | | 4 |
| | ____ | |

5. $\frac{86}{100} = 0{\cdot}86$. True or false? ____
6. 7l 635ml ÷ 5 = ____
7. Write as am or pm:
   20 past 6 in the evening. ____
8. 165cm = ____ m
9. Increase 135 by 20%. ____
10. Circle negative 2 on the number line.

$^{-}3 \quad ^{-}2 \quad ^{-}1 \quad 0 \quad ^{+}1 \quad ^{+}2 \quad ^{+}3$

11. What are the factors of 20? ____, ____, ____, ____, ____ and ____
12. A hexagonal prism has ____ edges.
13. The radius of a circle is 4cm.
    What is its diameter? ____
14. Write $0{\cdot}004$ as a fraction. ____
15. What percentage of the shape is coloured? ____

16. Tim's family wanted to buy a new television for €500 but the shopkeeper had to add on Value Added Tax of 20%. How much did the television cost the family then? ____
17. $\frac{3}{4}$ of a number is 27.
    What is the number? ____
18. Rory went to a concert at 7.45pm and came home at 11.20pm.
    How long was he away?
    ____ hours ____ minutes

/18

## Tuesday

1. Is 21 a composite number? ____
2. 53 + ____ = 61
3. 586 ÷ 10 = ____
4. Draw a right-angled triangle.

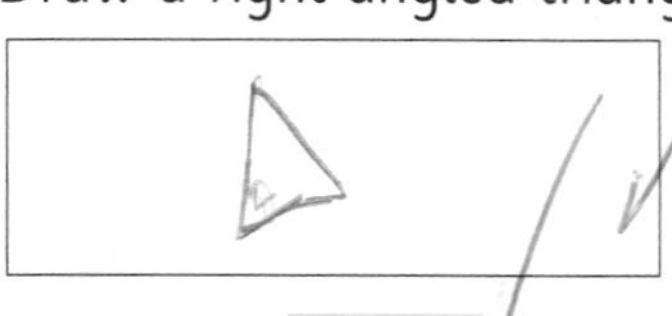

5. $95 \times 20 =$ ____

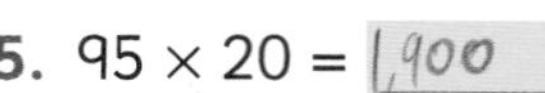

6. $63{,}428 - 19{,}000 =$ ____

7. What is the area of a rectangle with a width of 5cm and a perimeter of 36cm? ____
8. How many lines of symmetry has a rectangle? ____
9. $4{,}045\text{g} - 3{\cdot}095\text{kg} =$ ____
10. A hemisphere has ____ edges.
11. Write $\frac{17}{20}$ as a decimal fraction. ____
12. 10% of 640 = ____
13. $6\frac{1}{4} - 4\frac{5}{8} =$ ____
14. $4\overline{)984}$
15. $1\frac{3}{5}$ l = ____ ml

**John** works from 9am to 5pm Monday to Friday and earns **€9** per hour.

**Gretta** works from 8am to 3pm Monday to Friday and earns **€9·50** per hour.

**Jason** works from 7.30am to 4pm Monday to Friday and earns **€10** per hour.

Work out what each person earns per week.

16. John = ____
17. Gretta = ____

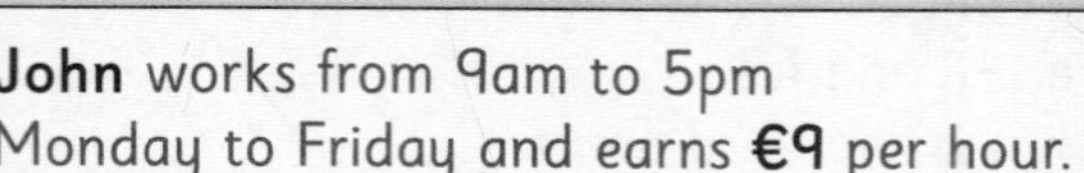

18. Jason = ____

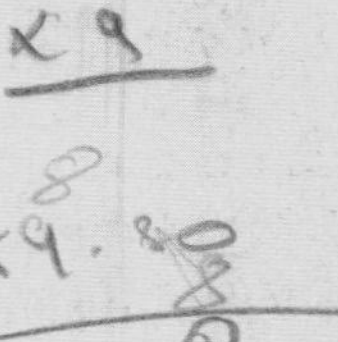

/18

## Wednesday

1. €4·25 x 3 =

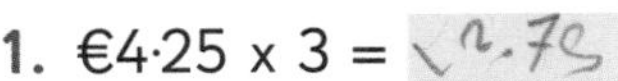

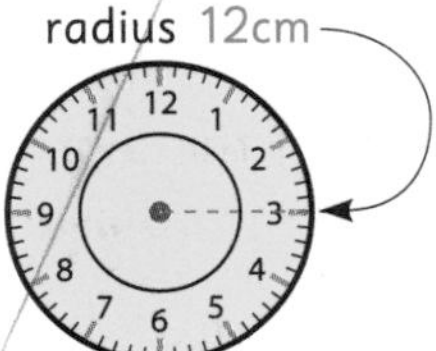


2. What is the diameter of this clock?
3. Write 2km 65m as a decimal. ______ km
4. $3{\cdot}46 \times 10 =$
5. How many hours and minutes are there from 08:45 to 10:15?
   ______ hour(s) ______ minutes
6. Decrease 752 by 25%.
7. $1\frac{3}{4}$kg = ______ g
8. $1\frac{1}{5} + 2\frac{6}{10} =$
9. $1{\cdot}11 \times 3 =$
10. Write $\frac{53}{9}$ as a mixed number.
11. $(11 \times 8) + 7 =$

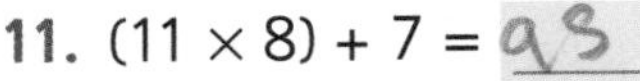

12. Complete the sequence.
    1, 4, 10, 19, ______
13. 

    The length of the rectangle is double its width. Find its perimeter.
14. Find the area of the rectangle.
15. $\frac{2}{5} =$ ______ %

16. Maurice's boss is giving him a 10% increase in his wages. Maurice earned €80 a day before the increase. How much will his weekly wage be after the increase (5-day week)?
17. There were 621 glasses in a box. 13 of them were damaged and had to be removed. The rest were placed on shelves in rows of 16. How many shelves did they fill?
18. Jim had €80. He spent 0·3 of it. How much did he spend?

/18

## Thursday

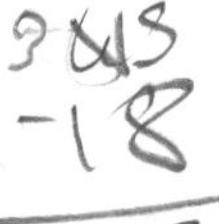

1. 76,345 – 18 =
2. $58 \div 100 =$
3. $1{\cdot}23 \times 10 =$
4. Find the whole number if $\frac{1}{8} = 12$.
5. Write $\frac{3}{20}$ as a decimal fraction.
6. Which of these is a multiple of 6: 13, 28, 35, 42, 53?
7. A pentagonal prism has ______ faces.

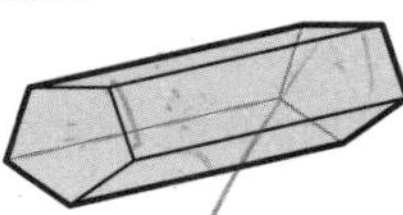

8. By how many degrees is $^{+}2°$ hotter than $^{-}4°$?
9. $(12 \times 9) + 7 =$
10. $8^2 =$
11. 214cm = ______ m
12. Find the value of **Y**. ______ °

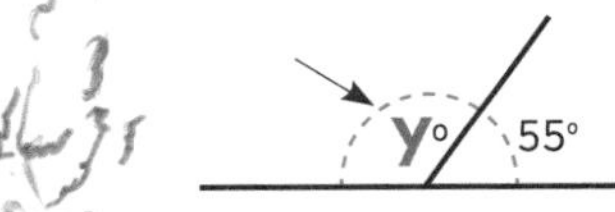


13. What is the value of the underlined digit: 5·00<u>6</u>?
14. $3{\cdot}52 + 9{\cdot}05 =$
15. Write $9\frac{7}{8}$ as an improper fraction.

16. If Frank had €5, what fraction had he of the cost of the hurley?
17. Write the price of the football as a percentage of the price of the tennis racket.
18. If Janet had €28, write this amount as a fraction of the total of the three items in its lowest terms.

/18

See page 90 for test.

## Monday

1. An octagon has ____ lines of symmetry.

2. Simplify $\frac{6}{8}$. ____
3. $100{,}000 - 10 =$ ____
4. $\frac{7}{10} =$ ____ %
5. $20\overline{)240}$
6. Are the numbers 5 and 9 both prime numbers? ____
7. Turn this arrow 90° anticlockwise and draw.
8. $3\frac{9}{12} - 1\frac{1}{4} =$ ____
9. Round 6·5 to the nearest whole number. ____
10. $(10 \times 20) + (4 \times 50) =$ ____
11. $6 \times 8 = 30 + \mathbf{x}$, so $\mathbf{x} =$ ____
12. Draw an equilateral triangle.

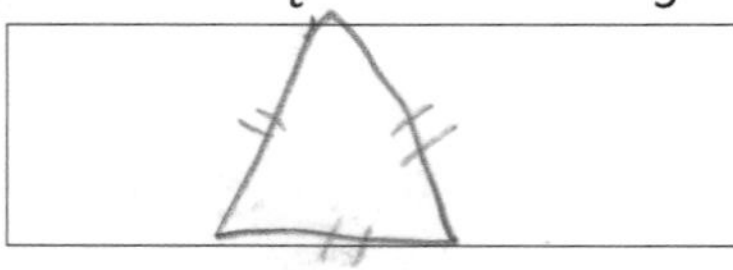

13. Write $6\frac{5}{9}$ as an improper fraction. ____
14. What part of the circle is the arrow pointing to? ____

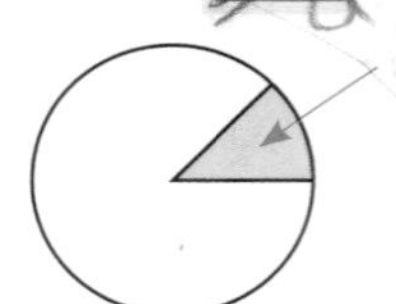

15. Round 16,582 to the nearest 1,000. ____

16. A farmer sold 25 of her 40 sheep. What fraction of her sheep did she sell (in its lowest terms)? ____

17. If 200g of tomatoes cost 80c, how much would 1·4kg of tomatoes cost? ____

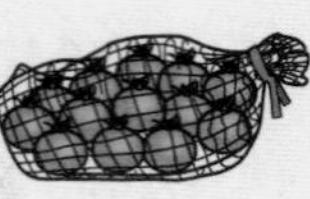

18. A train can carry 526 passengers. How many passengers can 12 trains hold? ____

/18

## Tuesday

1. $11^2 =$ ____
2. If the diameter of a circle is 10cm, its radius is ____.
3. A dishwasher costs €600. It is reduced by 20%. What is the new price? ____
4. $\frac{4}{9} + \frac{2}{9} + \frac{1}{9} =$ ____
5. Write $\frac{3}{20}$ as a percentage. ____
6. By how many degrees is $^{+}3°$ hotter than $^{-}1°$? ____
7. Show a 180° turn.

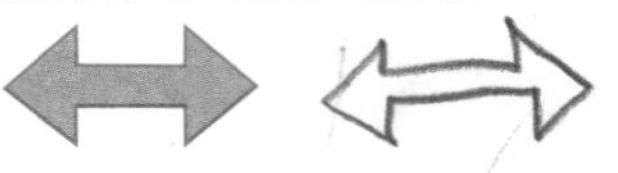

8. Find the area of the shape.

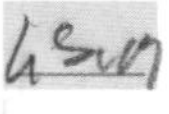

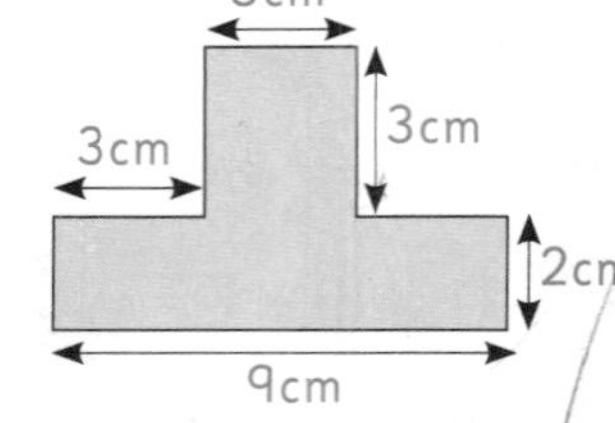


9. Find the perimeter of the shape. ____
10. €1·25 × 6 = ____
11. 1·7l = ____ ml

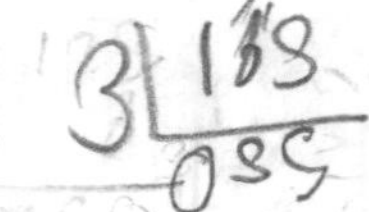

12. How many hours and minutes are there from 7.38pm to 9.15pm? ____ hour(s) ____ minutes
13. $117{,}000 - 19 =$ ____
14. $685 \div 10 =$ ____
15. $78 - 72 \div 9 =$ ____

It cost €1,650 to carpet the bedroom in a house. The carpet was €30 a square metre.

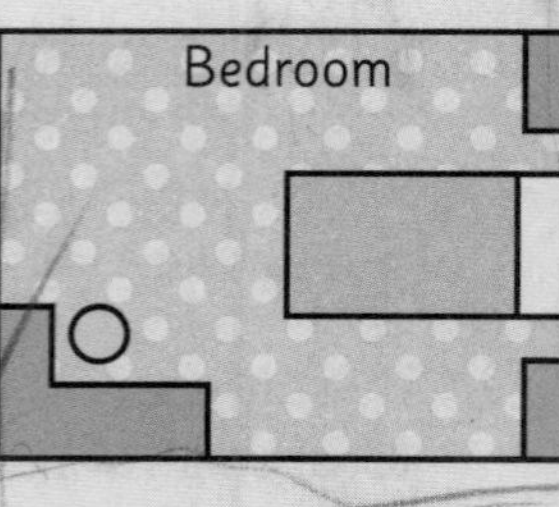


16. Find the area of the room. ____
17. If the length of the room is 11m, what would the width of the room be? ____
18. Find the perimeter of the room. ____

/18

## Wednesday

1. 8·42 + 8·04 = ____
2. Complete the sequence. 1, 3, 7, 13, ____
3. By how many degrees is $^{+}5°$ hotter than $^{-}3°$? ____
4. 500g of bananas are €1·20. How much for 3kg of bananas? ____

The following graph shows the amount of rain that fell in 5 days.

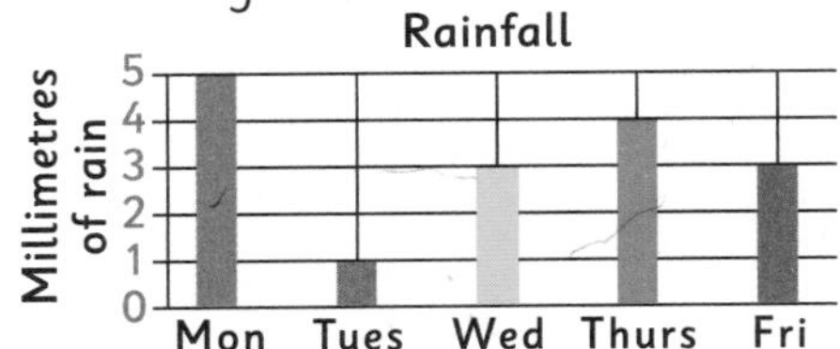


5. Which day had the most rain? ____
6. Which day had the least rain? ____
7. What was the total amount of rain that fell in the 5 days (answer in cm)? ____
8. What was the average amount of rain that fell over the 5 days (answer to nearest mm)? ____
9. 20,409 – 1,500 = ____
10. $6^2$ = ____
11. What part of the circle is the arrow pointing to? ____
12. Round 63,429 to the nearest 10. ____
13. Name the 2-D shape. ____

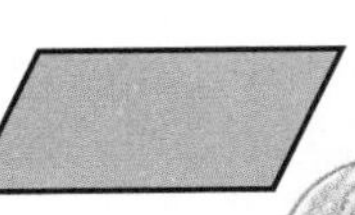

14. Write $\frac{43}{9}$ as a mixed number. ____
15. 48 × 3 = ____
16. What number is 5,093 greater than 63,489? ____
17. What is the difference between 16 times 526 and 15 times 482? ____
18. A newsagent had 100 newspapers. She sold $\frac{4}{5}$ of them. How many had she left? ____

/18

## Thursday

1. The square root of 64 is ____.
2. A parallelogram has ____ lines of symmetry.

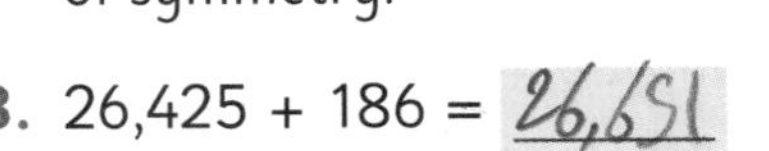

3. 26,425 + 186 = ____
4. 1·23 × 10 = ____
5. Write $\frac{39}{7}$ as a mixed number. ____
6. $\frac{3}{4}$ × 9 = ____
7. A pentagonal pyramid has ____ vertices.

8. Find the third angle. ____ °

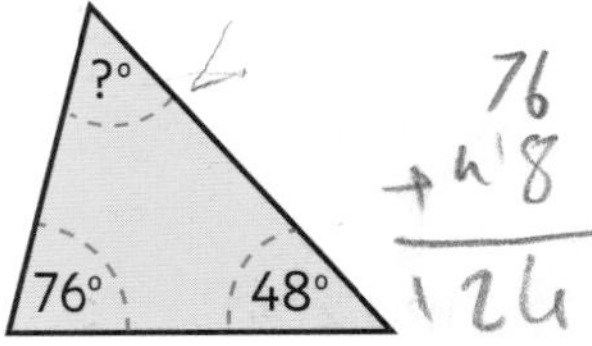


9. Write $\frac{1}{100}$ as a decimal fraction. ____
10. $\frac{3}{8} + \frac{3}{8} + \frac{1}{8}$ = ____
11. Colour the thermometer to $^{+}1$.
12. What are the chances of throwing an odd number on a die? ____ in ____
13. Which is nearer to 49,200: 48,500 or 50,000? ____

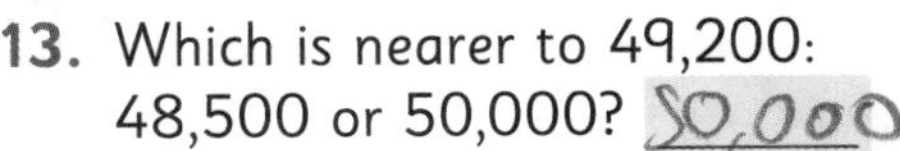

14. 6)192

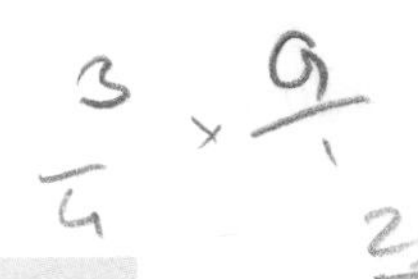

15. (7 × 9) – (4 × 8) = ____

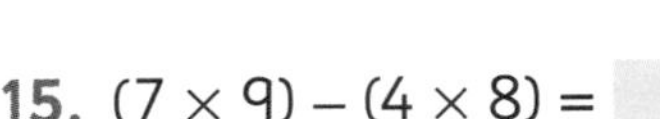

A carton of orange juice holds 250ml.
A large bottle of orange juice holds 1·5l.

16. How many bottles of orange juice are equal to 24 cartons of orange juice? ____
17. How much money would you save by buying the bottle at €2 if each carton costs 55c? ____
18. How much money would you save when buying 3l of each? ____

/18

See page 91 for test.

## Monday

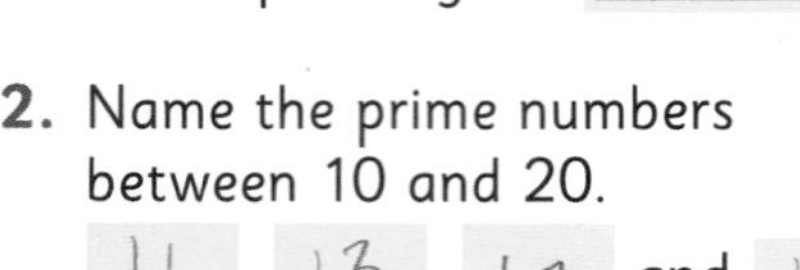

1. What part of the circle is the arrow pointing to? ______

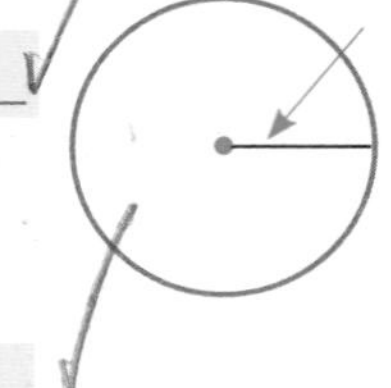

2. Name the prime numbers between 10 and 20.
   ____, ____, ____ and ____

3. What is the highest common factor of 24 and 36? ______

4. $11 \times \frac{3}{5}$ = ______

5. $5\frac{1}{3} - 2\frac{5}{6}$ = ______

6. 6)908
   ____ R ____

7. 180 ÷ 20 = ______

8. Write $\frac{78}{9}$ as a mixed number. ______

9. 5,970 – 140 = ______

10. Write 0·019 as a fraction. ______

11. The angle between the hands on a clock showing 7 o'clock is an ______ angle.

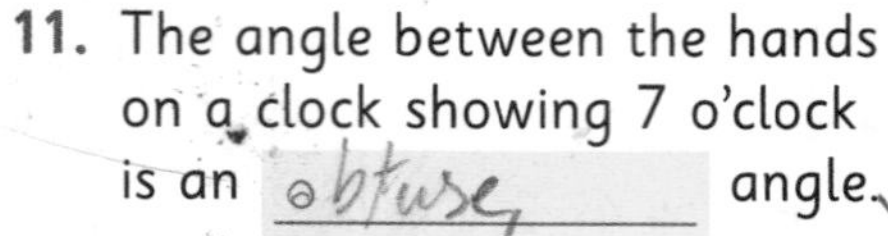

12. $\frac{3}{4}$ = ____ %

13. Put in order of size, starting with the smallest: 78%, $\frac{3}{4}$, 0·8.
    ____, ____, ____

14. Increase 295 by 40%. ______

15. $3\frac{7}{100}$l = ______ ml

16. Janet watched two programmes on television one Saturday, one from 1.20pm to 2.10pm and another from 5.15pm to 6.05pm. How long did she spend watching television? ______

17. A butcher sold a turkey weighing $8\frac{1}{2}$kg. If he sold it at €4·20 per kg, how much did he receive for the turkey? ______

18. Dervla weighs 40·365kg. If Noelle weighs 460g less than Dervla, what weight is Noelle? ______

/18

## Tuesday

1. If the diameter of a circle is 16cm, its radius is ______.

2. $\frac{1}{2}$ = ____ %

3. 6)7·458l

4. 60% of 25 = ______

5. The temperature is $^{+}4$°C. If it drops by 5°, what temperature will it be? ______

6. Write $\frac{34}{8}$ as a mixed number. ______

7. $\frac{3}{5} \times 7$ = ______

8. Find the area of a rectangle with a width of 11cm and a perimeter of 54cm. ______

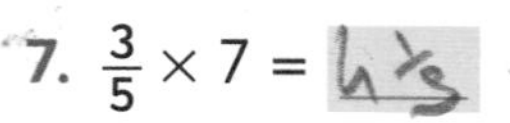

9. $\frac{5}{6} = \frac{\square}{12}$

10. 112 minutes = ____ hour(s) ____ minutes

11. Name the shape.

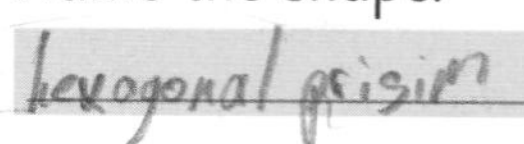

12. The square root of 9 = ______

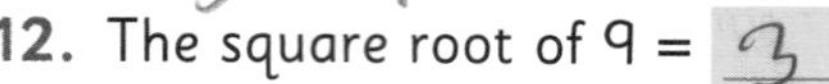

13. 3·462 × 7

14. Write $\frac{63}{1000}$ as a decimal fraction. ______

15. What is the value of 7 in 2·17? ______

The diameter of the €1 coin is 23·25mm.
The diameter of the €2 is 25·75mm.

23·25mm

25·75mm

16. What is the diameter of the €1 to the nearest cm? ______

17. What is the radius of the €2 coin to the nearest mm? ______

18. What is the length of four €1 coins? ______

/18

## Wednesday

1. Complete the sequence.
   4·68, 4·7, 4·74, 4·8, ____
2. Write $\frac{11}{100}$ as a decimal fraction. ____
3. Write $\frac{59}{7}$ as a mixed number. ____
4. $\frac{7}{8} \times 5 =$ ____
5. What fraction of this shape is shaded? ____

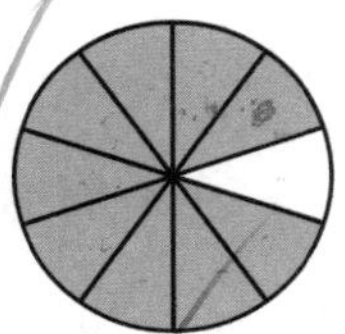

6. Increase 560 by 30%. ____
7. $4\frac{19}{1000}$ km = ____ m
8. 160 ÷ 20 = ____
9. 45,620 + 185 = ____
10. Write as am or pm:
    quarter to 11 in the evening. ____
11. 34 + 45 ÷ 5 = ____
12. By how many degrees is ⁻5° hotter than ⁻12°? ____
13. What are the chances of getting an odd number when I roll a die:
    0%, 50%, 100%? ____
14.

| | kg | g |
|---|---|---|
| | 2 | 562 |
| | 4 | 100 |
| + | 2 | 185 |
| | | |

15. What is the perimeter of an octagon with 2cm sides? ____

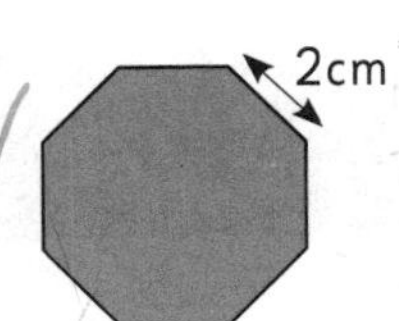


16. If 9 oranges cost €4·50, how much would 13 oranges cost? ____
17. Jamie can cycle 7km in 15 minutes. How far will he travel in 2 hours? ____
18. 0·45 of the children at a match were girls. If there were 81 girls, how many boys were there at the match? ____

/18

## Thursday

1. The outside part of a circle is called the ____.

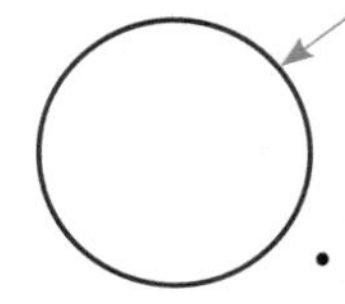

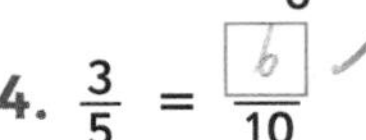

2. $6\frac{11}{12} - 3\frac{2}{3} =$ ____
3. Write $5\frac{5}{6}$ as an improper fraction. ____
4. $\frac{3}{5} = \frac{\square}{10}$
5. 647 ÷ 9 = ____ R ____
6. A ____ has 5 straight sides.
7. Draw the net of a triangular prism.

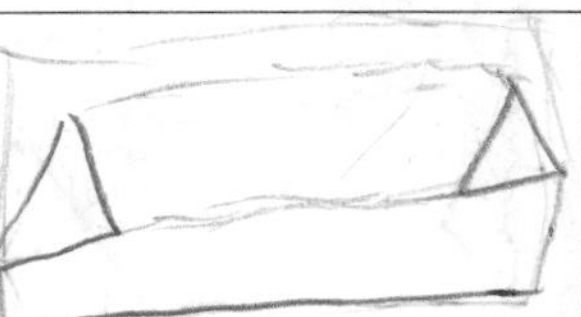

8. 16 × 20 = ____
9.

| |
|---|
| 81,492 |
| − 53,428 |
| |

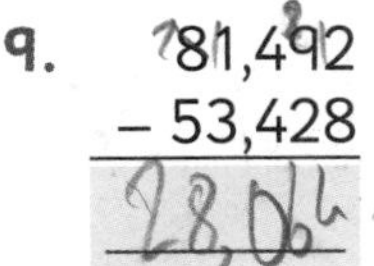

10. €10 − €4·28 = ____
11. 15% of 80 = ____
12. 2l 65ml = ____ ml

13. 24 ____ 7 = 31

14. 2·4km × 5 = ____ km
15.

| | hrs | mins |
|---|---|---|
| | 2 | 45 |
| × | | 4 |
| | | |

Jessie and her friends ordered 3 pizzas and ate the following amounts of pizza each:

Jessie = $\frac{1}{2}$

Liam = $\frac{2}{3}$

Brian = $\frac{3}{4}$

Sarah = $\frac{1}{2}$

16. How much pizza did Brian and Jessie eat between them? ____
17. How much pizza was eaten altogether? ____
18. How much pizza was left? ____

/18

See page 92 for test.

Week 28

## Monday

1. x + 14 = 30, so x = ____
2. 24 ÷ 4 ____ 36 ÷ 9 (<, > or =)
3. 30% of 430 = ____
4. A cylinder has ____ edges.
5. What part of the circle is the arrow pointing to? ____

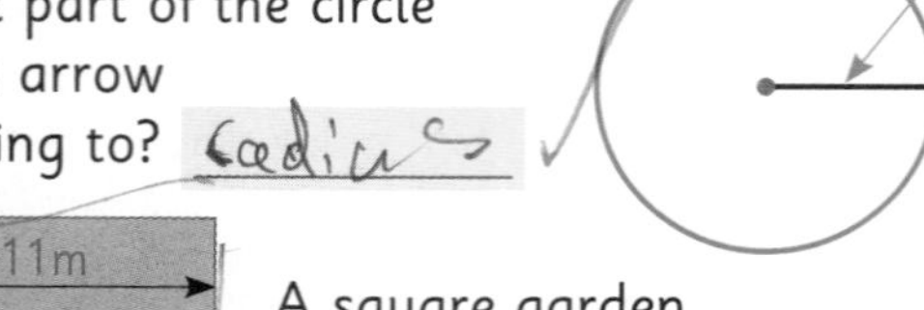

6. A square garden is 11m long. Find its area. ____

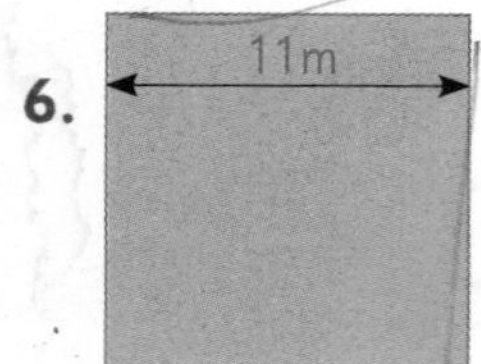


7. Find the perimeter of the garden. ____
8. hrs mins
   7 32
   − 3 48
   ____

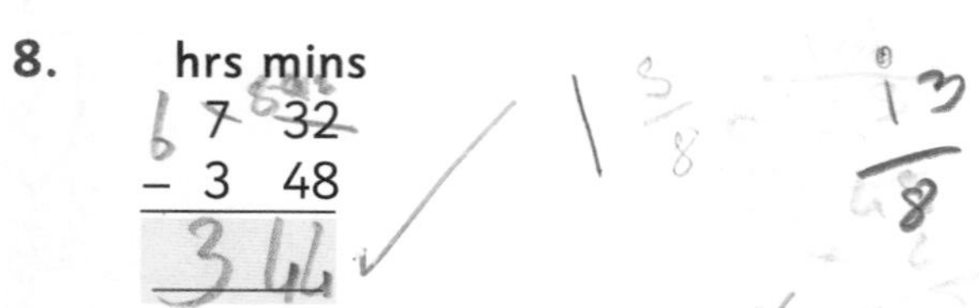

9. Increase 135 by 60%. ____
10. $\frac{1}{20}$ = ____ %

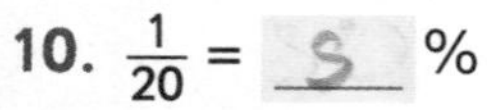

11. Put in order of size, starting with the smallest: $\frac{3}{5}$, 55%, 0·7.
    ____, ____, ____

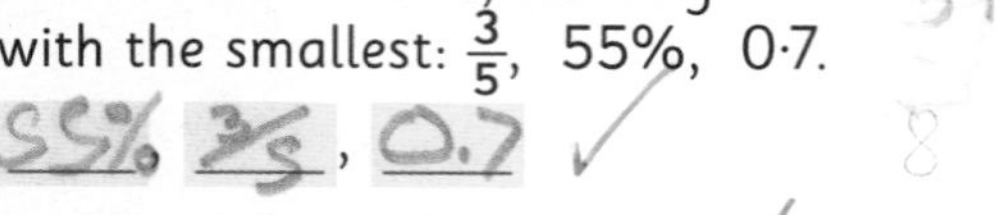

12. Are 15 and 16 both composite numbers? ____
13. What is the value of $x$? ____ °

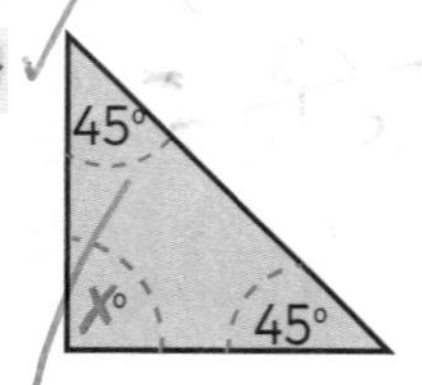


14. 32,168 – 204 = ____
15. If the temperature rises from $^-2$°C to $^+2$°C, by how many degrees did it rise? ____
16. What is the cost of 12kg of pasta if 1·5kg costs €2·40? ____
17. Joe spent $\frac{3}{4}$ of his money and Jason spent $\frac{7}{8}$ of his money. What fraction of their money did they spend between them? ____
18. The area of a rectangle is 132cm². If the length is 12cm, what is its perimeter? ____

/18

## Tuesday

1. Name the angle. ____

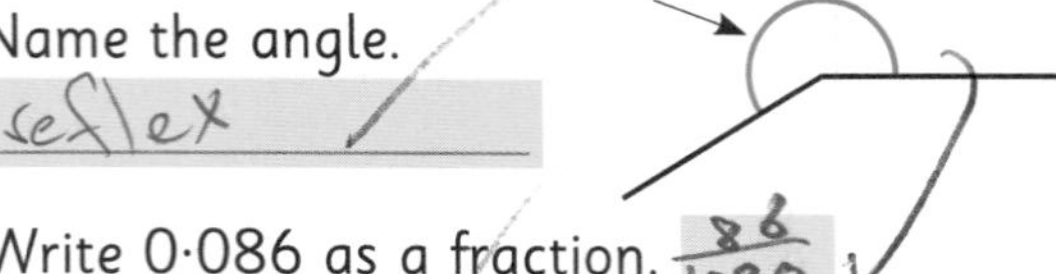

2. Write 0·086 as a fraction. ____
3. 75 × 4 = ____
4. What is the value of the underlined digit: 4·72<u>1</u>? ____
5. 3 × (4 + 6) = ____
6. What is the highest common factor of 18 and 27? ____
7. What fraction is shaded? ____

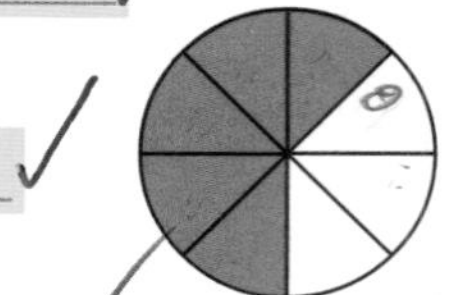

8. 4)835
   ____ R ____
9. $4 \times \frac{7}{9}$ = ____
10. Write $\frac{43}{12}$ as a mixed number. ____
11. 58ml × 2 = ____
12. By how many degrees is 0° hotter than $^-8$°? ____
13. 9kg 486g ÷ 2 = ____
14. 68mm = ____ cm
15. hrs mins
    3 27
    × 4
    ____

There are 360° in a full rotation.
There are 12 numbers on a clock face.

16. How many degrees are there between each number on the clock? (Hint: 360° ÷ 12) ____
17. How many degrees in half a rotation? ____
18. How many degrees between 1 and 6? ____

/18

## Wednesday

1. Find the area of the shape. ____

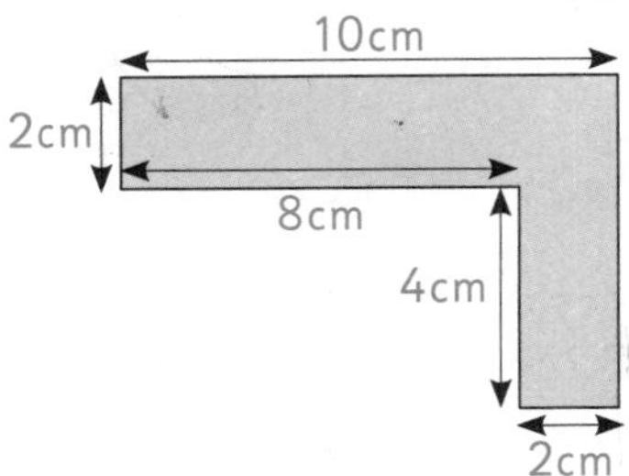


2. Find the perimeter of the shape. ____

3. (35 – 11) + ____ = 31

4. 8.15pm = ____:____

5. Write 1·07 as a fraction. ____

6. 
$$\begin{array}{r} 53{,}178 \\ -\ 28{,}297 \\ \hline \end{array}$$

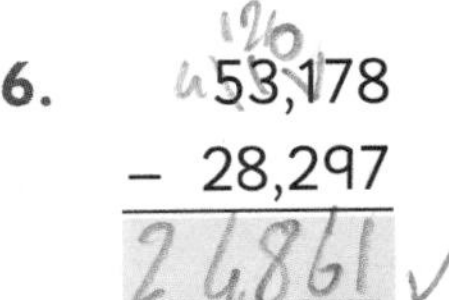

7. What is the square root of 121? ____

8. $5\frac{1}{5} - 1\frac{7}{10} =$ ____

9. Write $\frac{26}{3}$ as a mixed number. ____

10. Name the shape. ____

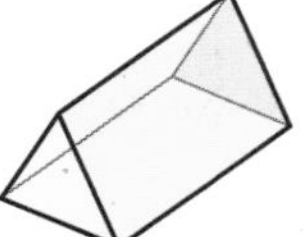

11. 17 × 20 = ____

12. $9\overline{)786}$ ____ R ____

13. If the diameter of a circle is 18cm, its radius is ____

14. €15 × 5 × 100 = ____

15. 9km 8m = ____ m

16. A computer cost €350. 10% Valued Added Tax had to be added on to the price. What is the new price? ____

17. A bakery that opens seven days a week sold 6,690 buns in the month of September. What was the average number of buns sold per day in September? ____

18. How many bags of 12 sweets can be made from 130 sweets? ____

/18

## Thursday

1. By how many degrees is ⁻2° hotter than ⁻10°? ____

2. 1·29 × 100 = ____

3. One turkey weighs $9\frac{7}{10}$kg. How much would seven weigh? ____

4. **x** ÷ 6 = 4, so **x** = ____

5. 0·25 of 28 = ____

6. 1·5l × 6 = ____

7. If one of the children that took part in the survey was asked to name their favourite fruit, what are the chances of it being apple? ____ in ____

| Favourite fruits of children | |
|---|---|
| **Apple** | 9 |
| **Banana** | 4 |
| **Orange** | 5 |
| **Grapes** | 2 |

8. What are the chances of it being grapes? ____ in ____

9. What are the chances of it being bananas or oranges? ____ in ____

10. Write 5% as a fraction in its lowest terms. ____

11. Increase 428 by 50%. ____

12. 21,483 – 7,000 = ____

13. 2.20am = ____:____

14. $\frac{4}{9} \times 5 =$ ____

15. Write $4\frac{5}{9}$ as an improper fraction. ____

**AT THE FUNFAIR**

| | |
|---|---|
| Rollercoaster | €1·25 |
| Teacups | €1·10 |
| Waltzer | €0·95 |

16. Karl had €10 going to the funfair. If he went on the Rollercoaster five times, how much money had he left? ____

17. Sinéad spent €6·65 on the Waltzer. How many times did she go on it? ____

18. How much change would I get from €5 if I went on all three rides? ____

/18

See page 93 for test.

## Monday

1. 25% of €160 = ____
2. A pentagon has ____ sides.
3. 4 + 0·1 + 0·02 = ____
4. 35·3 – 7·8 = ____
5. Which shape is symmetrical: **F**, **G** or **H**? ____
6. 700 ÷ 20 = ____
7. Name the 3-D shape. ____
8. Draw a 90° turn clockwise.

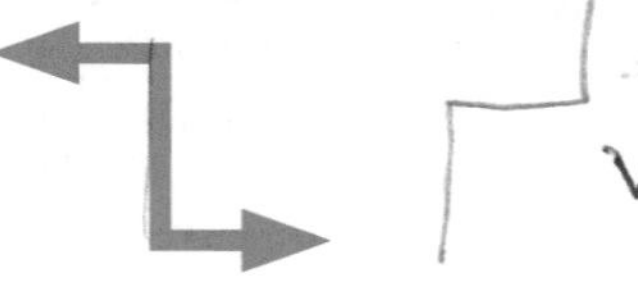

9. Put in order of size, starting with the smallest: 10%, 0·01, $\frac{3}{20}$. ____, ____, ____
10. $4\frac{2}{3} + 3\frac{5}{12}$ = ____
11. Write $\frac{49}{10}$ as a mixed number. ____
12. Write 2·19 as a fraction. ____
13. $6\overline{)8·34}$
14. 64,219 – 1,200 = ____
15. 5kg 19g = ____ g
16. A man was paid €10 an hour for every 8 hours he worked and got time and a half for every hour after that. If he worked from 9am to 6pm one day, how much did he earn? ____
17. Find the average capacity of these three containers: 26·725l, $30\frac{1}{2}$l and 20l 52ml. ____
18. Which is dearer and by how much,
    (a) a 1l bottle of water for €2·50 or
    (b) four 250ml bottles of water at €0·75 each? ____ by ____

/18

## Tuesday

1. 38 × 20 = ____
2. 46,215 + 2,100 = ____
3. 75% of 120 = ____
4. Put in order of size, starting with the largest: 19%, $\frac{1}{10}$, 0·2.

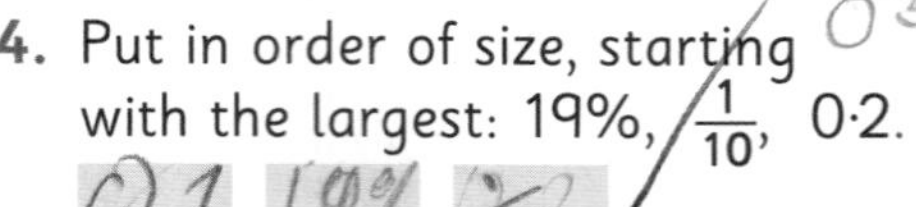

____, ____, ____

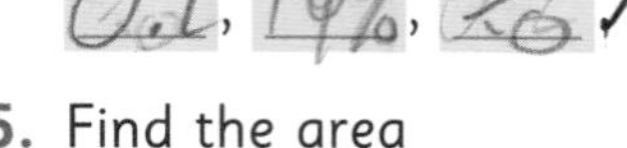

5. Find the area of this shape. ____

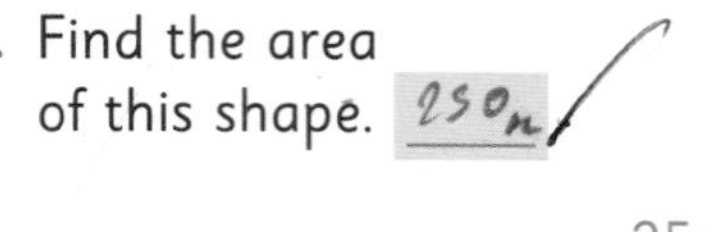

10m

25m

6. €13 × 4 × 10 = ____
7. $\frac{5}{6}$ of 42 = ____
8. $9\frac{1}{2}$m – 4m = ____
9. Find the average of 10, 11, 8, 9 and 12. ____
10. Lisa can run 5km in 20 minutes. How far will she run in an hour? ____
11. $2\frac{1}{4}$kg = ____ g
12. If the diameter of a circle is 15cm, what is its radius? ____
13. $12^2$ = ____
14. An octahedron has ____ vertices.
15. Draw the axes of symmetry on the pentagon.

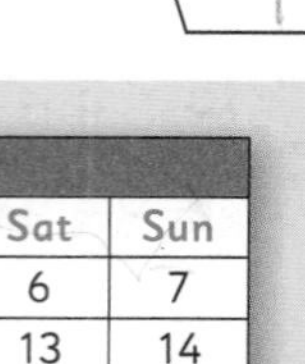

| JANUARY | | | | | | |
|---|---|---|---|---|---|---|
| Mon | Tue | Wed | Thur | Fri | Sat | Sun |
| 1 | 2 | 3 | 4 | 5 | 6 | 7 |
| 8 | 9 | 10 | 11 | 12 | 13 | 14 |
| 15 | 16 | 17 | 18 | 19 | 20 | 21 |
| 22 | 23 | 24 | 25 | 26 | 27 | 28 |
| 29 | 30 | 31 | | | | |

16. On what day will the 5th of February fall? ____
17. The last Sunday in December was on what date? ____
18. February the 14th will be on what day? ____

/18

## Wednesday

1. An octagonal prism has ______ surfaces.
2. $20 \times 30 =$ ______
3. 50% of 530 = ______
4. Put in order of size, starting with the smallest: 2·1, $2\frac{1}{100}$, 2%.
   ______, ______, ______
5. 7kg 24g ÷ 2 = ______
6. 3·5cm = ______ mm
7. How many hours and minutes are there from 13:00 to 15:05?
   ______ hours ______ minutes
8. What percentage of this shape is shaded? ______

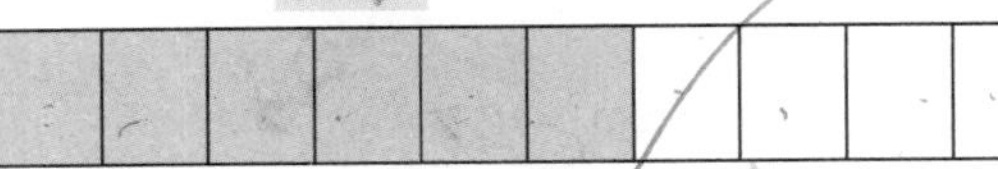

9. 82·3 ÷ 10 = ______
10. What part of the circle is the arrow pointing to? ______

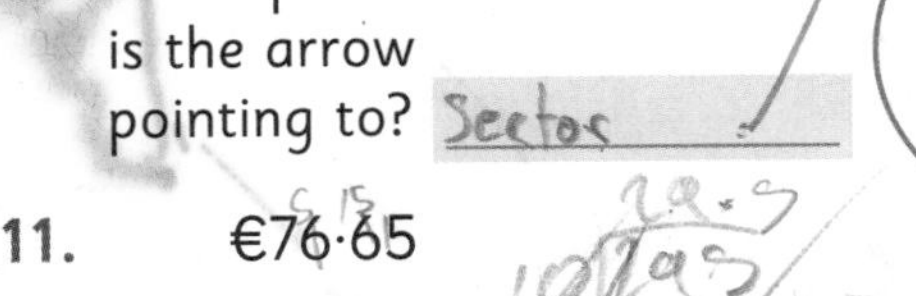

11. €76·65
    – €41·99

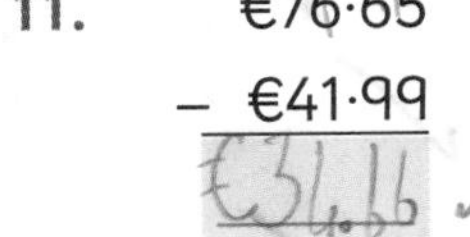

12. $6\frac{1}{2} - \frac{7}{12} =$ ______
13. Increase 295 by 80%. ______
14. Simplify $\frac{10}{15}$. ______
15. 7l 5ml = ______ ml

16. A stick is 10cm 4mm long. What is the total length of 9 sticks? ______
17. Three boys weigh a total of 106·5kg. If two of the boys weigh $36\frac{3}{4}$kg and 33·786kg, what weight is the third boy? ______
18. Maura has saved €486. She needs 5 times that amount to go on holiday. How much more does she need? ______

/18

## Thursday

1. $11 \times 40 =$ ______
2. 6·125
   4·913
   + 8·614

3. 76,412 – 7,100 = ______
4. $\frac{2}{3} + \frac{3}{4} =$ ______
5. What is the highest common factor of 24 and 30? ______
6. 0·3 of 490 = ______
7. Simplify $\frac{20}{24}$. ______
8. Find the area of this circle. (Each square represents 1cm$^2$.) ______

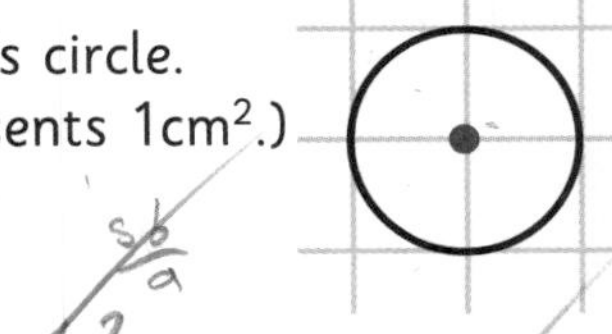

9. $7 \times \frac{8}{9} =$ ______
10. Write $\frac{76}{9}$ as a mixed number. ______

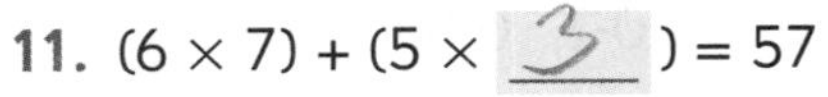

11. $(6 \times 7) + (5 \times$ ______ $) = 57$
12. A tetrahedron has ______ edges.

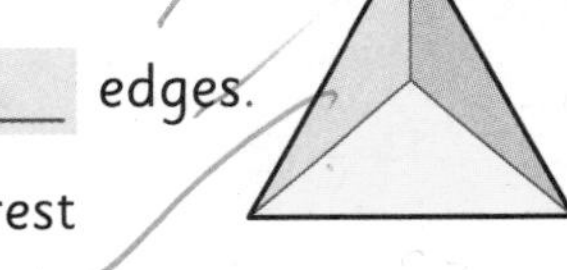

13. Round 6·2 to the nearest whole number. ______
14. Is 19 a composite number? ______
15. Write 7·007 as a fraction. ______

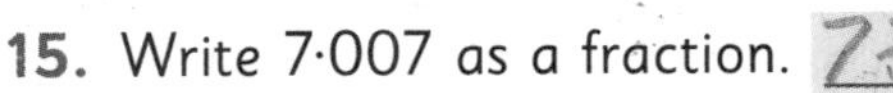

A pitch has a perimeter of 66m. The length of the pitch is 19m.

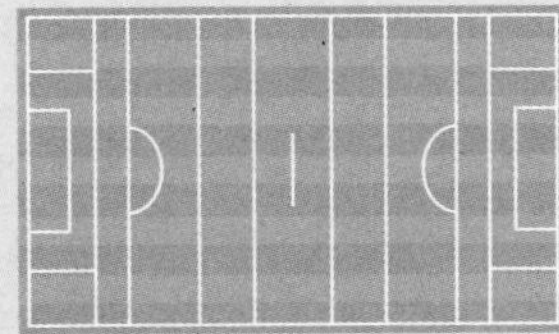

16. Find the area of the pitch. ______
17. If grass seed costs €2·90 per metre square, how much will it cost to seed the pitch? ______
18. The football club decided to put a 1-metre wide track around the pitch. What would the perimeter of the pitch and track be then? ______

/18

See page 94 for test.

## Monday

1. 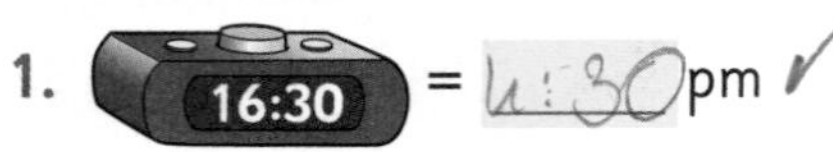 16:30 = ____ pm

2. 40% of 600 = ____

3. 6 + 0·2 + 0·01 = ____

4. 0·5 = ____ %

5. The angles in an octagon are all ____ angles.

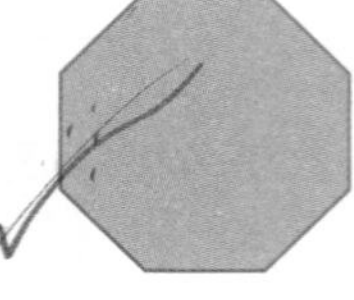

6. Circle the symmetrical letter.

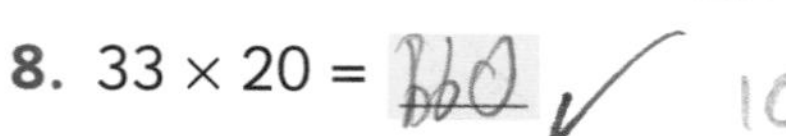

b c d e f

7. Is 33 a prime number? ____

8. 33 × 20 = ____

9. Draw the net of a cube.

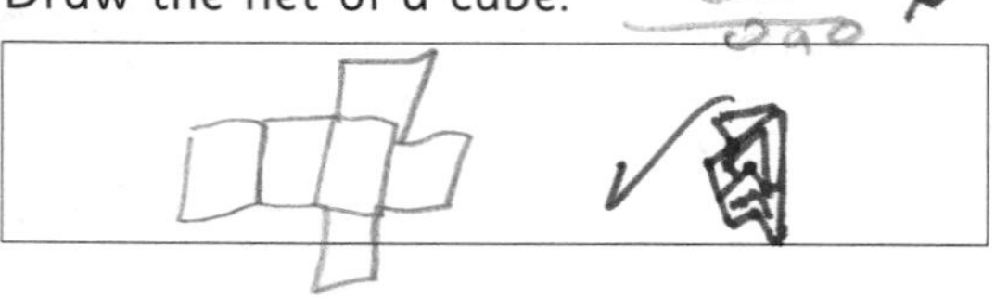

10. How many 50c coins make up €5? ____

11. Put in order of size, starting with the smallest: 0·2, 0·02, $\frac{1}{4}$.
____, ____, ____

12. 14 + (8 × 4) = ____

13. Round 18,762 to the nearest 1,000. ____

14. Will a semi-circle and a circle together tessellate? ____

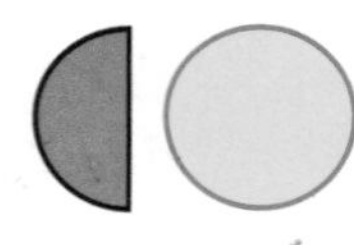

15. 63,421
− 5,362

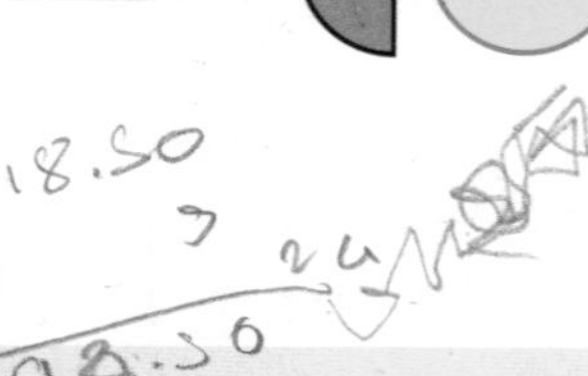

16. Bernie is paid €18·50 per hour. How much would she earn in a week (working 5 days) if she works from 9am to 5pm every day? ____

17. A cooker was priced at €590. During a sale, it was reduced by 20%. How much did it cost during the sale? ____

18. The distance from the shop to the school is 7km 45m. If Ger cycled 5,025m and walked the rest of the way from the shop to the school, how far did he walk? ____

/18

## Tuesday

1. If a girl can walk 5km in one hour, how far can she walk in $\frac{1}{4}$ of an hour? ____

2. 11 × 0·4 = ____

3. 16 ÷ 2 = 2 × **a**, so **a** = ____

4. Draw a 270° turn anticlockwise.

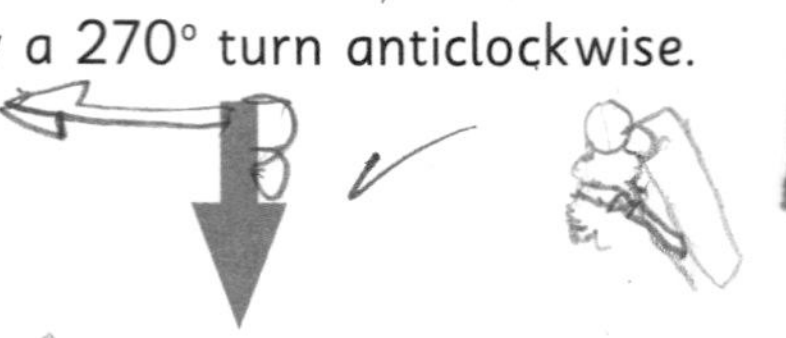

5. 4)2·064

6. 7 + 0·03 + 0·1 = ____

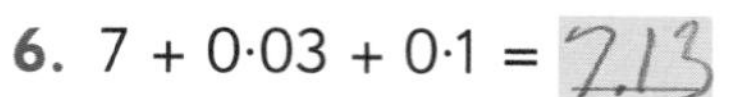

7. Find the area of this shape. ____

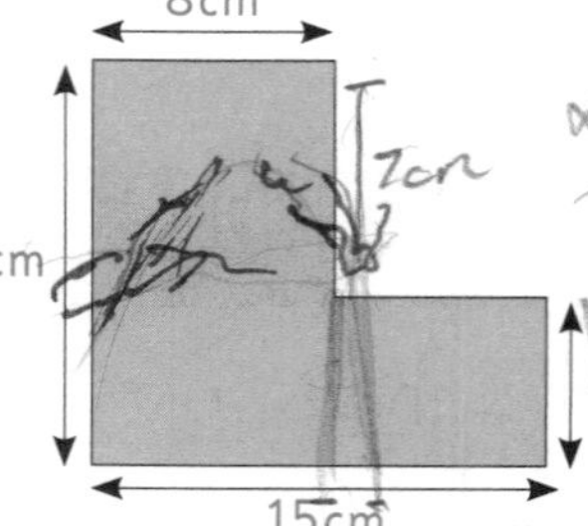


8. Find the perimeter of the shape. ____

9. This is a ____.

10. €6·45 + €9·16 = ____

11. 16,000 − 11,005 = ____

12. How many 20c coins make up €2? ____

13. 1,250m ÷ 2 = ____

14. Write $7\frac{7}{8}$ as an improper fraction. ____

15. 17:30 = ____ pm

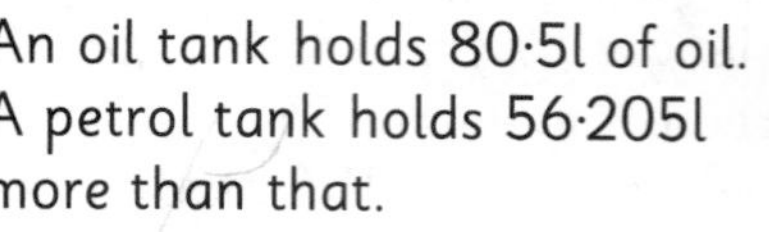

An oil tank holds 80·5l of oil. A petrol tank holds 56·205l more than that.

16. How much does the petrol tank hold? ____

17. How much would 5 oil tanks hold? ____

18. If oil costs €3 per litre, how much would it cost to fill the oil tank? ____

/18

## Wednesday

1. 96 × 100 = ____

2. 73,006 − 24,976 = ____

3. 150 × 7 = ____

4. This is a ____ .

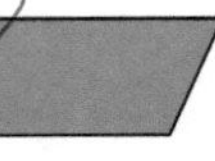

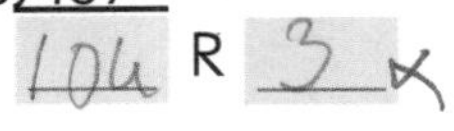

5. 8)967 ____ R ____

6. What is the value of x? ____

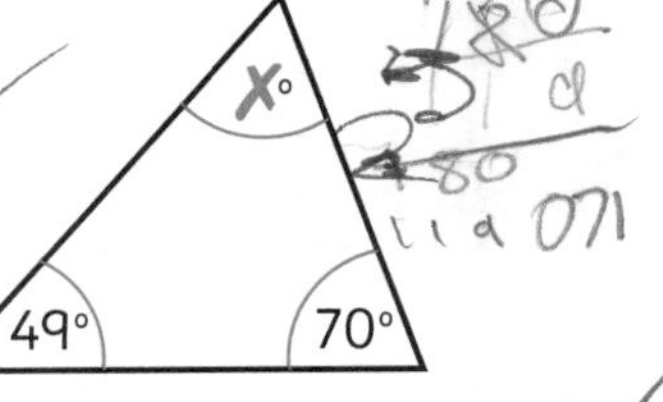


7. Write $9\frac{3}{4}$ as an improper fraction. ____

8. $7\frac{8}{9} - 1\frac{2}{3} =$ ____

9. If the diameter of a circle is 34cm, its radius is ____ .

10. The value of 3 in 3·425 is ____

11. The angle made by the hands of the clock at 9 o'clock is ____ °.

12. The square root of 81 is ____ .

13. $\frac{1}{20} = \frac{?}{100} =$ ____ %

14. Write as am or pm: 10 past 9 in the evening. ____

15. 4km 68m = ____ m

16. The perimeter of a rectangular room is 70m. If the length of the room is 25m, what is the area of the room? ____

17. A school paid €825 for 33 helmets. How much did each helmet cost? ____

18. A concert began at 16:45 and lasted for 3 hours 10 minutes. At what time did it end? ____ : ____

/18

## Thursday

1. 1·003km × 6 = ____

2. Find the area of a square that has a perimeter of 36cm. ____

3. How much hotter is $^{+}14°$ than $^{-}8°$? ____

4. 56 ÷ 7 − 4 = ____

5.

| | hrs | mins |
|---|---|---|
| | 6 | 14 |
| − | 2 | 37 |
| | ____ | ____ |

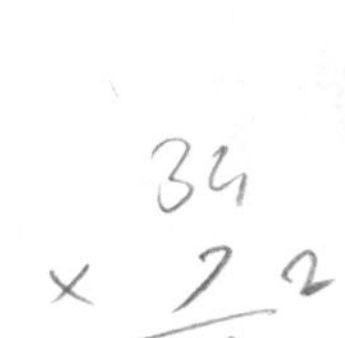

6. Increase 340 by 70%. ____

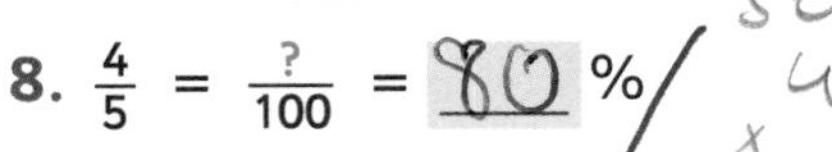

7. Put in order of size, starting with the smallest: 65%, $\frac{3}{5}$, 0·69.
____ , ____ , ____

8. $\frac{4}{5} = \frac{?}{100} =$ ____ %

9. 67 × 20 = ____

10. How many degrees are there between north and east? ____ °

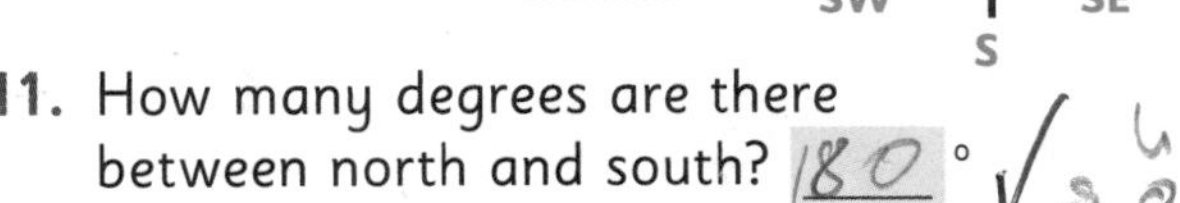


11. How many degrees are there between north and south? ____ °

12. If I turn 135° clockwise from north, where would I land? ____

13. Write $\frac{77}{8}$ as a mixed number. ____

14. 42,165 + 500 = ____

15. €10 − €7·63 = ____

| Library opening times | |
|---|---|
| **Monday to Friday** | **Late opening** |
| Opens at 9.30am | Thursday until 7.00pm |
| Closes at 5.45pm | |

16. How many minutes does the library open for on a Monday? ____

17. How many hours does it stay open for on a Thursday? ____

18. Write the closing time on a Wednesday as 24-hour time. ____ : ____

/18

See page 95 for test.

# Week 1 Test

1. (4 + 8) – 7 = 5

2. Round 4,259 to the nearest 10. 4,260

3. Round 1,268 to the nearest 100. 1,308

4. 5,122 + 3,847 = 8,464

5. $\frac{1}{4}$ of 28 = 7

6. What fraction of the shape is shaded? 5/8

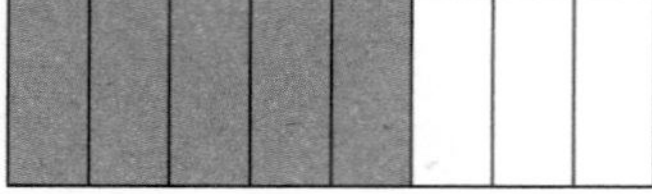

7. Complete the sequence.
356, 357, 358, 354, 360

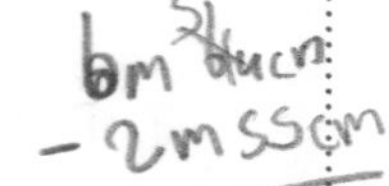

8. 6m 64cm – 2m 55cm = 4m09cm

9. 1·2km = 1200 m

10. Find the perimeter of the following shape. 20

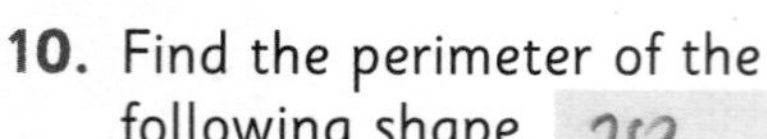

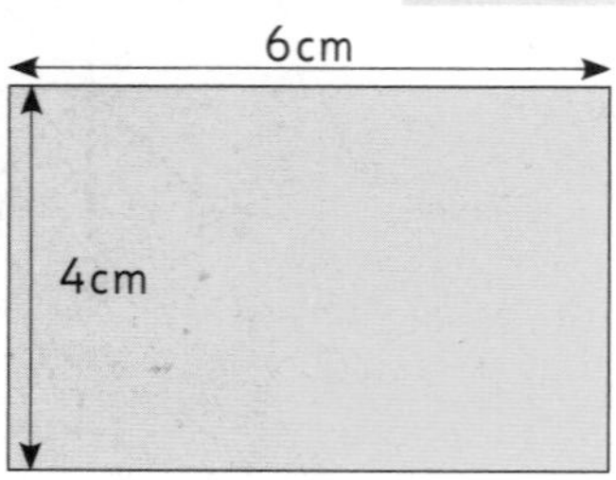


11. Write this time in digital form. 01:35

12. Name the 2-D shape. Pentagon

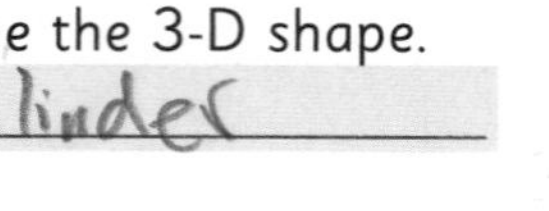

13. Name the 3-D shape. cylinder

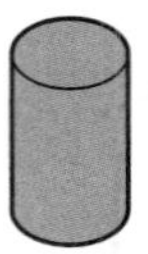

14.
| | hrs | mins |
|---|---|---|
| | 3 | 28 |
| + | 2 | 43 |
| | 6 | 11 |

15. (9 × 4) + 7 = 43

16. 0·7 of 60 = 42

17. 438 ÷ 9 = 48 R 6

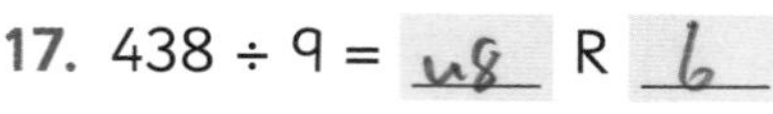

18. 1kg + 250g = 1,250g

19. Write 0·25 as a fraction. $\frac{25}{100}$

20. This is a right angle.

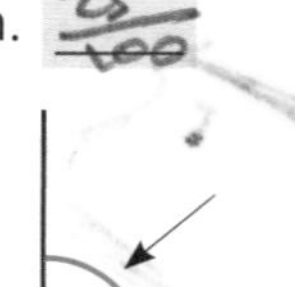

## Problems

21. A farmer has 58 sheep, 96 cattle and 8 horses.
How many animals has the farmer altogether? 162

22. A washing machine costs €499·25.
A dishwasher costs €346·99.
How much more does the washing machine cost? 152.26

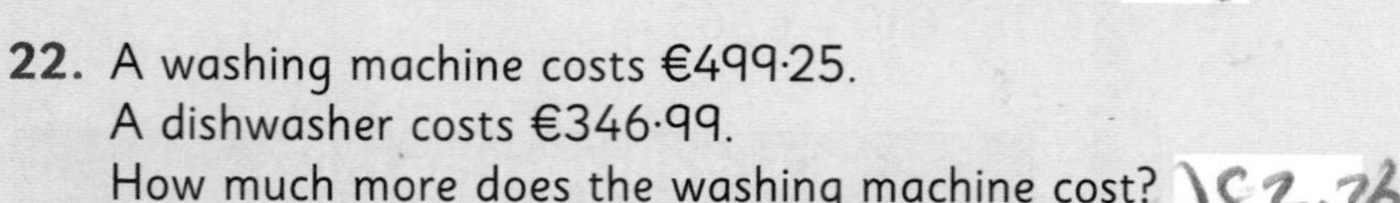

23. Paul has €6·80. Laura has €2·50 more than Paul.
How much money has Laura? 9.20

24. Frank has 56 cards.
He gives $\frac{1}{8}$ of them to his friend.
How many has he left? 49

25. 5 chocolate bars cost €5·75.
How much would one bar cost? 1.15

/25

# Week 2 Test

1. Complete the sequence.
   4,008, 4,009, 4,010, ____

2. Write the number three thousand four hundred and fifty. ____

3. €2·06 = ____ c

4. 8)295
   ____ R ____

5. $\frac{2}{5}$ of 40 = ____

6. Write this time in digital form. ____ : ____

7. What fraction of the shape is coloured? ____

8. 46 × 100 = ____

9. (6 × 9) + 8 = ____

10. 2,466 – 2,000 = ____

11. Round 1,009 to the nearest 10. ____

12. How likely is it that a new student will join our class next year? ____
    (likely, unlikely, certain, impossible)

13.

| | hrs | mins |
|---|---|---|
| | 3 | 47 |
| + | 1 | 35 |
| | ____ | ____ |

14. Name the 2-D shape. ____

15. Name the 3-D shape. ____

16. 4·32m + 1·65m = ____

17. This is a ____ angle.

18. 4kg 100g = ____ g

19. 2l 400ml = ____ ml

20. Find the perimeter of this shape. ____

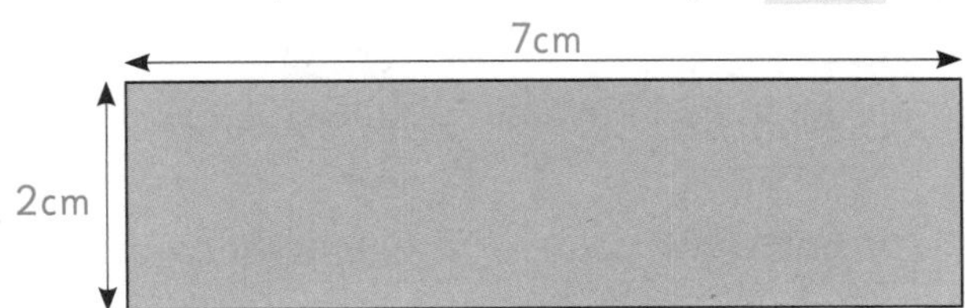


## Problems

21. Jane had 208 grapes.
    She shared them equally among 8 children.
    How many grapes did each child get? ____

22. One newspaper costs €2·50.
    How much would 9 newspapers cost? ____

23. Frank bought socks for €3·95, a t-shirt for €7·80 and a cap for €5·10.
    How much change did he get from €20? ____

24. There were 96 cups on a shelf. $\frac{1}{8}$ of them broke.
    How many were left? ____

25. 

    Mary has to go to the dentist in 25 minutes' time.
    At what time does she have to go to the dentist?
    ____ : ____

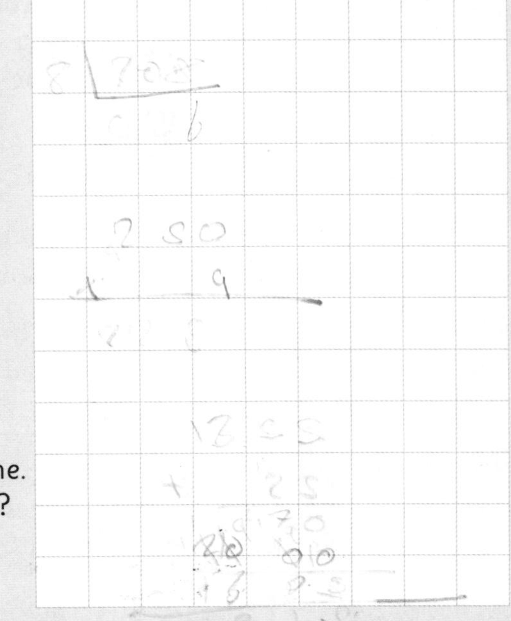

/25

# Week 3 Test

1. Complete the sequence.
   5,014, 5,016, 5,018, ______

2. (7 × 7) + 9 = ______

3. 27 × 10 = ______

4. Write $\frac{3}{100}$ as a decimal fraction. ______

5. Write the digital time shown on the clock. [ : ]

6. 6·23
   × 4
   ______

7. Name the 2-D shape. ______

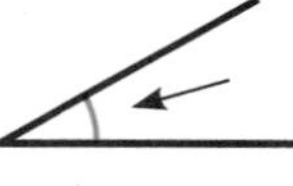

8. Name the type of angle. ______

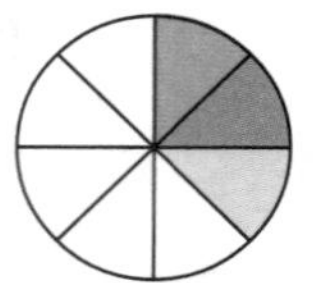

9. What fraction of the shape is shaded? ______

10. What is the value of the underlined digit: <u>7</u>6,248? ______

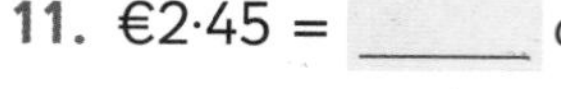

11. €2·45 = ______ c

12. Find the perimeter of the rectangle. ______

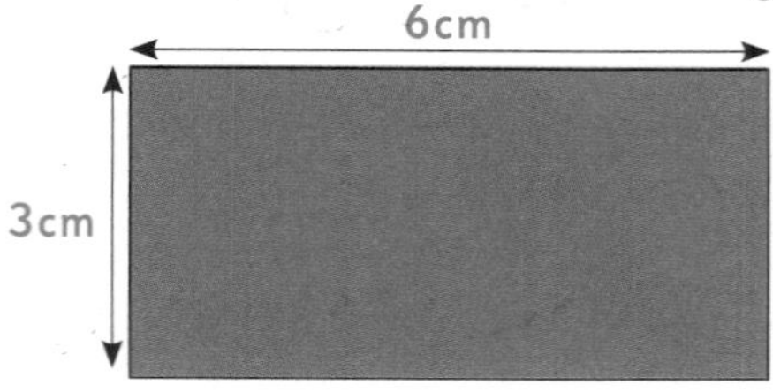


13. Find the area of the rectangle. ______

14. 18 + ______ = 35

15. Name the 3-D shape. ______

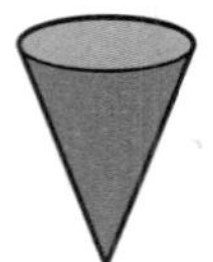

16. How likely is it that you will be on two weeks' holidays from school over Easter?
    ______
    (likely, unlikely, certain, impossible)

17. 3l 250ml
    × 5
    ______

18. 74,165 + 100 = ______

19. 6,225 + 1,250 + 1,050 = ______

20. 6)263
    ______ R ______

## Problems

21. John lives 3·25km from the railway station. Daniel lives 2·34km further away from the railway station. How far does Daniel live from the train station? ______

22. A football jersey costs €52·75. How much would six jerseys cost? ______

23. Three sticks of equal length were lying in a straight line on the ground. If the three sticks measure 4m 86cm in length, how long is each stick? ______

24. A film started at [8:35]. It lasted for 2 hours 25 minutes. At what time did the film end? [ : ]

25. Shauna's book had 280 pages. If she read $\frac{1}{4}$ of it on Monday, 0·1 of it on Tuesday and 50 pages on Wednesday, how many pages did she read altogether? ______

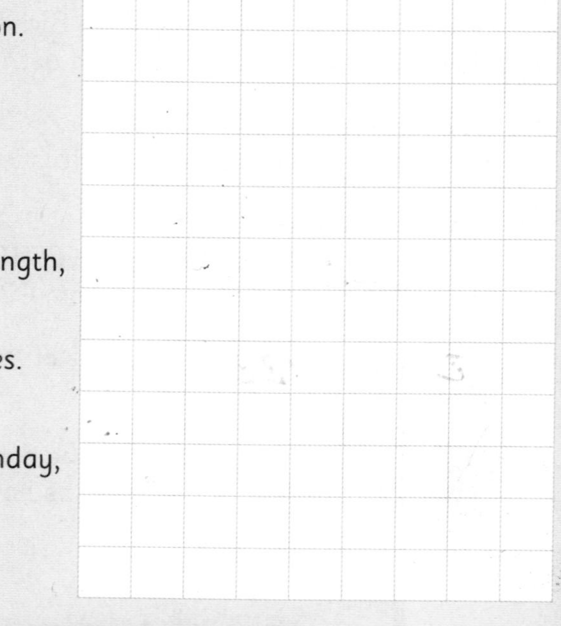

/25

# Week 4 Test

1. Complete the sequence.
5,087, 5,091, 5,095, ______

2. Put the following numbers in order of size, starting with the smallest:
44,387, 30,080, 33,768, 19,423.
______, ______, ______, ______

3. This is an ______ angle.

4. 51,455 + 28,392

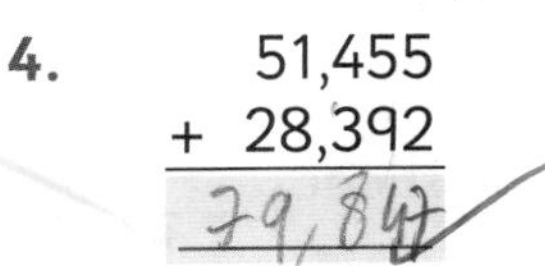

5. m cm
10 45
− 6 96

6. (6 × 6) + ______ = 43

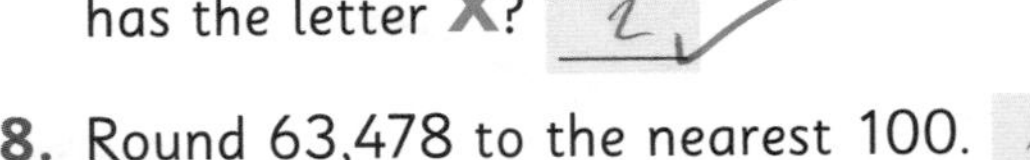

7. How many lines of symmetry has the letter **X**? ______

8. Round 63,478 to the nearest 100. ______

9. What time will it be 25 minutes later than the time shown on the clock? ______

10. Write $\frac{7}{100}$ as a decimal fraction. ______

11. Find the perimeter of this shape. ______

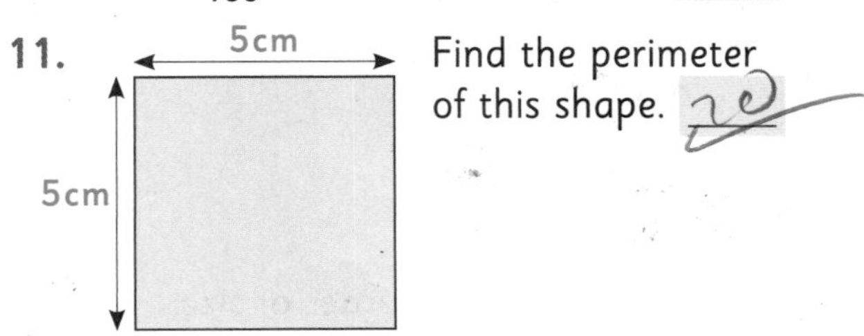


12. A pentagon has ______ sides.

13. This is the net of a ______.

14. 20 × 44 = ______

15. How likely is it that it will rain today?
______
(likely, unlikely, certain, impossible)

16. €4·15 = ______

17. 70,099 − 100 = ______

18. 6)8·82l

19. 2kg 450g = ______ g

20. Measure the line. ______ cm

## Problems

21. Robert has €40.
He buys runners costing €24·65.
How much money has he left? ______

22. How many minutes are in $\frac{1}{4}$ of an hour? ______

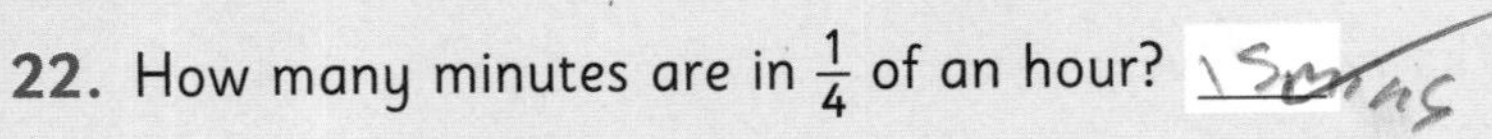

23. Jane had €24. She spent $\frac{3}{4}$ of it.
How much money has she left? ______

24. If a film begins at 2:25 and ends at 4:10, how many hours and minutes does it last for?
______ hour(s) ______ minutes

25. A kettle holds 3l 225ml.
A large container holds 4 times that amount.
How much does the large container hold? ______

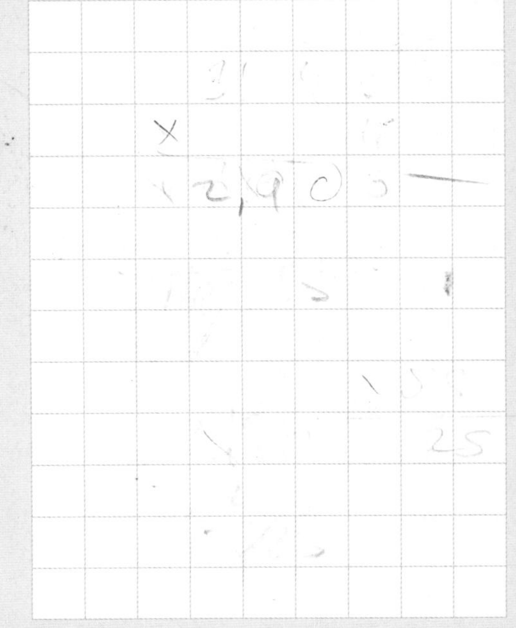

/25

# Week 5 Test

1. Complete the sequence.
7,200, 7,600, 8,000, ____

2. $\begin{array}{r} 63{,}420 \\ -\ 17{,}999 \\ \hline \end{array}$
____

3. Put these numbers in order of size, starting with the smallest:
13,003, 17,062, 15,900, 11,045.
____, ____, ____, ____

4. Name the angle. ____

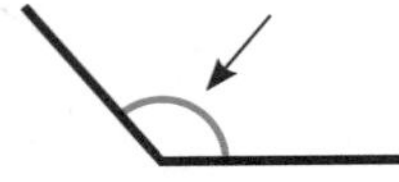

5. Write a letter that has more than one line of symmetry. ____

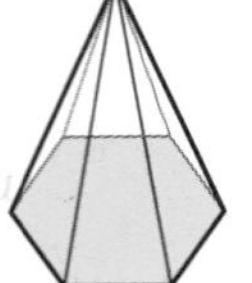

6. This is a ____ pyramid.

7. Find the average of the following amounts:
€6, €8, €5, €9. ____

8. Round 68,555 to the nearest 1,000. ____

9. 

| km | m |
|---|---|
| 5 | 680 |
| × | 4 |

____

10. $7\overline{)485}$
____ R ____

11. $\frac{1}{2} \times 50 =$ ____

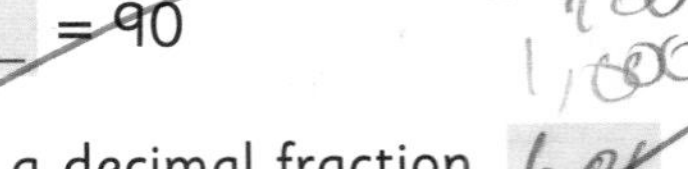

12. $(9 \times 9) +$ ____ $= 90$

13. Write $6\frac{1}{100}$ as a decimal fraction. ____

14. 23,465 – 1,000 = ____

15. An octagon has ____ sides.

16. Find the perimeter of the shape. ____

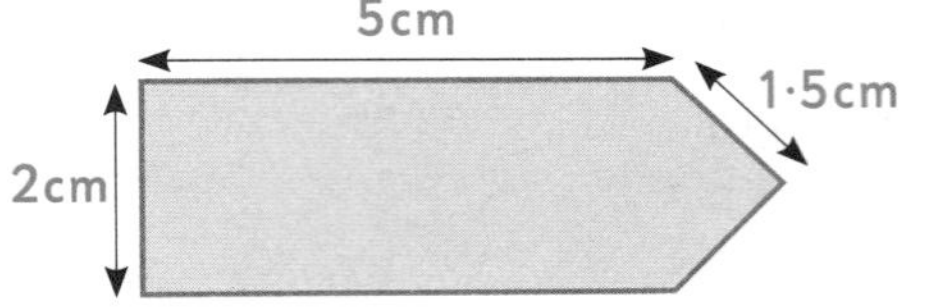


17. Write 0·01 as a fraction. ____

18. What is the value of the underlined digit:
7<u>1</u>,289? ____

19. $22 \times 100 =$ ____

20. What time will it be 35 minutes later than the time shown on the clock? ____ : ____

## Problems

21. Declan wrote down the number 785 instead of 587.
What was the difference between the number he wrote and the correct number? ____

22. Three children weighed 45kg, 63kg and 57kg respectively.
What was the average weight of the children? ____

23. There are 20 books on each shelf in the library.
There are 45 shelves in the library.
How many books are there altogether? ____

24. There are 280 fence posts around the school grounds.
$\frac{1}{4}$ of them are painted green. The rest are painted black.
How many black posts are there? ____

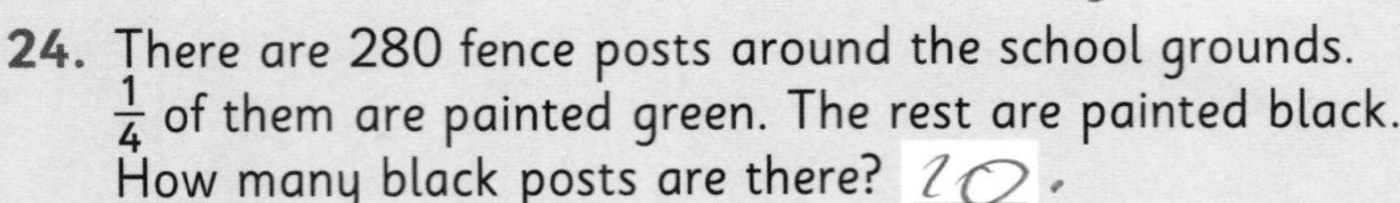

25. Kate had €240. She spent $\frac{1}{5}$ of it.
How much money did she spend? ____

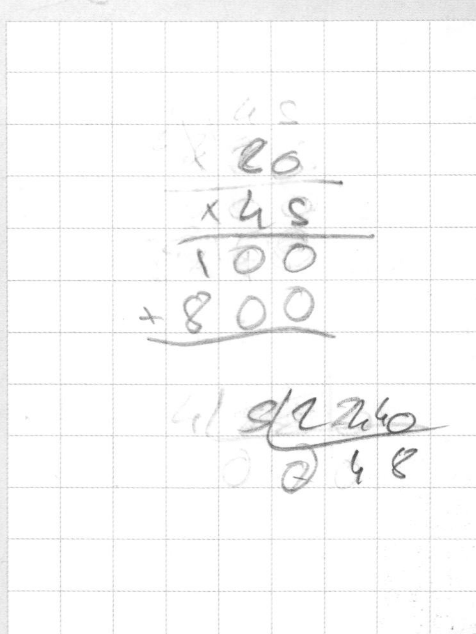

/25

# Week 6 Test

1. Complete the sequence.
4,350, 4,650, 4,950, ______

2. Find the perimeter of this shape. ______

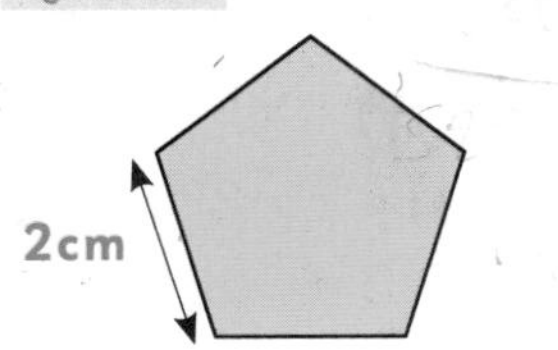


3. Name the 2-D shape above. ______

4. What is the value of the underlined digit: 65,1<u>2</u>4? ______

5. How many glasses each with a capacity of 500ml can be filled from a 2l bottle? ______

6. 300 ÷ 7 = ______ R ______

7. 102 – 56 = ______

8. Round 47,263 to the nearest 1,000. ______

9. €3·11 = ______ c

10. Write the time 40 minutes later than the time shown on the clock. ___ : ___

11. (8 × 3) + ______ = 31

12. By how much is 54 greater than 7 × 7? ______

13.

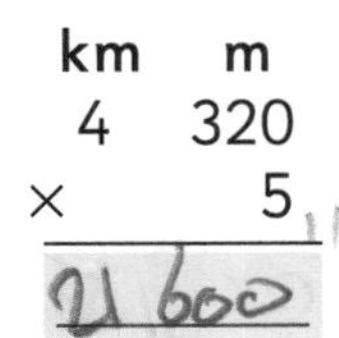

| km | m |
|---|---|
| 4 | 320 |
| × | 5 |
| | |

14. How likely is it that Christmas Day will happen during summer? ______
(likely, unlikely, certain, impossible)

15. Which is heavier: 140g or 4kg? ______

16. Draw a line of symmetry.

17. Turn the shape 90° clockwise and draw.

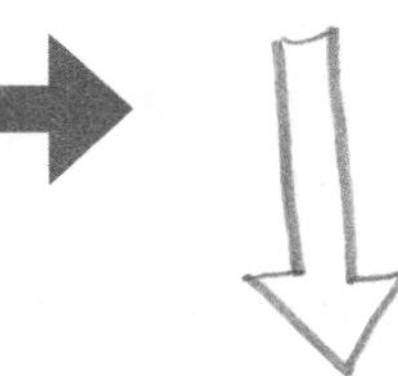

18. Write $6\frac{1}{100}$ as a decimal fraction. ______

19. Put in order of size, starting with the largest: 54,021, 29,999, 55,622, 44,250.
______, ______, ______, ______

20. Is the letter **R** symmetrical? ______

## Problems

21. A plank 7m 44cm long was cut into six equal pieces. How long was each piece? ______

22. Mary drinks 2·2l of water every day. How many litres would she drink in a week? ______

23. What must be added to the sum of 45,339 and 21,465 to make 70,000? ______

24. Gerry walked 2km 245m. Emma walked 750m further than that. How far did Emma walk? ______

25. Each side of a square field measures 15m. How many metres of fence would a farmer need to fence around the field? ______
(Hint: find the perimeter.)

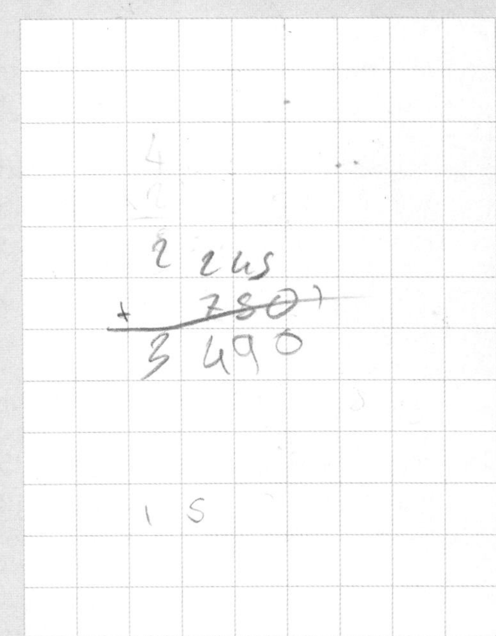

/25

# Week 7 Test

1. Complete the sequence. 68, 59, 50, ______

2. What is the value of the underlined digit: <u>8</u>5,226? ______

3. This is the net of a ______

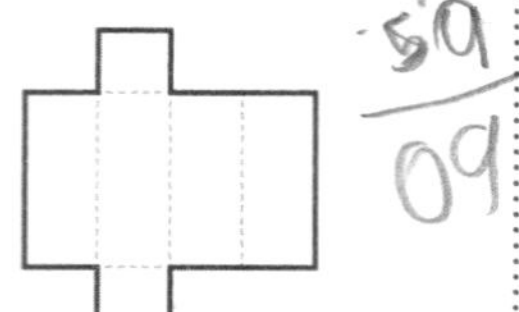

4. Find the area of the following shape. ______

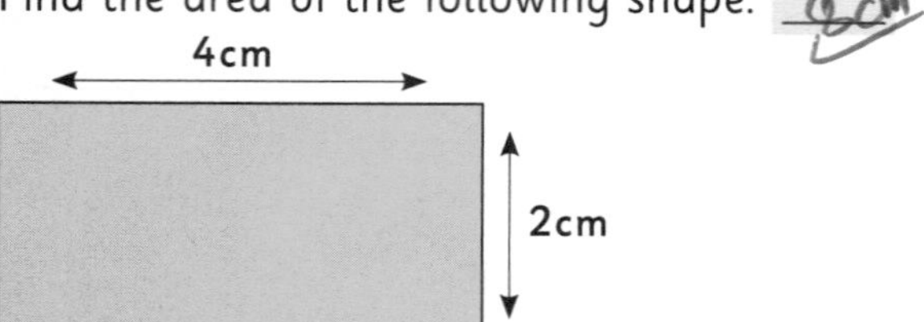



5. Find the perimeter of the rectangle above. ______

6. Round 96,554 to the nearest 1,000. ______

7. (7 × ______) + 8 = 64

8. 269 × 10 = ______

9. 3)219

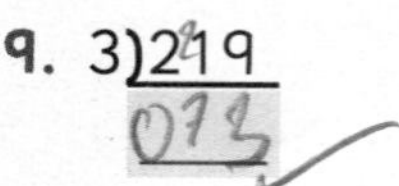

10. What are the chances of rolling a 5 on one die? ______ in ______

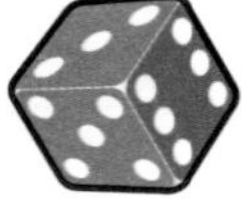

11. Write $\frac{1}{4}$ as a decimal fraction. ______

12. Which unit of measurement would you use to weigh a pile of bricks? ☐ g ☐ kg

13. Name the 2-D shape. ______

14. Name the angle. ______

15. Find the average of the following ages: 8, 9, 4, 6, 3. ______

16. $\frac{2}{5} - \frac{1}{10} =$ ______

17. Draw the line of symmetry.

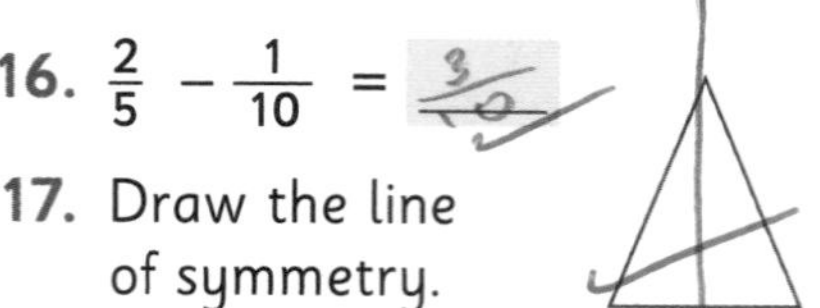

18. What are the factors of 8? ______, ______, ______ and ______

19. 41,329 + 36,699 = ______

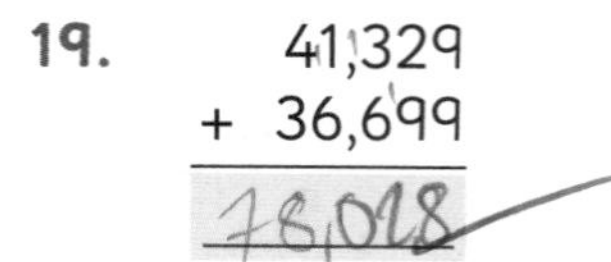

20. 1km 430m = ______ m

## Problems

21. The population of Newtown is 31,798. Oldtown's population is 12,438 more than Newtown's. How many people are living in Oldtown? ______

22. 60,422 people attended a concert on Monday night. 4,253 fewer than that attended the concert on Tuesday night. How many attended the concert on Tuesday night? ______

23. If 6 eggs cost €1·26, how much would two eggs cost? ______

24. There are 70 apples in a box. How many apples are there in 9 boxes? ______

25. Martin was asked to multiply 125 by 26 but instead he multiplied 125 by 62. By how much was his answer too big? ______

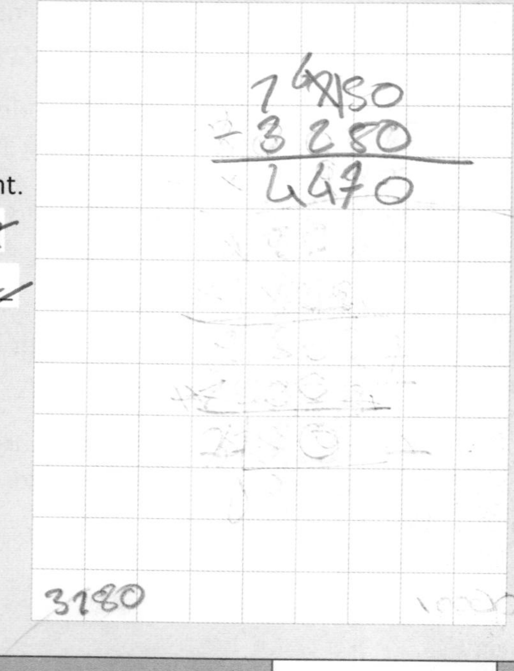

/25

# Week 8 Test

1. Complete the sequence. 61, 49, 37, ____

2. How many minutes are there in $\frac{3}{4}$ of an hour? ____

3. Round 39,658 to the nearest 1,000. ____

4. Name the 2-D shape.
____

5. €25 – €12·50 = ____

6. Measure the line. ____ cm

7. What is the value of the underlined digit: <u>4</u>1,233? ____

8. What is the value of the missing angle? ____

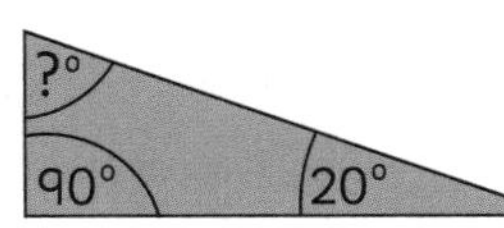


9. $\frac{1}{2}$ ____ $\frac{1}{8}$ (<, > or =)

10. 8·648km ÷ 4 = ____

11. 4·36 × 10 = ____

12. This is a ____ pyramid.

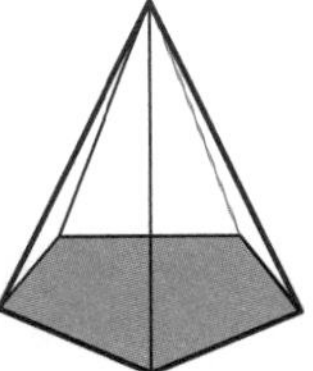

13. 635 ÷ 6 = ____ R ____

14. Write $\frac{3}{100}$ as a decimal fraction. ____

15. What are the chances of rolling a 1 or a 6 on one die?
____ in ____

16. Find the average of the following ages: 20, 24, 22, 18, 16. ____

17. Which unit of measurement would you use to measure the amount of water in a cup? ☐ ml ☐ l

18. A semi-circle has ____ line(s) of symmetry.

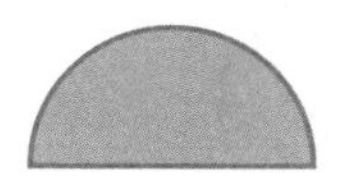

19. Put in order of size, starting with the largest: 18,625, 11,416, 18,111, 14,861.
____, ____, ____, ____

20.
$$\begin{array}{r} 62{\cdot}86 \\ \times \quad 4 \\ \hline \end{array}$$
____

## Problems

21. If one copybook costs €1·45, how much would 8 copybooks cost? ____

22. There are 15 sweets in a packet. James bought 9 packets. How many sweets less than 200 does James have? ____

23. Margaret has €64.
Niamh has $\frac{7}{8}$ of that amount.
How much money has Niamh? ____

24. A farmer had 180 sheep.
He sold $\frac{1}{5}$ of them.
How many has he left? ____

25. John had €50.
He spent 0·1 of it buying a t-shirt.
How much did he spend? ____

/25

# Week 9 Test

1. Complete the sequence.
0·4, 0·8, 1·2, ______

2. What is the value of the underlined digit:
7<u>8</u>,524? ______

3. Put in order of size, starting with the smallest:
75,420, 7,542, 7,052, 57,425.
______, ______, ______, ______

4. Turn the following shape 180° clockwise and draw.

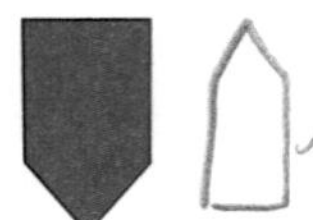

5.

$$\begin{array}{r} 512 \\ \times \quad 8 \\ \hline \end{array}$$

6. $560 \div 10 =$ ______

7. $(6 \times 8) + (4 \times 3) =$ ______

8. Name the 3-D shape.

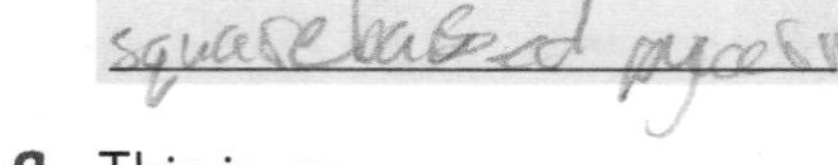

9. This is an

triangle.

10. The factors of 14 are

______, ______, ______ and ______.

11. $\frac{1}{9} + \frac{1}{3} =$ ______

12. The chances of rolling an odd number on a die are ______ in ______.

13. Which is better value for money?

(a) 8 pens at €5·60 (b) 10 pens at €8

14. How many glasses with a capacity of 200ml can be filled from a 2l jug? ______

15. How many hours and minutes are there from 3:45 to 6:20? ______

16. Will a circle and a triangle together tessellate? ______

17. $542 \div 6 =$ ______ R ______

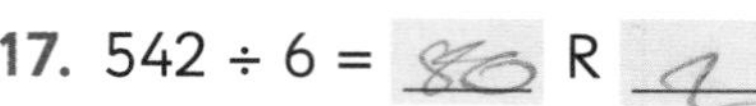

18. Write $\frac{17}{100}$ as a decimal fraction. ______

19. Find the average of the following numbers:
8, 6, 7, 5, 9. ______

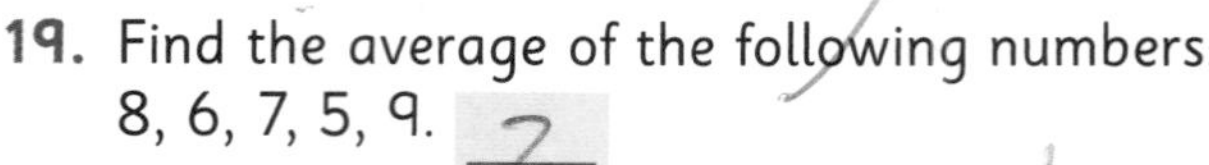

20. Round 19,630 to the nearest 1,000. ______

## Problems

21. It takes 10 biscuits to fill a packet.
How many packets can be filled from 420 biscuits? ______

22. Carl had €500.
He spent $\frac{3}{10}$ of his money on new runners.
How much did he spend? ______

23. Kate has read $\frac{3}{8}$ of her book.
What fraction of her book has she still to read? ______

24. A train can carry 520 passengers.
How many passengers can 12 trains hold? ______

25. What is the difference between 72,318 and 41,963? ______

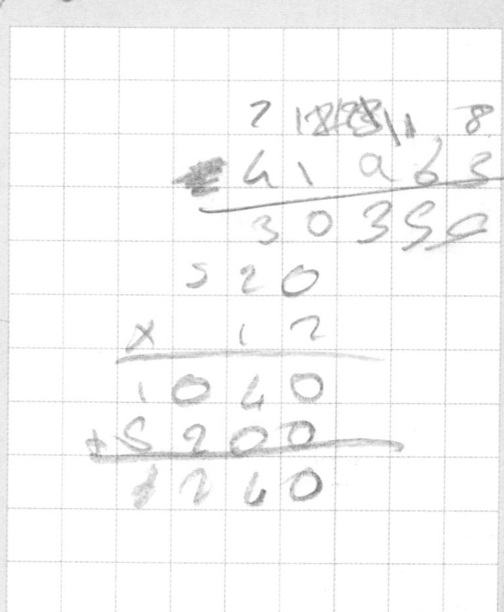

/25

# Week 10 Test

1. Complete the sequence.
   4·0, 3·7, 3·4, ______

2. What is the value of the underlined digits:
   61,251? ______

3. Put these fractions in order of size, starting with the largest: $\frac{1}{2}$, $\frac{5}{8}$, $\frac{1}{4}$, $\frac{3}{4}$, $\frac{3}{8}$.
   ______, ______, ______, ______, ______.

4. What is the perimeter of this triangle? ______

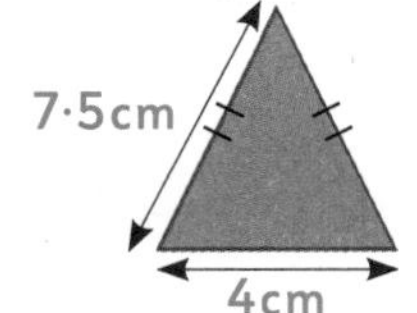


5. Name the type of triangle above. ______

6. What are the chances of landing on heads when throwing one coin?
   ______ in ______

7. $\frac{3}{4} < \frac{10}{12}$. True or false? ______.

8. A pentagonal prism has ______ edges.

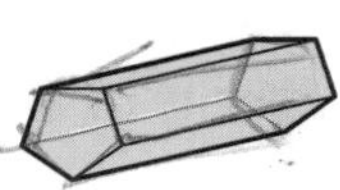

9. 1:10 = ______ past ______

10. 45·1 – 22·4 = ______

11. $\frac{6}{8} - \frac{1}{4}$ = ______.

12. Which is better value for money? ______
    (a) 7 bananas at €1·75
    (b) 6 bananas at €1·80

13. (4 × 7) + (6 × 8) = ______.

14. Which unit of measurement would be the best to measure the weight of a baby? ☐ g ☐ kg

15. Is this angle about 10°, 70° or 110°? ______

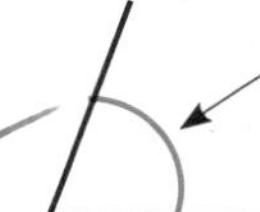

16. If a glass holds 400ml, how many litres will 8 glasses hold? ______

17. Round 25,425 to the nearest 100. ______

18. Which 2-D shape has 6 sides?
    ______

19. 6·33 × 10 = ______

20. Write the time 45 minutes earlier than the time shown on the clock. ______ : ______

## Problems

21. A minibus can carry 12 people. How many minibuses are needed to carry 70 people? ______.

22. There are 12 squares in a bar of chocolate. James ate $\frac{1}{4}$ of the bar. How many squares did he eat? ______.

23. A shop sold 120l of milk each day. How many litres would it sell in a week (7 days)? ______

24. What must be added to the product of 45 and 10 to make 500? ______.

25. A garage sold 12,835 cars in one year. They sold 1,263 less the following year. How many cars did it sell that year? ______

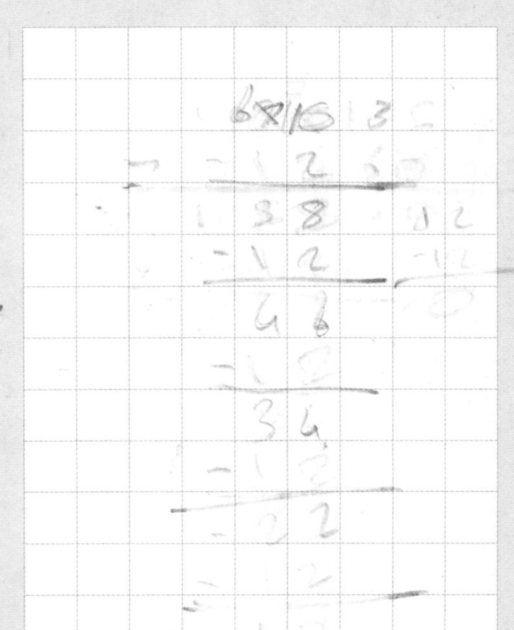

/25

# Week 11 Test

1. Put in order of size, starting with the smallest: $\frac{1}{2}$, $\frac{3}{8}$, $\frac{3}{4}$, $\frac{1}{4}$, $\frac{5}{8}$.
   ____, ____, ____, ____, ____

2. Round 85,323 to the nearest 10. ____

3. How many sides has an octagon? ____

4. Write $\frac{22}{7}$ as a mixed number. ____

5. This is a ______________ angle.

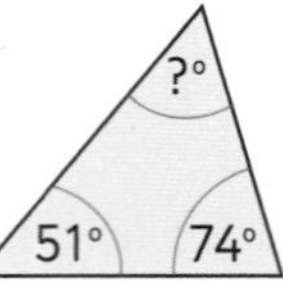

6. A hexagonal pyramid has ____ faces.

7. Find the value of the missing angle. ____

?°
51°
74°

8. 45·6 + 22·2 = ____

9. 450 ÷ 100 = ____

10. 2·3km = ____ m

11. Put in order of size, starting with the smallest: 0·2, 0·45, 1·2, 0·1, 0·85.
    ____, ____, ____, ____, ____

12. Rotate this shape 90° clockwise and draw.

13. $\frac{1}{5} = \frac{\square}{10}$

14. 10:35 = ____ to ____

15. €30 – €14·25 = ____

16. What are the chances of picking a diamond from a pack of cards?
    ____ in ____

17. Find the perimeter of the triangle. ____

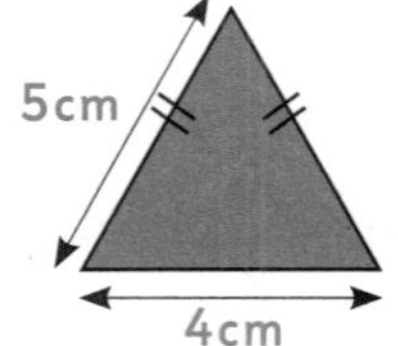


18. How many lines of symmetry has a rectangle? ____

19. Which is better value for money? ____
    (a) 5 pencils at €4·35
    (b) 7 pencils at €5·25

20. (6 × 3) + (9 × 5) = ____

## Problems

21. A packet of sweets costs €1·25.
    How much change would I get from €10 if I bought 3 packets of sweets? ____

22. If a car travels 9km in 10 minutes, how far will it travel in an hour? ____

23. A farmer had 40 cows.
    He sold 0·25 of them.
    How many did he sell? ____

24. $\frac{1}{2}$ of Jim's money is €16·25.
    How much money has Jim altogether? ____

25. Liam ran 1·8km.
    Peter ran 2,150m.
    How much further did Peter run? ____

/25

# Week 12 Test

1. Complete the sequence.
   1, 5, 13, 25, ____.

2. How many hours and minutes are there from 10:35 to 2:24?
   ____ hours ____ minutes

3. 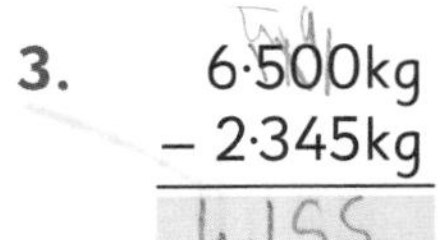

$$\begin{array}{r} 6{\cdot}500\text{kg} \\ -\ 2{\cdot}345\text{kg} \\ \hline \end{array}$$

4. This is a ____.

5. What are the chances of picking a king from a pack of cards?
   ____ in ____

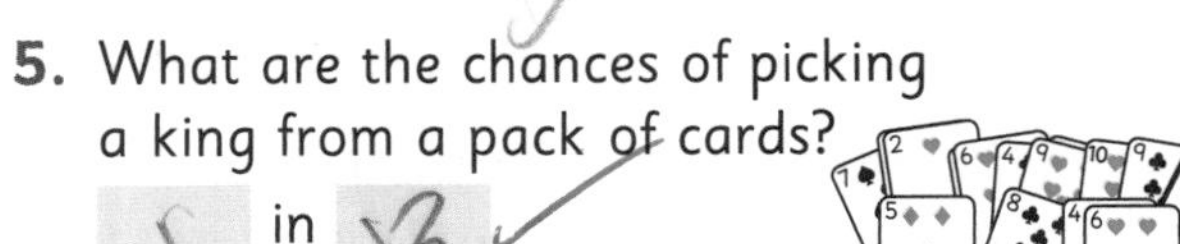

6. $0{\cdot}45 =$ ____%

7. The factors of 20 are ____, ____, ____, ____, ____ and ____.

8. Each angle in a square is ____°.

9. $4\frac{1}{2}l - 1\frac{1}{4}l =$ ____

10. $85 \times 20 =$ ____.

11. $870 \div 100 =$ ____

12. Write the time 32 minutes later than the time shown on the clock. ____ : ____.

13. Find the value of the missing angle. ____

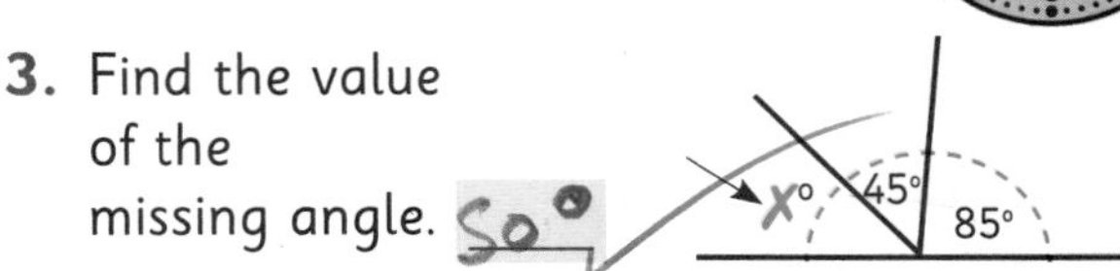


14. How many vertices has a cube? ____.

15. Round 5,369 to the nearest 10. ____

16. Measure the line. ____ cm

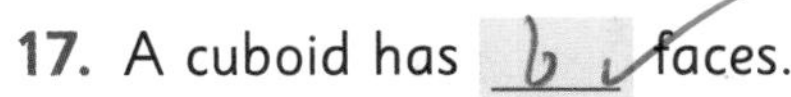

17. A cuboid has ____ faces.

18. €30 – €6·30 = ____

19. 25,435 + 1,000 = ____

20. 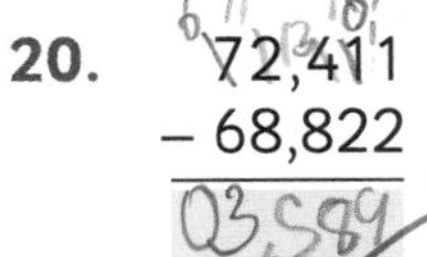

$$\begin{array}{r} 72{,}411 \\ -\ 68{,}822 \\ \hline \end{array}$$

## Problems

21. A jacket cost €225.
    A jumper cost €98·45.
    How much more did the jacket cost? ____

22. The sides of an equilateral triangle add up to 36cm.
    What is the length of each side? ____

23. Jill had €595.
    She spent $\frac{3}{5}$ of it.
    How much had she left? ____

24. A field is 80 metres long and 40 metres wide.
    What is the perimeter of the field? ____

25. What is the area of the above field? ____

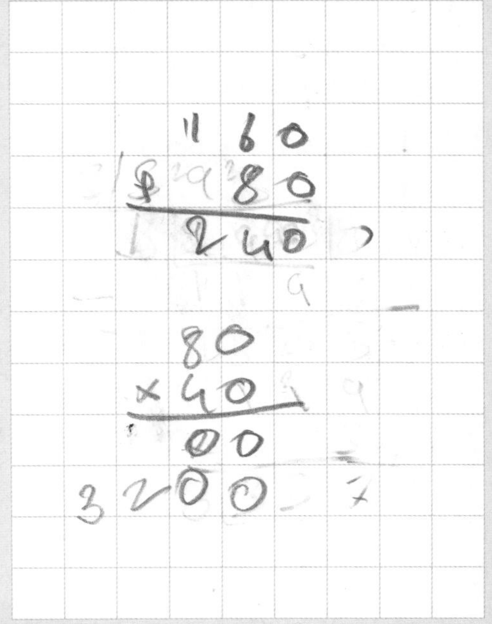

/25

# Week 13 Test

1. Complete the sequence.
   3, 3·05, 3·1, 3·15, ____
2. $\frac{1}{7} + \frac{2}{7} =$ ____
3. 8 + ____ → 24 – 6
4. €40·00
   – €18·50
   ____
5. Write the time that is 20 minutes later than the time shown on the clock. ____

6. Find the value of the missing angle. ____

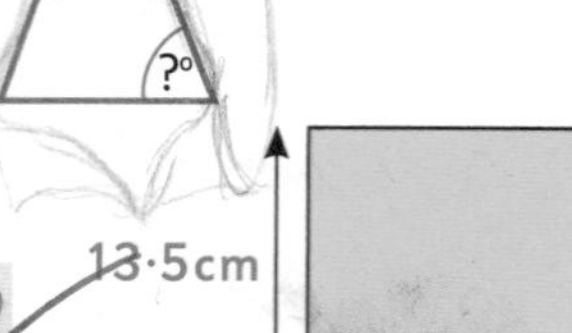

7. Find the perimeter of a square with a side of 13·5cm. ____

8. 680 ÷ 100 = ____
9. What must be added to 720ml to make 1l? ____

10. How many faces has a square-based pyramid? ____
11. 3,000 + 250 + 40 + 7 = ____
12. This is the net of a ____.

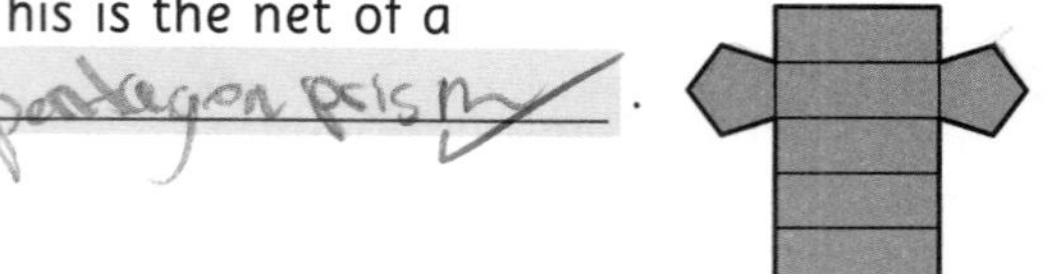

13. 4·44 × 2 = ____
14. Write 60% as a decimal fraction. ____
15. What are the chances of picking an odd numbered card from a pack of cards?
    ____ in ____.

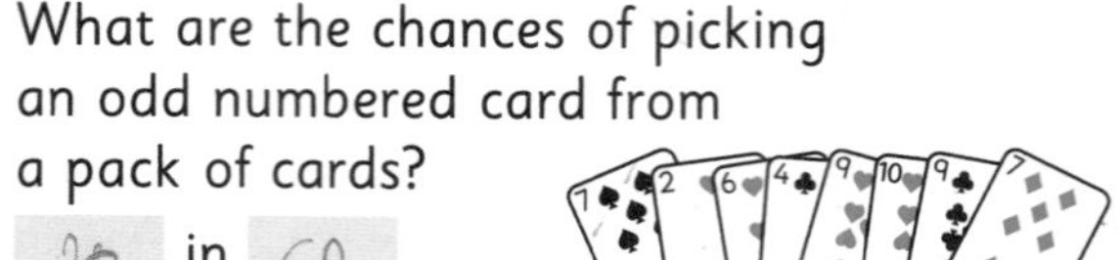

16. If two of the angles in a triangle are 65° and 40°, what is the measure of the third angle? ____.
17. $\frac{5}{9}$ of 36 = ____
18. The factors of 12 are
    ____, ____, ____, ____, ____ and ____.

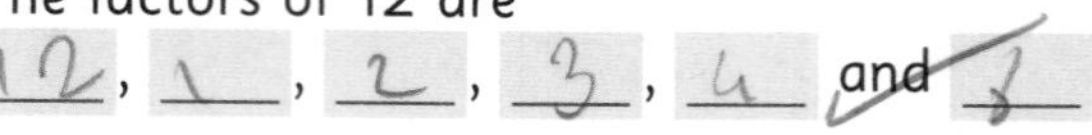

19. $\frac{3}{7} = \frac{\square}{14}$
20. Round 3,957 to the nearest 100. ____

## Problems

21. Evelyn cycled 6·345km.
    Joan cycled 750m further than that.
    How far did Joan cycle? ____
22. How far did Joan and Evelyn cycle altogether? ____
23. Seven of the ten pens in a box are blue.
    What fraction is not blue? ____

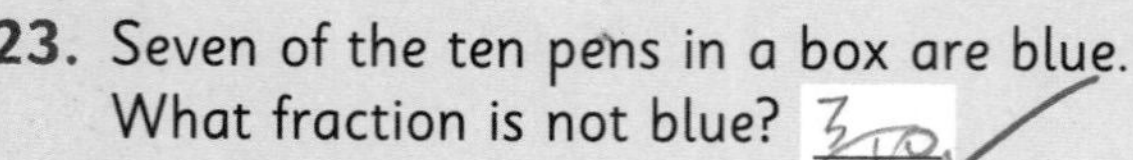

24. $\frac{2}{3}$ of the animals on a farm are cows.
    If there are 230 cows, how many animals are on the farm altogether? ____
25. How many minutes are there in $5\frac{1}{4}$ hours? ____

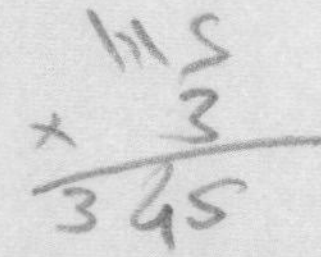

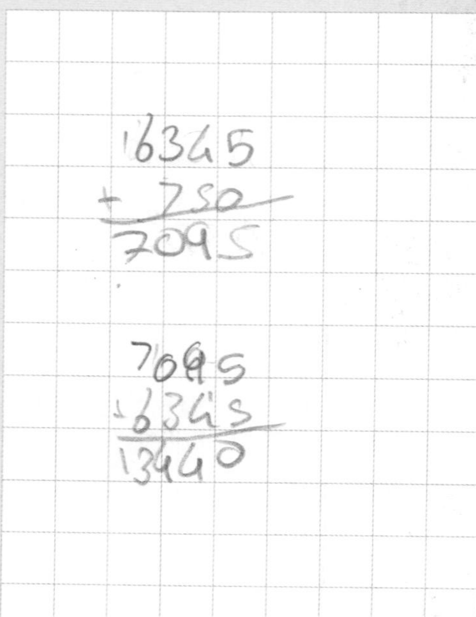

/25

# Week 14 Test

1. Complete the sequence.
   80·3, 78·2, 76·1, ____

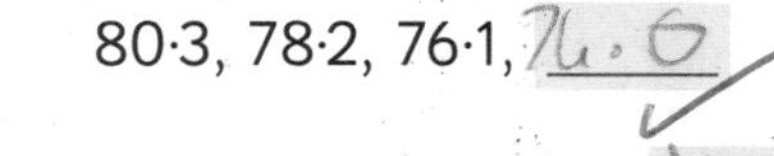

2. (14 + 20 + 8) ÷ 3 = ____

3. Write the time 35 minutes earlier than the time shown on the clock. [ : ]

4. 5·06l = ____ ml

5. 645 ÷ 4 = ____ R ____

6. Which is nearer to 70,000: 69,500 or 71,000? ____

7. Find the whole number if $\frac{9}{10}$ = 450. ____

8. Write the composite numbers from 0–11.
   ____, ____, ____, ____, ____

9. $\frac{5}{6} + \frac{1}{12} =$ ____

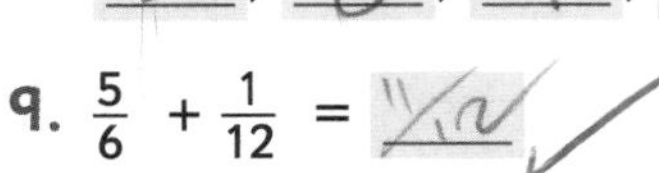

10. Draw the net of a cylinder.

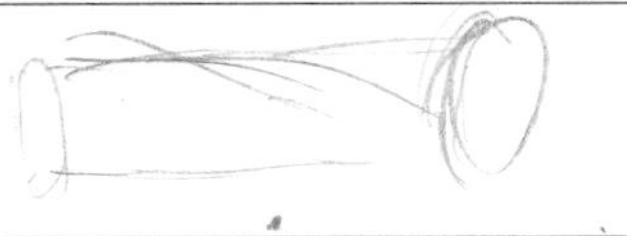

11. 62 × 4 = ____

12. Write 7% as a decimal fraction. ____

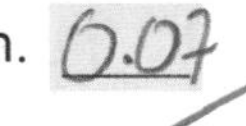

13. How likely is it that tomorrow will be Saturday: 0%, 50% or 100%? ____

14. How many 500g are there in 6kg? ____

15. Find the perimeter of a rectangle 8cm by 3cm. ____

16. 12 + (9 × 5) = ____

17. Find the average of 4, 8, 12, 7 and 9. ____

18. What fraction of this shape is shaded? ____

19. Is 7 a prime number? ____

20.

| | hrs | mins |
|---|---|---|
| | 4 | 31 |
| – | 2 | 13 |
| | | |

## Problems

21. Joey ran the following distances over three days: 21·125km, 23·441km and 18·963km. How many kilometres did he run altogether? ____

22. A kettle holds 2·124l of water. How many ml of water needs to be added to make 3l? ____

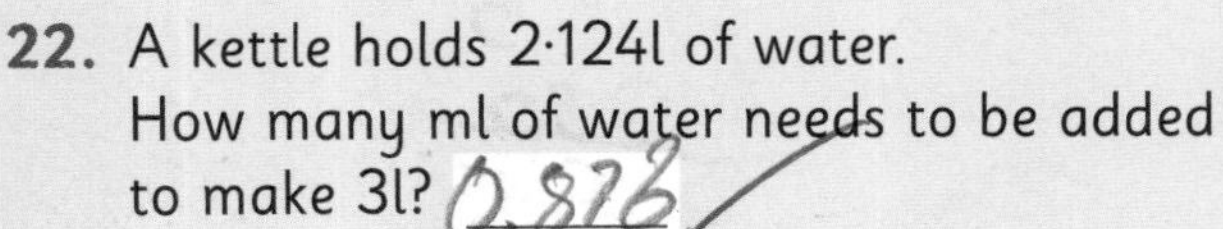

23. Petrol costs 96c per litre. How much would 50l cost? ____

24. 500ml of paint costs €5·80. How much would 2l of paint cost? ____

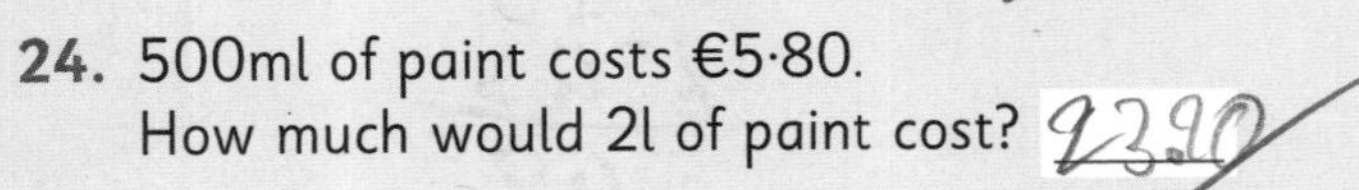

25. There are 5 children in a family. 3 of them are boys. What percentage of the children are boys? ____

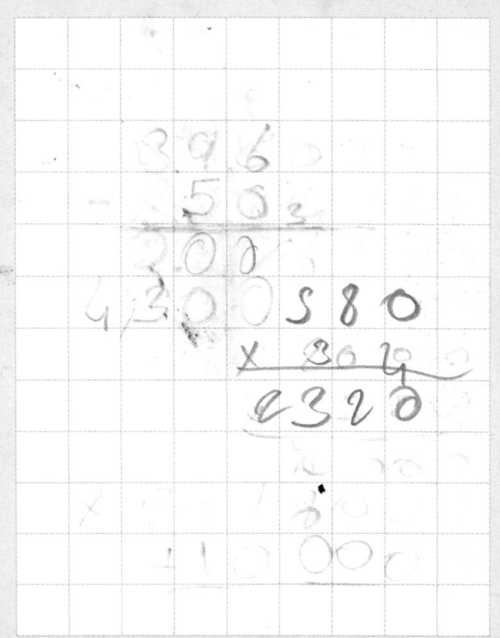

/25

# Week 15 Test

1. $\frac{2}{3}$, $1\frac{1}{3}$, 2, ____
2. $\frac{5}{6} + \frac{1}{12} =$ ____
3. Is 8 a composite number? ____
4. This is the net of a ____.
5. $\frac{2}{5} =$ ____ %
6. $81 - (6 \times 7) =$ ____
7. Which is nearer to 80,000: 80,400 or 79,800? ____
8. €26·40 If one tracksuit costs €26·40, how much would 6 tracksuits cost? ____
9. How many hours and minutes are there from 4:33 to 7:51? ____ hours ____ minutes
10. $711 \div 8 =$ ____ R ____
11. 4·5m = ____ cm
12. $360 \div 100 =$ ____
13. Measure the line. ____ cm
14. Find the perimeter of this shape. ____

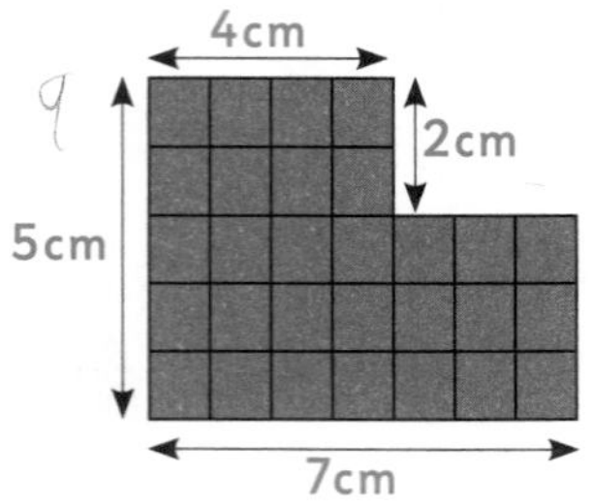


15. This is a ____.

16. If eight pairs of trousers cost €116, how much would one pair cost? ____
17. The factors of 15 are ____, ____, ____ and ____.
18. Find the value of the missing angle. ____

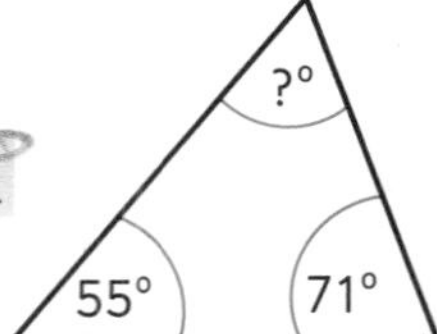


19. 8 + ____ = $7 \times 4$
20. $\frac{1}{3}$ of 3,087 = ____

## Problems

21. How many 125g are there in 2kg? ____
22. What is the perimeter of a room 8m long and 5m wide? ____
23. A television set cost €935 before the sale. In the sale, it was reduced by 20%. What was the price of the television then? ____
24. 0·4 of a cake costs 60c. How much would the full cake cost? ____
25. A bus can carry 15 people. How many buses are needed to carry 100 people? ____

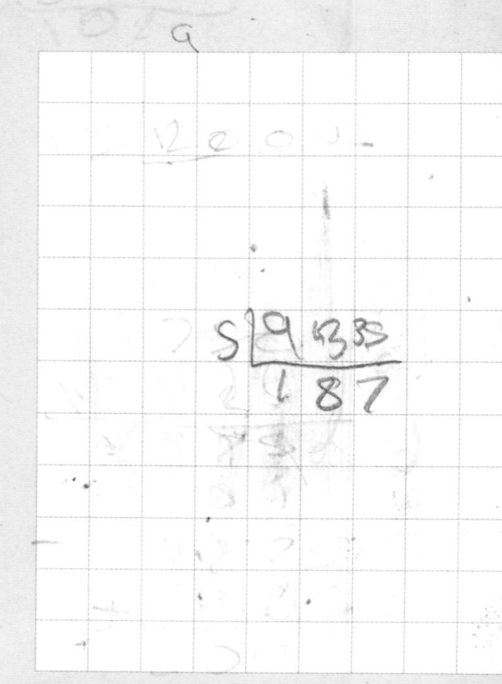

____ /25

# Week 16 Test

1. Complete the sequence.
   1·01, 2·11, 3·21, ____
2. (7 × 9) – (4 × 6) = ____
3. Is 18:00 = ☐ 6.00am ☐ 6.00pm?
4. Draw the net of a cube.

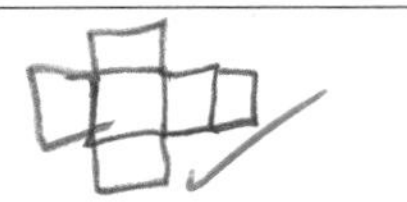

5. Name this 2-D shape.

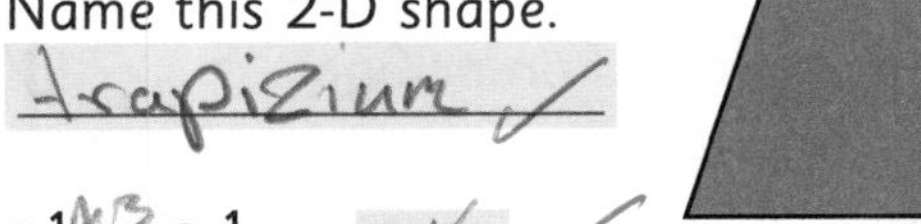

6. $3\frac{1}{4} + 2\frac{1}{12}$ = ____
7. Find $\frac{3}{7}$ of 84. ____
8. Which is nearer to 39,000: 38,250 or 39,500? ____
9. Find the perimeter of the following triangle. ____

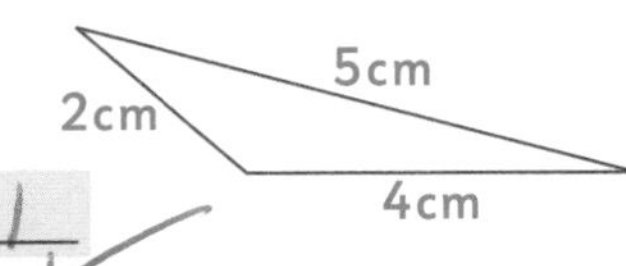


10. What are the chances of picking a blue cube from a bag containing 5 red cubes, 2 green cubes and 3 blue cubes?
    ____ in ____

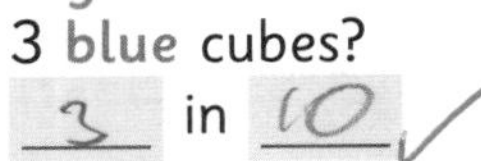

11. 7·02kg = ____ g
12. Is 18 a prime number? ____
13. 0·007 = $\frac{\square}{\square}$

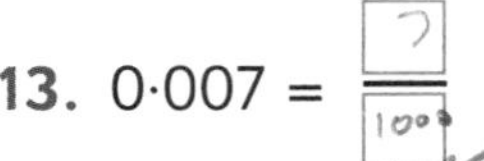

14. Name the angle. ____
15. Write $2\frac{1}{5}$ as a decimal fraction. ____

16. How many hours and minutes are there from 09:05 to 11:55?
    ____ hours ____ minutes

17. Will a triangle and a square together tessellate? ____
18. Find the whole number if $\frac{3}{5}$ = 1,032. ____
19. 502ml × 7 = ____
20. Round 84,275 to the nearest 10. ____

## Problems

21. A garage sold 24,239 cars one year. It sold 2,499 less the next year. How many cars did it sell over the two years? ____

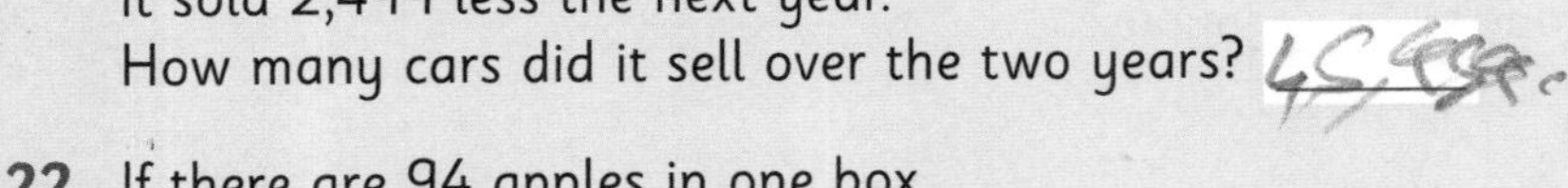

22. If there are 94 apples in one box, how many apples are there in 12 boxes? ____
23. How many boxes of 48 crayons can be made from 930 crayons and how many crayons are left over? ____ R ____

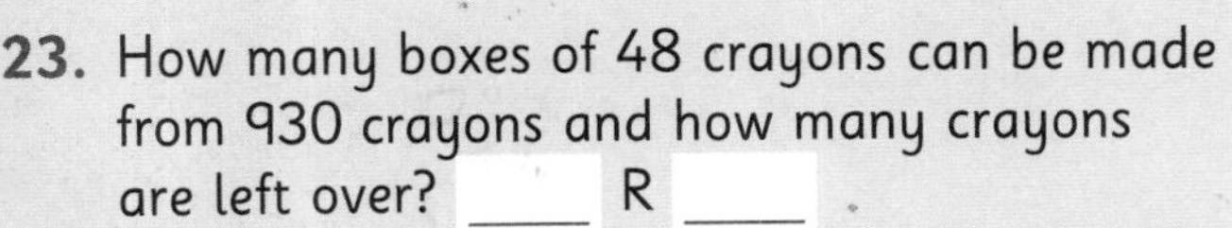

24. How many quarter pizzas can I make from $2\frac{3}{4}$ pizzas? ____
25. 500ml of shampoo costs €3·85. How much change would I get back from €20 if I buy 2l of shampoo? ____

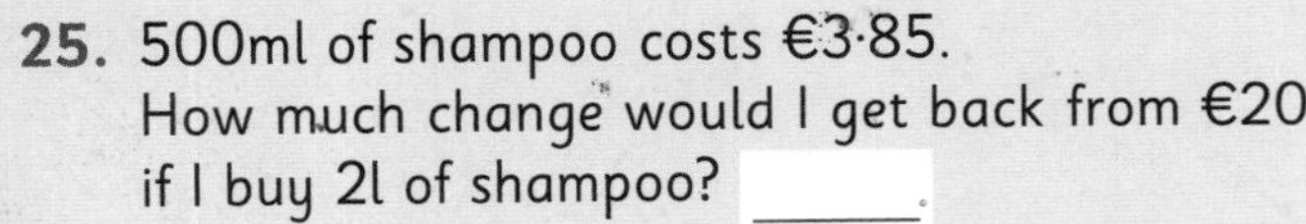

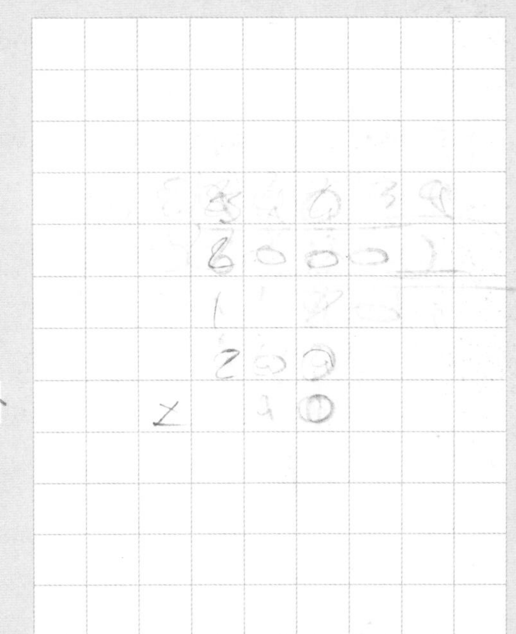

/25

# Week 17 Test

1. Complete the sequence. 600, 60, 6, ____

2. €8·23
 × 7
 ____

3. What are the chances of picking an even numbered card from a pack of cards? ____ in ____

4. (9 × 7) – (6 × 3) = ____

5. Write $\frac{9}{1000}$ as a decimal fraction. ____

6. 2,100g = ____ kg

7. Is 09:30 = ☐ 9.30am ☐ 9.30pm?

8. Which is nearer to 25,250: 24,500 or 26,500? ____

9. $9\frac{3}{8} - 4\frac{1}{4} =$ ____

10. How many faces has a cube? ____

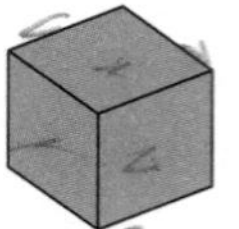

11. Will a circle and a rectangle together tessellate? ____

12. 9·6 × 10 = ____

13. An angle greater than 90° and less than 180° is called an ____ angle.

14. Write $\frac{19}{5}$ as a mixed number. ____

15. The factors of 16 are ____, ____, ____, ____ and ____.

16. The perimeter of an octagon with each side measuring 2cm is ____.

17. How many 300ml are there in 3l? ____

18. Draw the line of symmetry in the trapezium.

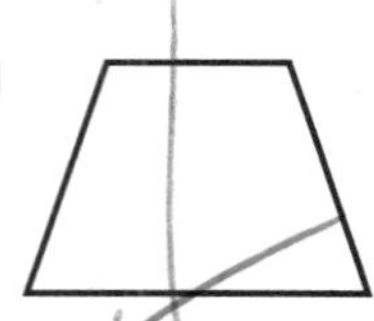

19. 5)225

20. Find the value of the missing angle. ____

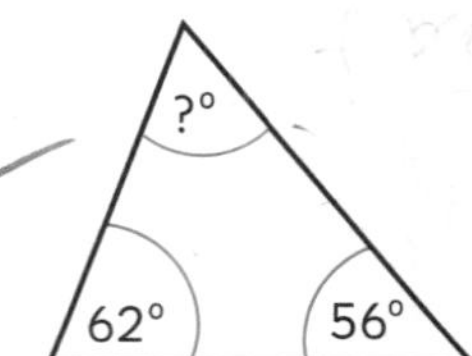


## Problems

21. A film started at 18:25 and finished at 20:05.
How long did the film last? ____ hour(s) ____ minutes

22. A piece of string 9m 84cm long was cut into four equal pieces.
What length was each piece? ____

23. How much would 2kg of flour cost if 250g cost €1·05? ____

24. A piece of wood measures 3m 35cm.
What would be the total length of 6 such pieces? ____

25. John had $3\frac{1}{4}$ bars of chocolate.
He ate $1\frac{1}{8}$ bars.
How many bars of chocolate had he left? ____

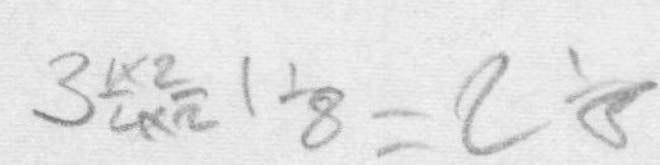

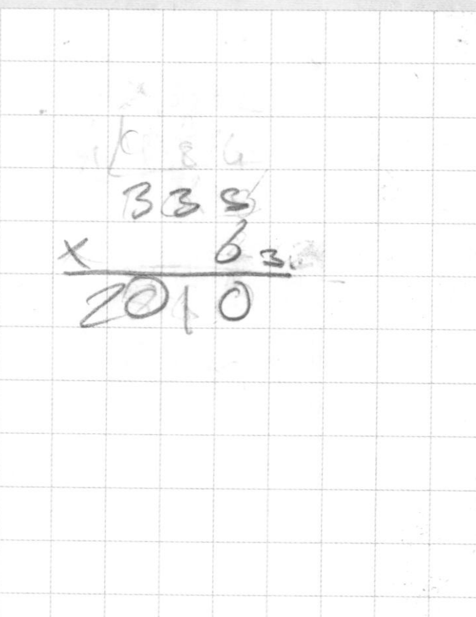



/25

# Week 18 Test

1. $\frac{1}{4}$, $\frac{1}{2}$, $\frac{3}{4}$, ______

2. Draw the net of a cone.

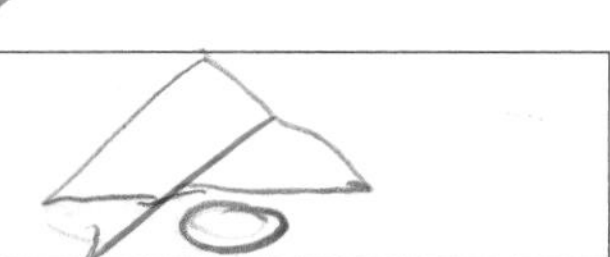

3. Find the perimeter of the following shape. ______

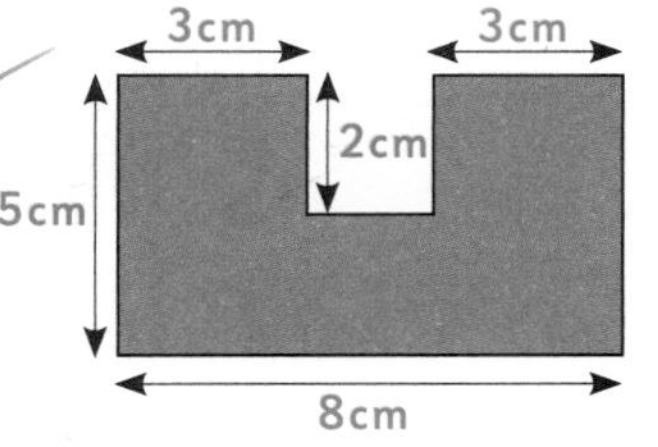


4. How many hours and minutes are there from 14:35 to 18:52?
   ______ hours ______ minutes

5. What are the outcomes of tossing two coins?
   heads and ______
   ______ and ______
   ______ and ______

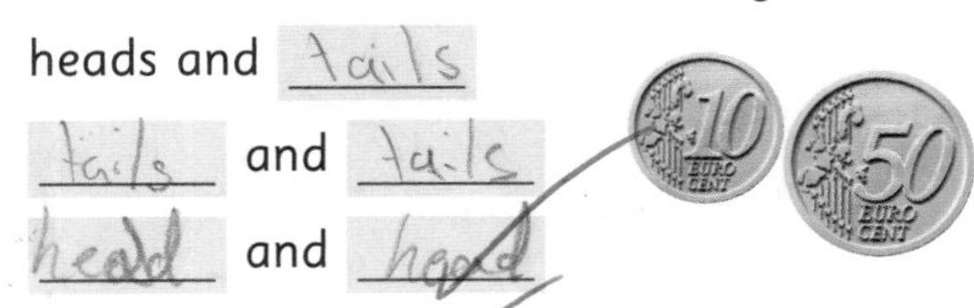

6. $6 \div \frac{1}{2} =$ ______

7. 6.45pm = ___ : ___

8. 85 – (7 × 8) = ______

9. $\frac{2}{3} = \frac{\square}{12}$

10. Draw an obtuse angle.

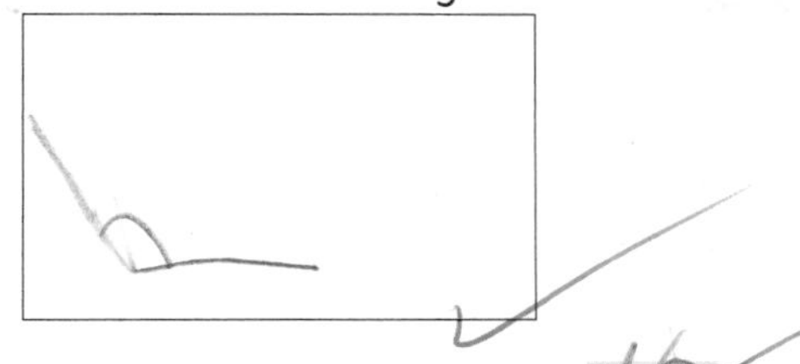

11. Is 5 a composite number? ______

12. 1·235 × 100 = ______

13. How many 250m are there in 5km? ______

14. 6·24kg = ______g

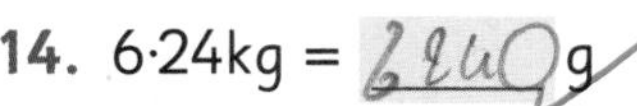

15. $7\frac{1}{2} - 2\frac{3}{8} =$ ______

16. Write 5·03 as a mixed number. ______

17. 3)453

18. Round 85,239 to the nearest 1,000. ______

19. $\frac{3}{5}$ of 765 = ______

20. Name the shape.
    ______

## Problems

21. How many bags of 9 sweets can be filled from a box of 88 sweets and how many sweets will be left over? ______ R ______

22. Gerard got 86 marks out of 100 in his history test. Write his score in decimal form. ______

23. Joe spent 0·8 of his money and had €24 left. How much money had he at first? ______

24. A coat cost €480. It was reduced by 30% in a sale. How much was the coat then? ______

25. If the perimeter of a square is 44cm, what is the length of one side? ______

______ /25

# Week 19 Test

1. $\frac{7}{8} = \frac{\square}{16}$

2. Is 15 a composite number? ______

3. $(4 \times 9) + (6 \times 8) =$ ______

4. Circle the prime number.
63 45 47 39

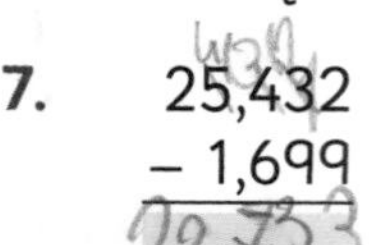

5. $6\frac{1}{5} - 2\frac{3}{10} =$ ______

6. How many axes of symmetry has a square? ______

7. 25,432
− 1,699

8. $7{\cdot}89 \times 10 =$ ______

9. 9·008l = ______ ml

10. Which is nearer to 96,300: 96,000 or 96,500? ______

11. Draw a line of symmetry on the triangle.

12. 0·32 = ______ %

13. Find the perimeter of this shape. ______

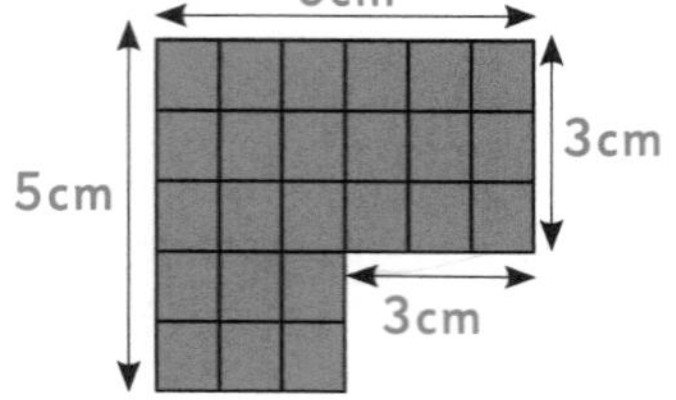



14. Increase €40 by 50%. ______

15. 2·354
× 5

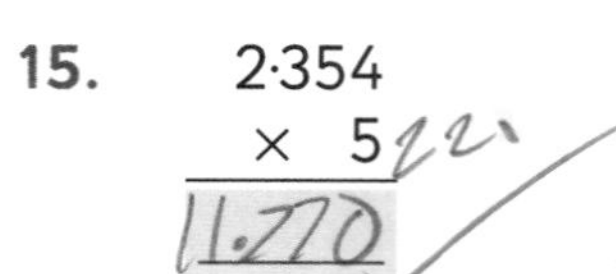

16. 10.05pm = ______ : ______

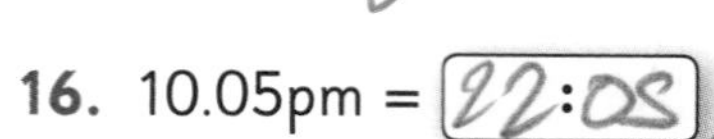

17. This is the net of a ______.

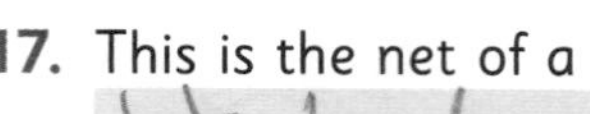

18. 25% of 6,540 = ______

19. Find the area of the rectangle. ______

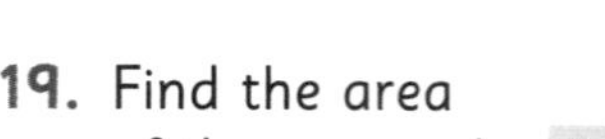

20. $65 - 7 \times 4 =$ ______

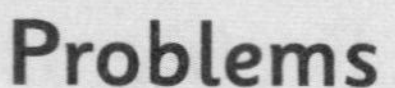

## Problems

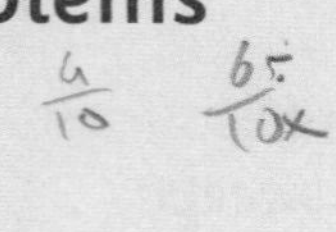

21. There were 160 apples in a box.
$\frac{3}{8}$ of them were rotten.
How many were rotten? ______

22. A farmer sold 0·4 of his animals and had 156 left.
How many had he at first? ______

23. Paul has 50 stamps.
Declan has 10% more than that.
How many stamps has Declan? ______

24. Eight packets of nuts cost €9·36.
How much would six packets cost? ______

25. Grapes cost €2 per kg.
How much would 750g of grapes cost? ______

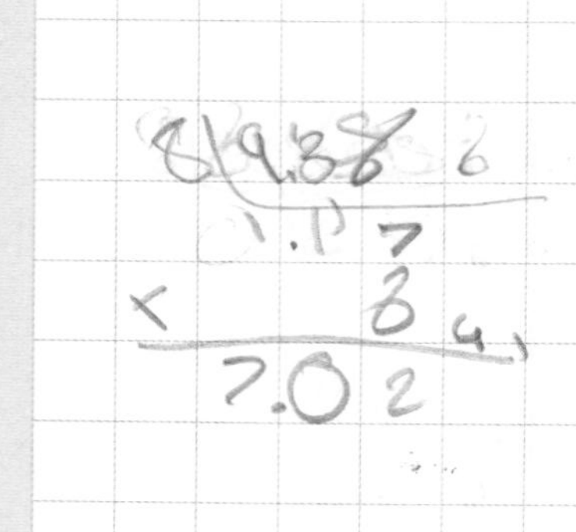

/25

# Week 20 Test

1. Write $\frac{41}{9}$ as a mixed number.

2. Name the triangle.

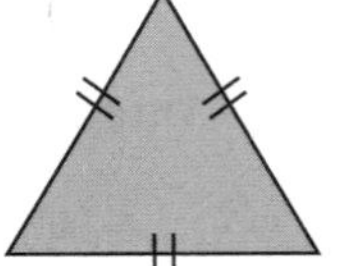

3. €5·25 × 7 =

4. 1·25 + 2·55 =

5. Draw a reflex angle.

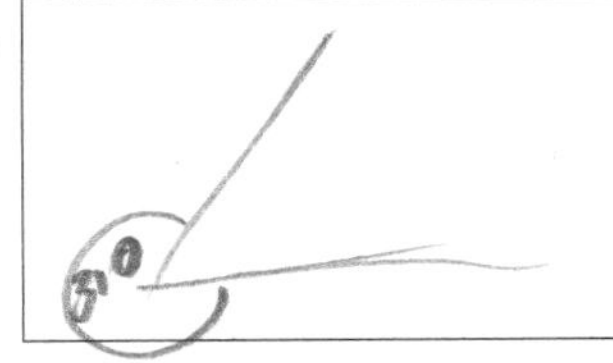

6. Write 29% as a decimal fraction.

7. Turn this shape 90° clockwise and draw.

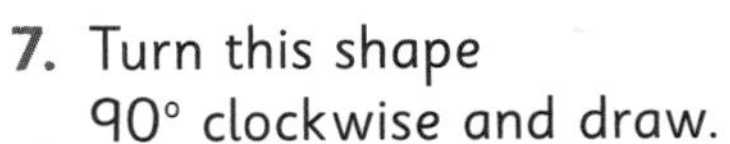

8. 70% of 110 =

9.

| | hrs | mins |
|---|---|---|
| | 3 | 20 |
| × | | 6 |

10. Round 45,263 to the nearest 100.

11. 6·32 × 10 =

12. $7\frac{2}{3} - 2\frac{5}{12} =$

13. Find the area of a square that has a side of 4cm.

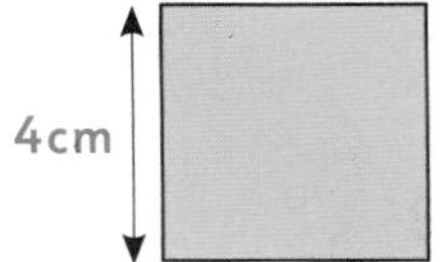


14. Colour 0·8 of this shape.

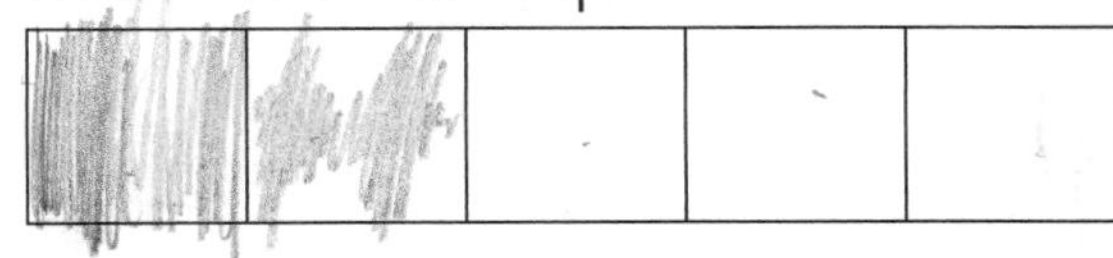

15. Which of the following is a prime number: 27, 28, 29?

16. How many minutes are in $\frac{1}{6}$ of an hour?

17. $2\frac{1}{4}$kg + $1\frac{1}{2}$kg + 4,025g = ______ kg

18. 81 – 8 × 7 =

19. Name this 2-D shape.

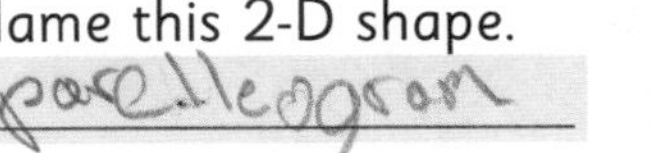

20. 340 ÷ 10 =

## Problems

21. A bicycle costs €176·90.
Ann has €91·20 and her mother gives her €50.
How much more does she need to buy the bicycle?

22. What must be added to the sum of 17,625 and 24,369 to make 50,360?

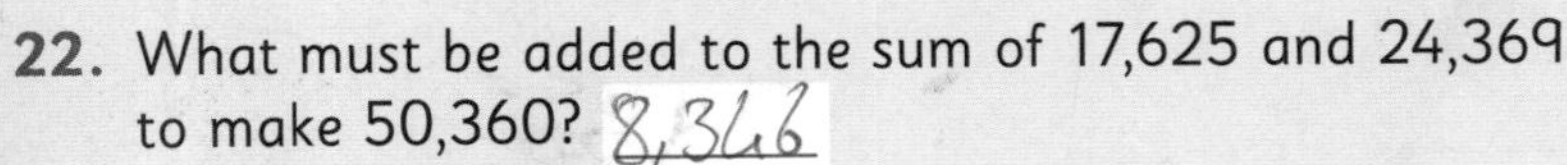

23. There are 24 oranges in a box.
How many oranges are in 7 boxes?

24. John has read $\frac{5}{9}$ of the 81 pages in his book.
How many pages has he still to read?

25. A train left the station at 18:35.
The journey lasted for 2 hours 30 minutes.
At what time did the train arrive at its destination?

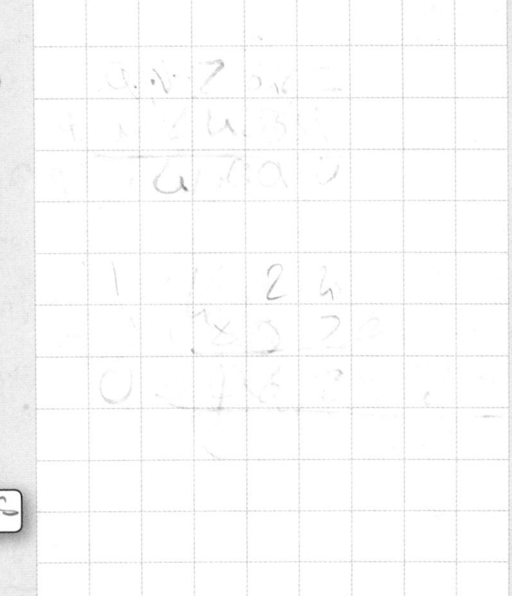

/25

# Week 21 Test

1. $\frac{2}{5}$ = ______ %

2. Put in order of size, starting with the smallest: 0·3, 29%, $\frac{1}{4}$.
______, ______, ______

3. $\frac{11}{12} - \frac{5}{6} =$ ______

4. 63,425 – 8,000 = ______

5. How many hours and minutes are there from 10:55 to 13:20?
______ hours ______ minutes

6. 45 × 20 = ______

7. Circle positive 2 on the number line.

8. $4\frac{1}{4}$kg = ______ g

9. Turn this shape 270° clockwise and draw.

10. 80% of 90 = ______

11. 45·3 × 10 = ______

12. Write as am or pm:
$\frac{1}{4}$ to 6 in the morning. ______

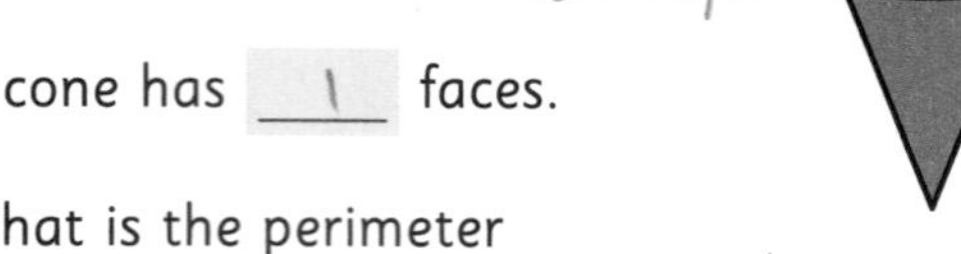

13. A cone has ______ faces.

14. What is the perimeter of a rectangle 6cm by 4cm? ______

15. What is the area of the same rectangle? ______

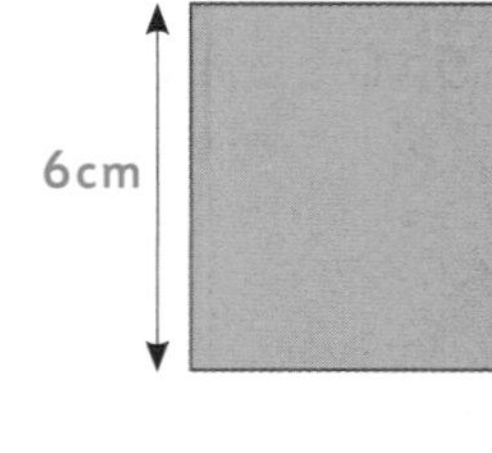


16.
$$\begin{array}{r} 58{,}695 \\ -\ 22{,}821 \\ \hline \end{array}$$

17. What is the value of 4 in 6·42? ______

18. Which of the following is a prime number: 21, 22, 23? ______

19. $1\frac{3}{4}$km + 1,085m = ______ km

20. Calculate the value of the missing angle. ______

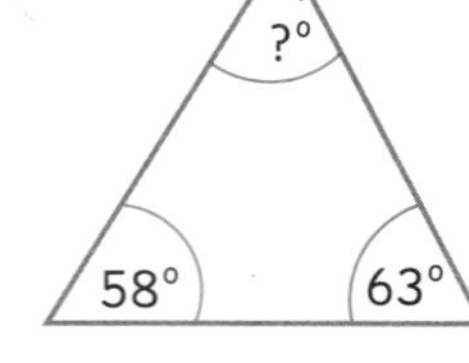


## Problems

21. Susan works 5 days a week from 9.00am to 5.00pm at €9·50 an hour. How much does she earn in one week? ______

22. Five lunch boxes cost €25·80. How much would 8 lunch boxes cost? ______

23. Yvonne had 20·85l of petrol in her car. The car used 6·32l going to work. How many litres of petrol were left in the car? ______

24. If Grainne's mother weighs 50·35kg and Grainne is 18·369kg lighter, what weight is Grainne? ______

25. Seán leaves for school at 8.55am and arrives home at 3.30pm. How many hours and minutes is he away from home?
______ hours ______ minutes

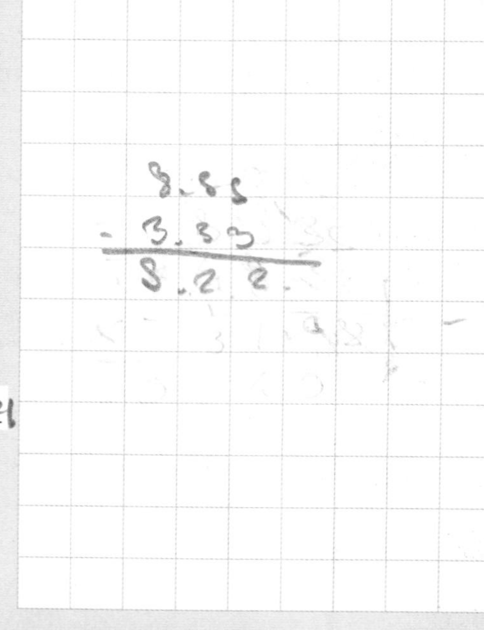

/25

# Week 22 Test

1. $\frac{7}{20}$ = ____ %

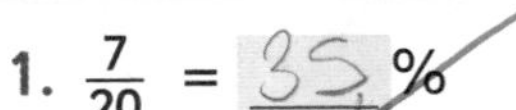

2. 60% of 565 = ____

3. How many lines of symmetry has a trapezium? ____

4. If two angles in a triangle are 55° and 68°, what is the value of the third angle? ____

5. Write $6\frac{5}{8}$ as an improper fraction. ____

6. Which of these is a prime number: 31, 32, 33? ____

7. What is the area of this rectangle? ____

4cm

perimeter 22cm

8. 2·25km × 3 = ____

9. Write the number negative 3. ____

10. A sphere has ____ edges.

11. 763 ÷ 10 = ____

12. 56,548 + 6,000 = ____

13.

| | hrs | mins |
|---|---|---|
| | 6 | 15 |
| – | 2 | 37 |

14. $5\frac{1}{3} - 2\frac{2}{9}$ = ____

15. $\frac{5}{8} \times 6$ = ____

16. **a** + 14 = 26, so **a** = ____

17. Put in order of size, starting with the smallest: $\frac{1}{5}$, 15%, 0·21.

____, ____, ____

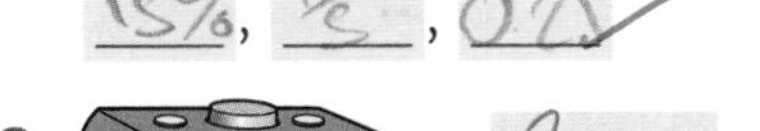

18. 

= ____ pm

19. 5)623

____ R ____

20. Find the perimeter of this shape. ____

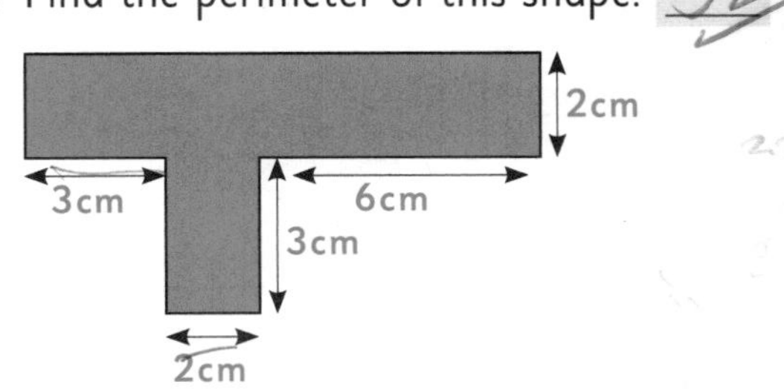


## Problems

21. One night, the temperature in Ireland was ⁻2°C. It was 20°C warmer in Valencia. What temperature was it in Valencia? ____

22. 8 children ate $\frac{3}{4}$ of a bar of chocolate each. How many bars did they eat altogether? ____

23. Jane works from 8.45am to 5.00pm every day. How many hours does she work every week (5 days)? ____

24. A family uses 2l of milk every day. How much would it cost them for a week if a litre of milk costs 90c? ____

25. A jumper cost €65 before the sale. If it was reduced by 20% in the sale, how much would the jumper cost then? ____

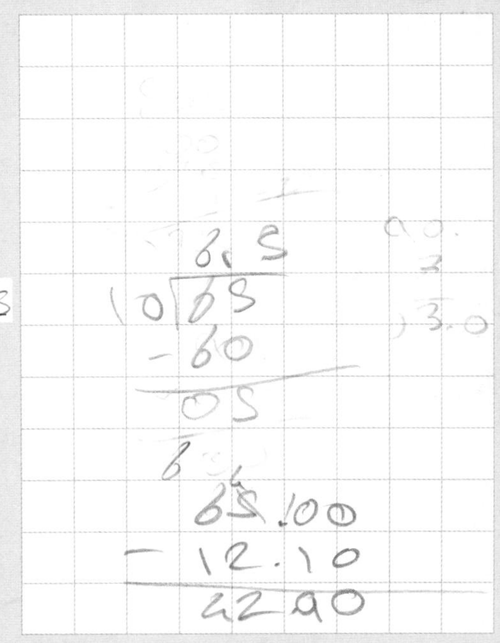

/25

# Week 23 Test

1. 65,239 − 1,860 = ____

2. $\frac{3}{8} \times 7 =$ ____

3. Put in order of size, starting with the smallest: 0·652, $\frac{3}{5}$, 64%.
____, ____, ____

4. 0·3 of 70 = ____

5. $8\frac{3}{10} - 4\frac{4}{5} =$ ____

6. 52 – 6 × 7 = ____

7. Write $\frac{52}{9}$ as a mixed number. ____

8. 640 ÷ 20 = ____

9. Double 6·2. ____

10. What are the chances of it raining today?
____ (likely, unlikely, certain, impossible)

11. Find the area of this shape. ____

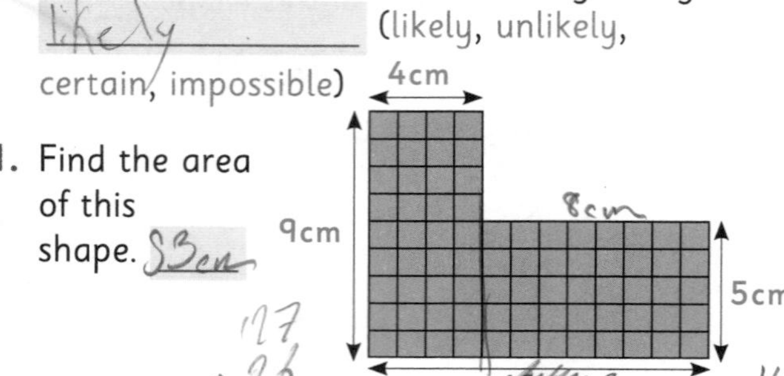


12. If a car can travel 35km in 30 minutes, how far can it travel in an hour? ____

13. Find the whole number if 25% = 32. ____

14. 4,085m + 3km 45m = ____

15. Circle negative 3 on the number line.

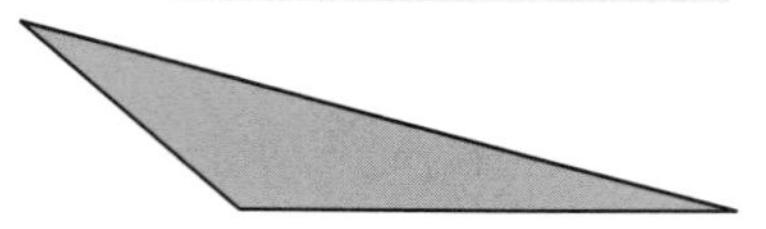


16. This is a ____ triangle.

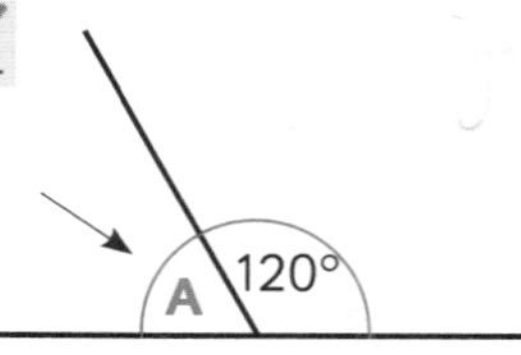

17. What is the value of angle **A**? ____

18. 4·2kg = ____ g

19. A tetrahedron has ____ vertices.

20. | hrs | mins |
|---|---|
| 3 | 42 |
| × | 6 |

## Problems

21. Anne spent 75% of her money on a bicycle and had €60 left.
How much was the bicycle? ____

22. Jenny had $2\frac{7}{8}$ punnets of strawberries.
She ate $1\frac{1}{4}$ punnets.
How many punnets had she left? ____

23. How many bags each holding 26 apples can I make from 390 apples? ____

24. There are 28 colouring pencils in a box.
How many would there be in 14 boxes? ____

25. Colin left his house at 15:45.
He arrived back at 17:19.
How long was he away? ____ hour(s) ____ minutes

/25

# Week 24 Test

1. Draw a line of symmetry through this leaf.

2. 25,865 – 17,000 = ____

3. Write $\frac{9}{20}$ as a decimal fraction. ____

4. Draw the net of a cube.

5. $8 \times \frac{7}{9}$ = ____

6. Name this 2-D shape.

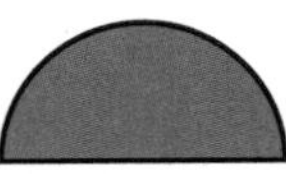

____

7. Write $\frac{46}{9}$ as a mixed number. ____

8. Find the perimeter of this shape. ____

9m

area $27m^2$

9. 980 ÷ 10 = ____

10. Which of these is a multiple of 8: 14, 23, 32, 45, 50? ____

11. Round 7·6 to the nearest whole number. ____

12. 3·870km × 5 ____

13. $3\frac{1}{4}$ hours = ____ minutes

14. 75% of 2,024 = ____

15. 4)267 ____ R ____

16. $5\frac{1}{4} + 1\frac{7}{8}$ = ____

17. 2·36 + 1·15 = ____

18. What is the radius of a circle if its diameter is 10cm? ____

19. $12^2$ = ____

20. 30% off a €200 jacket. New price = ____

## Problems

21. A bucket was holding 15l of water. When 3·5l and 2·01l were taken away, how much water was left in the bucket? ____

22. Claire spent $\frac{3}{4}$ of her money. Margaret spent $\frac{1}{12}$ of her money. What fraction of their money did they both spend altogether? ____

23. Liam ran for 75% of an hour. How many minutes did he run for? ____

24. James had €14·80. Andrew had 30% less than that. How much had they altogether? ____

25. 50% of Mark's money is €17·80. How much money has he in total? ____

/25

# Week 25 Test

1. (11 + ____ ) – 5 = 10

2. Colour to $^{+}2$ on the thermometer.

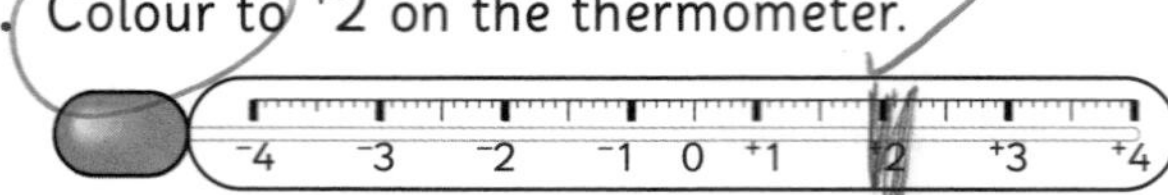


3. Write $\frac{29}{5}$ as a mixed number. ____

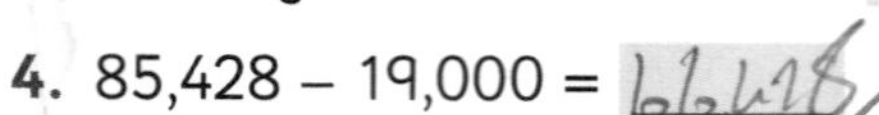

4. 85,428 – 19,000 = ____

5. Which part of the circle is the arrow pointing to? ____

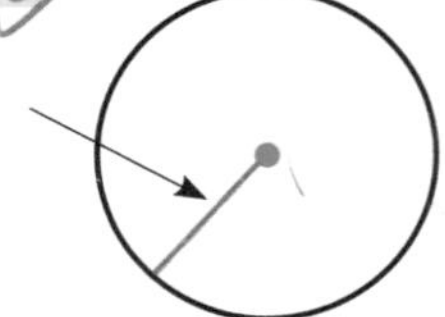

6. Increase 645 by 20%. ____

7. 104cm = ____ m

8.

| | cm | mm |
|---|---|---|
| | 5 | 7 |
| × | | 5 |

9. Name the triangle. ____

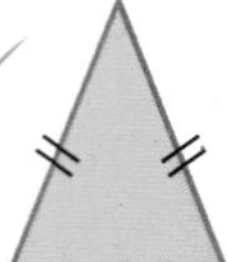

10. How many faces has a hemisphere? ____

11. Is 49 a composite number? ____

12. 4)768

13. Write $\frac{19}{20}$ as a decimal fraction. ____

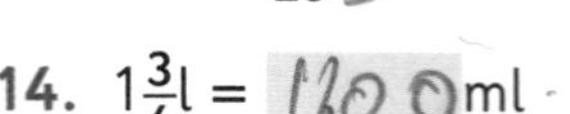

14. $1\frac{3}{4}$l = ____ ml

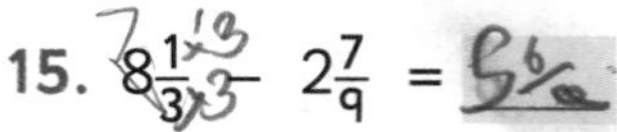

15. $8\frac{1}{3}$ – $2\frac{7}{9}$ = ____

16. 0·2 of 80 = ____

17. How many hours and minutes are there from 8.45pm to 11.20pm? ____ hours ____ minutes

18. What is the perimeter of a hexagon with 3cm sides? ____

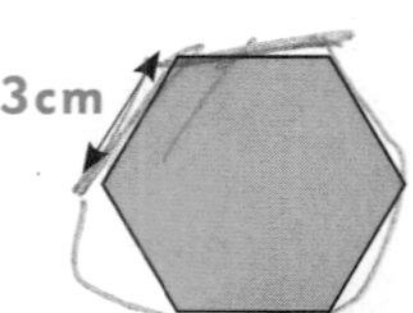


19. What are the factors of 30? ____, ____, ____, ____, ____, ____, ____ and ____

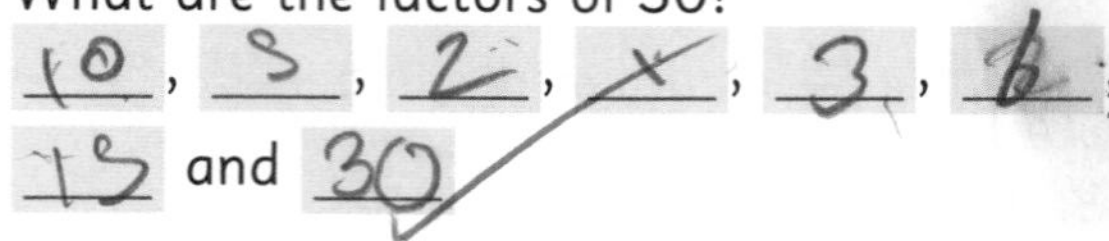

20. Find the value of **Y**. ____°

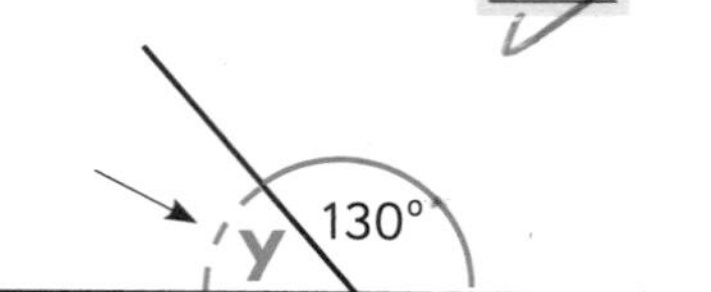


## Problems

21. I spent 0·15 of my money in one shop and $\frac{3}{5}$ of it in another. What percentage of my money had I left? ____

22. 8 lollipops cost €3·20. How much would 16 cost? ____

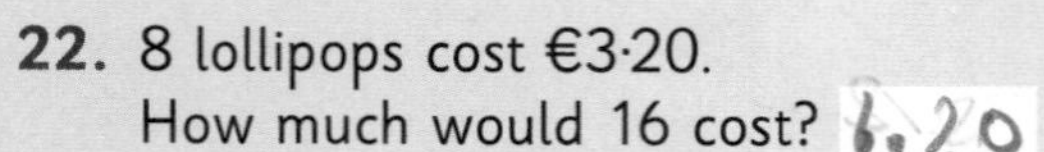

23. What change would Danielle get from €50 if she bought 7 footballs at €6·50 each? ____

24. Last year, a jumper cost €60. This year, it is 20% more expensive. What price is it this year? ____

25. A box weighs $10\frac{2}{5}$kg. How many grammes does it weigh? ____

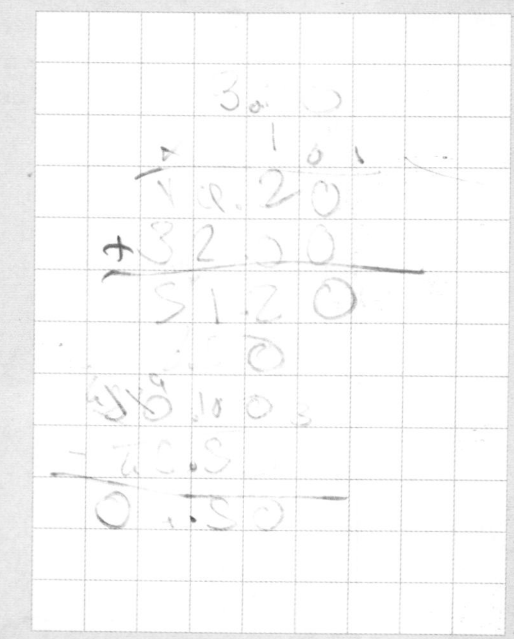

/25

# Week 26 Test

1. $\frac{6}{10}$ = ___%

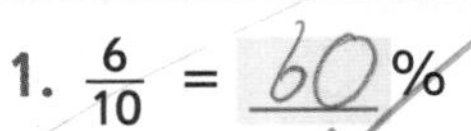

2. Turn this arrow 90° clockwise and draw.

3. 21,000 – 100 = ___

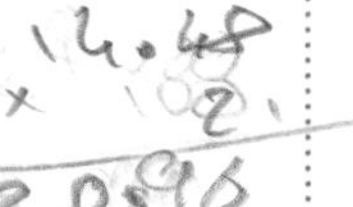

4. €14·48 × 2 = ___

5. Write as am or pm:
10 to 7 in the evening. ___

6. $\frac{3}{7} + \frac{2}{7} + \frac{1}{7}$ = ___

7. 1·6kg = ___g

8. Write $7\frac{7}{9}$ as an improper fraction. ___

9. $6\frac{1}{4} - 2\frac{7}{8}$ = ___

10. Draw the net of a triangular prism.

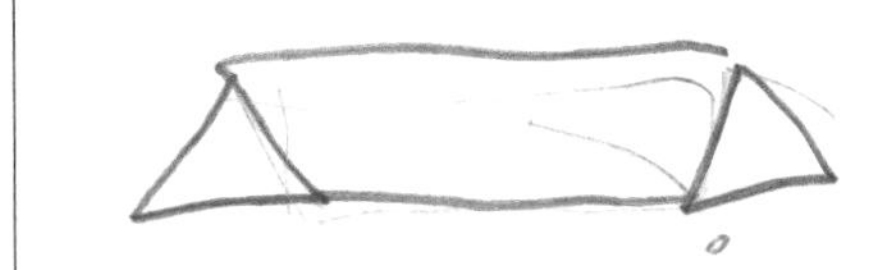

11. 40% of 925 = ___

12. Complete the sequence.
3, 5, 9, 15, ___

13. Find the area of this shape. ___

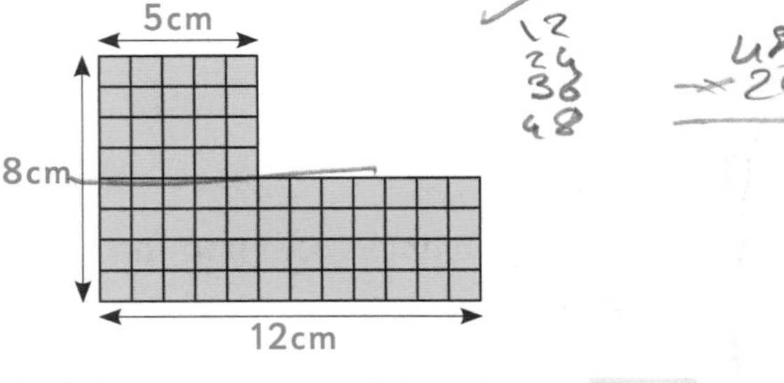


14. Find the perimeter of this shape. ___

15. How many places are there from $^{-}2$ to $^{+}2$? ___

16. Which is nearer to 21,200:
19,500 or 23,000? ___

17. The square root of 49 is ___.

18. 6·3 × 10 = ___

19. What are the chances of throwing an even number on a die? ___ in ___

20. Name the 2-D shape.

## Problems

21. 

John and Eileen are saving for a washing machine.
John has €125·69 and Eileen has €248·21.
How much more do they need? ___

22. A field is 38m long and 26m wide.
Find the area of the field. ___

23. When two numbers were multiplied together, the answer was 2,491. If one of the numbers was 47, what was the other number? ___

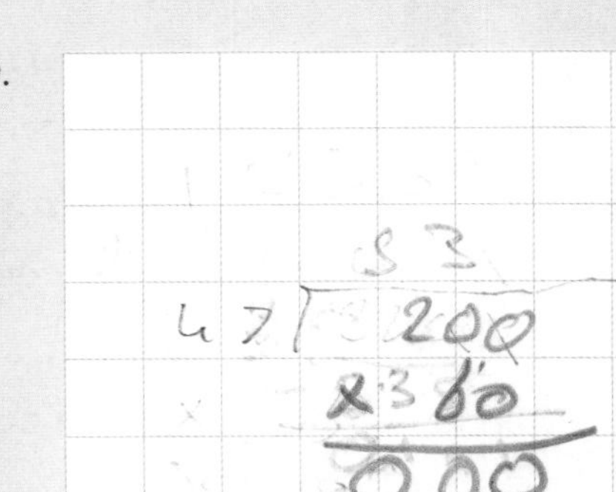

24. A circular garden has a diameter of 24m.
What is the radius of the garden? ___

25. Mark can run 200m in 1 minute.
How many km would he run in 1 hour? ___

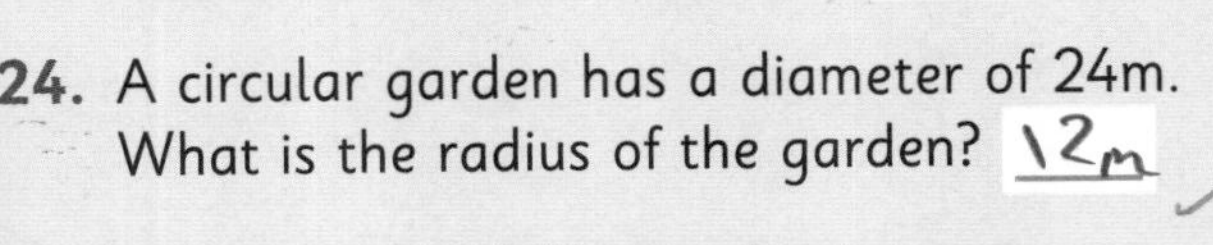

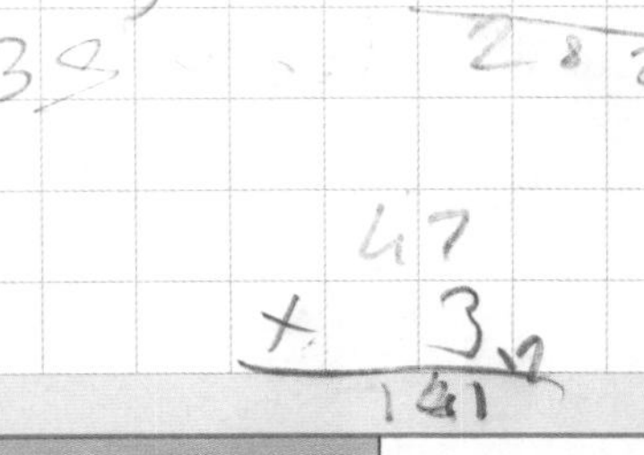

/25

# Week 27 Test

1. If the diameter of a circle is 12cm, the radius is 6 cm.

2. $6\frac{1}{2} + 1\frac{3}{8}$ = 1 7/8

3. 6,842 – 520 = 6322

4. $12 \times \frac{3}{8}$ = 5

5. What is the highest common factor of 15 and 20? 3/5

6. $\frac{1}{4}$ = 25 %

7. $4\frac{9}{1000}$ l = 0.009 ml

8. 360 ÷ 20 = 18

9. 80% of 120 = 100

10. How many hours and minutes are there in 165 minutes?
2 hours 45 minutes

11. The angle between the hands on a clock showing 10 past 12 is an acute angle.

12. Write $\frac{60}{8}$ as a mixed number. 7 4/8

13. Name the shape. pentagonal prism

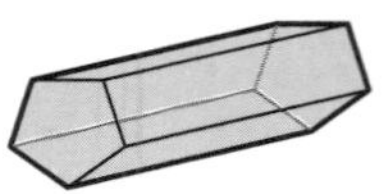

14. The square root of 121 = 11

15. What is the perimeter of this shape? 30cm

12m

area 48m²

16. 3km 7m = 3.07 m

17. €28·45 ÷ 5 = 05.69

18. Write $\frac{13}{100}$ as a decimal fraction. 0.13

19. What are the chances of throwing an even number on a die: 0%, 50%, 100%? 50%

20. The temperature is ⁻2.
If it rises by 4°,
what temperature will it be? +2

## Problems

21. A bus can carry 45 passengers. How many buses are needed to carry 820 passengers? 19

22. 4 children each ate $\frac{3}{8}$ of a bar of chocolate. How many bars did they eat altogether? 4/0

23. A trip to Spain costs €425. If John has €326·24, how much more does he need to pay for his holiday? 98.76

24. Sarah filled her oil tank with 980l of oil. After one month, there was 20% less oil in her tank. How much oil does Sarah have left? 196

25. A running track is 750m. If an athlete ran around the track 5 times, how many km did he run? 3km750m

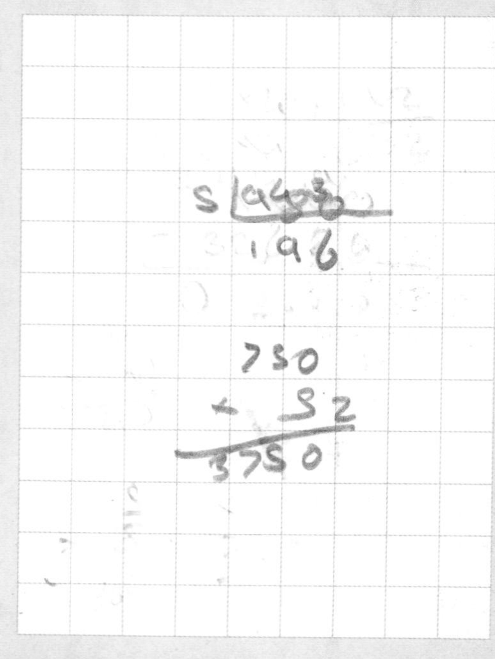



/25

# Week 28 Test

1. $\frac{7}{20}$ = ____ %

2. 25% of 624 = ____

3. Are 7 and 9 both prime numbers? ____

4. Decrease 700 by 40%. ____

5. A square garden is 18m long. Find the area of the garden. ____

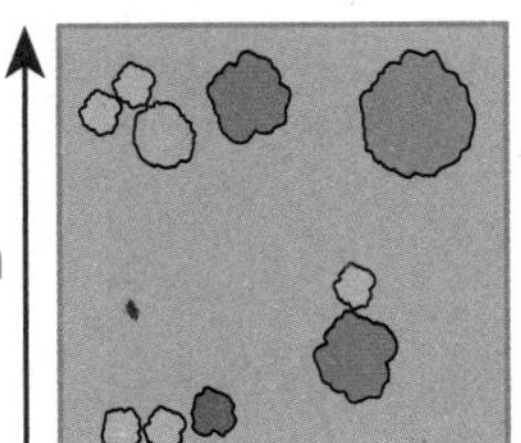

6. Find the perimeter of the garden. ____

7. Write $\frac{61}{8}$ as a mixed number. ____

8. 
$$\begin{array}{r} 8{\cdot}236 \\ \times \quad 4 \\ \hline \end{array}$$

9. $7 \times \frac{5}{8}$ = ____

10. 3,765g – 2,565g = ____ kg

11. Put in order of size, starting with the smallest: $\frac{1}{2}$, $\frac{2}{5}$, 0·55.
____, ____, ____

12. By how many degrees is $^{-}1°$ hotter than $^{-}9°$? ____

13. What is the value of 9 in 4·936? ____

14. Name the angle. ____

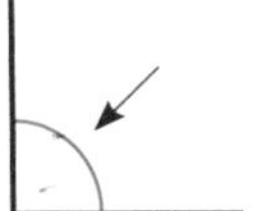

15. 
$$\begin{array}{r} 58{,}321 \\ -\ 45{,}179 \\ \hline \end{array}$$

16. What is the value of X? ____

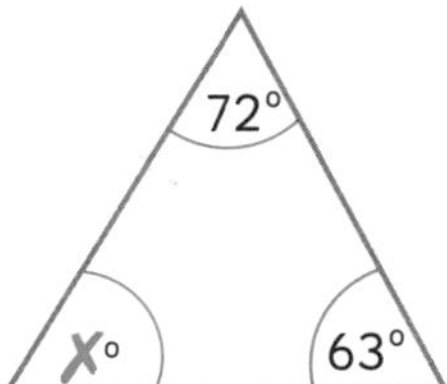


17. Write 1·007 as a fraction. ____

18. If the radius of a circle is 20cm, what is its diameter? ____

19. 5km 7m = ____ m

20. What is the highest common factor of 20 and 25? ____

## Problems

21. A film ended at 17:50. It lasted for 2 hours 15 minutes. At what time did it start? ____ : ____

22. The total capacity of 5 buckets is 20·365l. What is the average capacity of one bucket? ____

23. During a sale, a watch was reduced by 20%. If the normal price was €645, what was the sale price? ____

24. Linda spent 0·4 of her money on clothes. If she has €66 left, how much did she spend on clothes? ____

25. If a car travels 20km on 1 litre of petrol, how many litres does it use on a journey of 140km? ____

/25

# Week 29 Test

1. 25% of €600 = ____

2. 600 ÷ 20 = ____

3. A pentagon has ____ sides.

4. Put in order of size, starting with the smallest: $\frac{7}{10}$, $\frac{3}{5}$, $\frac{3}{4}$.
   ____, ____, ____

5. What percentage of this shape is shaded? ____

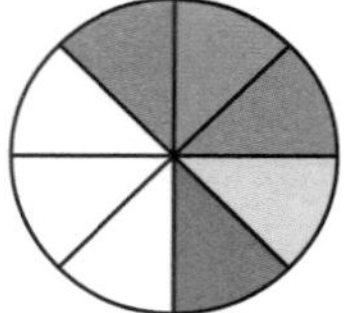

6. Write 2·01 as a fraction. ____

7. 75·32 – 25·10 = ____

8. 7kg 45g = ____ g

9. 84 × 20 = ____

10. Find the perimeter of this rectangle. ____

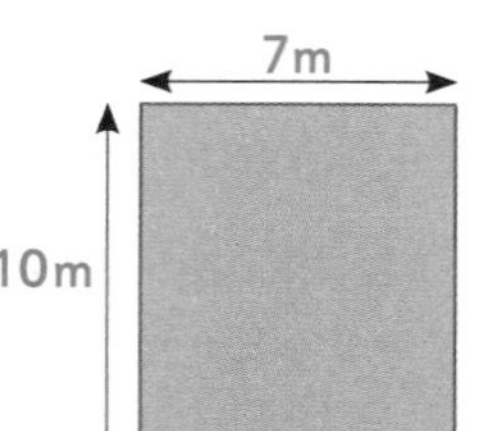


11. Find the area of the rectangle. ____

12. By how many degrees is 0° hotter than ⁻6°? ____

13. Find the average of 20, 23, 21, 22 and 24. ____

14. What part of the circle is the arrow pointing to? ____

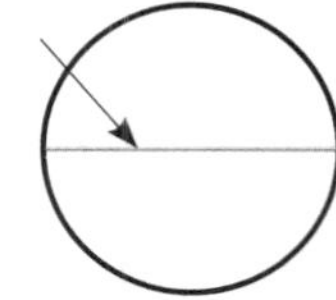

15. $11^2$ = ____

16. Increase 415 by 20%. ____

17. How many hours and minutes are there from 13:45 to 17:10?
    ____ hours ____ minutes

18. An octahedron has ____ edges.

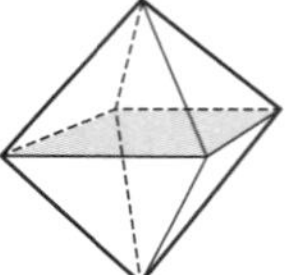

19. (6 × 8) – (7 × 3) = ____

20.
```
  21·86
  34·37
+ 41·92
-------
```
____

## Problems

21. Tea costs €2·65 per 500g.
    How much change would I get from €20 if I bought 1·5kg of tea? ____

22. A car travels 11km on 1 litre of petrol.
    What is the cost of petrol for a journey of 99km if petrol costs €1·10 per litre? ____

23. Having eaten 0·75 of her bag of grapes, Julia had 24 left.
    How many grapes had she at first? ____

24. The perimeter of a rectangle is 38m.
    If its length is 11m, what is its area? ____

25. A jug has 1·635l of water in it.
    How many ml of water must be added to make 2l? ____

/25

# Week 30 Test

1. 15:45 = ______ pm
2. $8 + 0{\cdot}03 + 0{\cdot}2 =$ ______
3. $0{\cdot}6 =$ ______ %
4. Find the area of this shape. ______

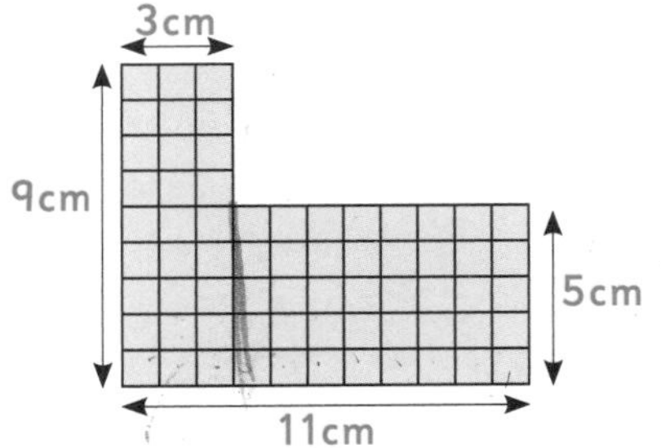


5. Circle the symmetrical letter: x, y, z.
6. What part of the circle is the arrow pointing to? ______
7. Put in order of size, from smallest to largest: $\frac{1}{2}$, 0·45, 55%. ______, ______, ______
8. $45 - 56 \div 7 =$ ______
9. How many 10c coins make up €3? ______
10. This is a ______

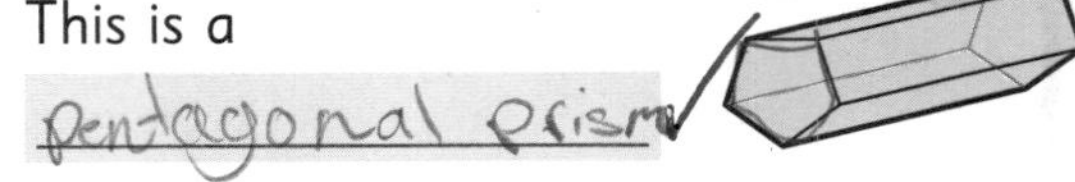

11. Will a square and a rectangle together tessellate? ______
12. Find the perimeter of an octagon with 3cm sides. ______

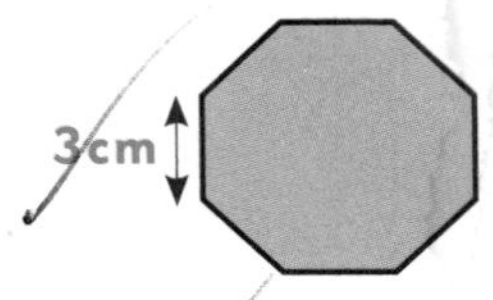


13. By how many degrees is $^{-}2°$ hotter than $^{-}6°$? ______
14. $\begin{array}{r} 45{,}325 \\ -\ 18{,}900 \\ \hline \end{array}$
15. $\frac{3}{5} = \frac{?}{100} =$ ______ %
16. 4kg 45g = ______ g
17. The square root of 64 is ______.
18. The value of 3 in 4·365 is ______.
19. $\frac{3}{8} \times 7 =$ ______
20. $(7 \times 5) + (3 \times 4) =$ ______

## Problems

21. 300ml of juice costs €1·10. How much would 3l cost? ______
22. Leo has 7 stickers. Patrick has 28 stickers. Express Leo's stickers as a percentage of Patrick's. ______
23. During a sale, a jersey normally costing €240 was reduced by 20%. What was the sale price? ______
24. 60% of the apples in a box were green. If there were 42 green apples, how many apples were there altogether? ______
25. When a runner had completed 750m of a 1km race, what fraction (in its lowest terms) had she still to run? ______

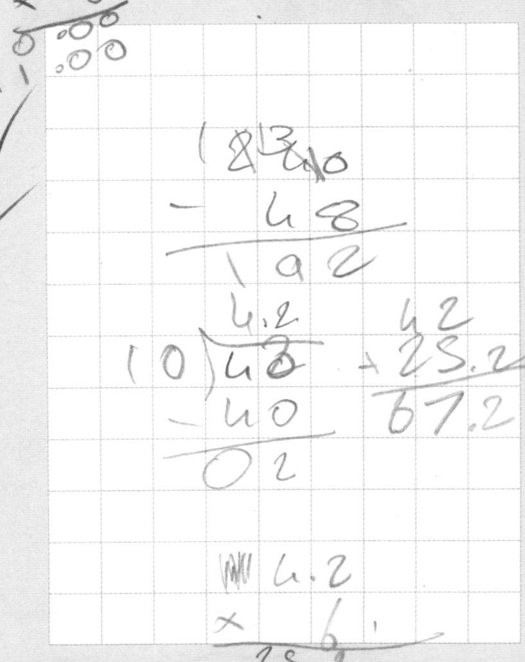

/25

635
+150
785
+21
706
704
635